FREDDIE
MERCURY
The Biography

About the Author

Laura Jackson is a bestselling rock and film biographer who has interviewed many of the world's leading celebrities. For twenty years she has tracked the lives of the stars and gained access to their inner circles to produce a series of critically acclaimed biographies. To find out more, visit www.laurajacksonbooks.com.

Laura's books include:

Brian Jones: The Untold Life and Mysterious Death of a Rock Legend

Steven Tyler: The Biography

Brian May: The Definitive Biography

Jon Bon Jovi: The Biography

Kiefer Sutherland: The Biography

The Eagles: Flying High

Neil Diamond: The Biography

Bono: The Biography

Queen: The Definitive Biography

Paul Simon: The Definitive Biography

Sean Bean: The Biography

FREDDIE
MERCURY
The Biography

Laura Jackson

piatkus

PIATKUS

First published in Great Britain in 1996 by Smith Gryphon Limited
as *Mercury King of Queen*
This paperback edition published in 2011 by Piatkus

A CIP catalogue record for this book
is available from the British Library.

ISBN 978-0-7499-5608-0

Typeset in Bembo by M Rules
Printed and bound in Great Britain by
Clays Ltd, St Ives plc

Papers used by Piatkus are from well-managed forests
and other responsible sources.

MIX
Paper from
responsible sources
FSC® C104740

Piatkus
An imprint of
Little, Brown Book Group
100 Victoria Embankment
London EC4Y 0DY

An Hachette UK Company
www.hachette.co.uk

www.piatkus.co.uk

This book is dedicated to my remarkable husband, David

Contents

Acknowledgements

Grateful appreciation to everyone whom I interviewed for this book, for their honesty in talking openly of the Freddie Mercury they each remember. My thanks for all contributions go to: Michael Appleton; Simon Bates; Mike Bersin; Tony Blackman; John Boylan; Tony Brainsby; Sir Richard Branson; Pete Brown; Michael Buerk; Lady Chryssie Cobbold; Derek Deane; Bruce Dickinson; Wayne Eagling; Spike Edney; Joe Elliott; Elizabeth Emanuel; David Essex; Fish; Dudley Fishburn; Scott Gorham; Mike Grose; Jo Gurnett; Bob Harris; Geoff Higgins; Mandla Langa; Gary Langhan; Malcolm McLaren; Barry Mitchell; Mike Moran; Chris O'Donnell; Tony Pike; Andy Powell; Donald Quinlan; Dr Ken Reay; Zandra Rhodes; Sir Tim Rice; Sir Cliff Richard; Pino Sagliocco; Tim Staffell; Peter Stringfellow; Dick Taylor; Ken Testi; Barbara Valentin; Terry Yeadon; Susannah York; Paul Young.

Also thanks to: BBC Radio; BBC TV; British Library, Gail Imlach and Elgin Library staff; Secretary to Governor of Maharashtra; Lady Olivier; Alistair, David and Andrew of Moray Business and Computer Centre, Elgin; Elizabeth Taylor.

Special thanks to David for his eternal support and to Zoe Goodkin and all at Piatkus and the Little, Brown Book Group.

ONE

A Star is Born

Freddie Mercury is one of rock music's greatest legends. As Queen's unique front man he had captivating stage presence and his public persona was polished, proud and unparalleled in its fantastic egotism. His character was extreme. By turns, he could be funny and cruel and his frequent use of cocaine heightened his tendency to excess and fuelled his rampant sexual appetites. Mercury was unable to be faithful to those homosexual relationships that were important to him, while remaining constant in his love for Mary Austin whom he had known before fame swept him up into the stratosphere. His reckless gay lifestyle – sometimes sinking into the sordid realms of rough street trade – led to his tragic death from Aids, aged forty-five, in 1991. Not since the murder of John Lennon had a rock star's demise made such an impact worldwide.

On the flipside of the coin, Mercury was also a cultured, intelligent and well-read man with a wide knowledge of the arts. A terrific raconteur, he was the master of risqué repartee and capable of extending great kindness, loyalty and generosity to a small, select group of friends. He showed incredible strength and heartbreaking courage as he faced his traumatic illness and death. No surprise, then, that such a paradoxical, larger-than-life character should attract attention from film makers and when news broke that a big-screen biopic of

Freddie Mercury was due to go into production in 2011, with Sacha Baron Cohen in the lead role, it ignited intense excitement and anticipation among Queen's legions of devoted fans.

When once asked how he would like to be remembered, the irrepressible singer had tossed back with a flick of his wrist, 'Oh, I don't know. When I'm dead, who cares? I don't.' The truth is, to be immortalised on the silver screen in a major movie would, to Freddie, be no more than his just desserts. But behind the flippancy and flamboyance, who was the *real* Freddie Mercury?

Freddie Mercury was born Farrokh Bulsara, on 5 September 1946 at the Government Hospital on the spice island of Zanzibar in the Indian Ocean. He was the pride and joy of Jer and Bomi Bulsara, who doted on their first child. Of Persian descent, his father Bomi was cashier at the British Colonial Office. When he finished work each day, in the early afternoon, the family would go to the beach to teach their son to swim or for a walk in the city's exotic gardens.

This idyllic way of life, however, began to disintegrate in 1951, when he was enrolled at the island's missionary school, run by strict British nuns. Months later, after having spent six years as an only child, a baby sister, Kashmira, arrived, and Freddie was no longer the focus of attention at home. As he was struggling to adapt to this new state of affairs, his father's reappointment to India heralded a major upheaval for the family when they were required to leave Zanzibar for Bombay.

The sudden change suited the Bulsaras. Bomi and Jer were devout Parsees – the modern descendants of ancient Zoroastrianism – and although the faith was once dominant in Persian Iran before its Muslim conquest, since the seventeenth century Parsees have largely concentrated in and around Bombay. In addition to the security of being among their own people, Mercury's parents believed this was the best place to provide their son with a good education. Furthermore, although the family lived comfortably in a substantial house staffed with servants, there was now some unpredictability about Bomi Bulsara's job, and it was thought best to send their eldest child, just seven years old, to boarding school.

St Peter's School was a type of British public school in Panchgani, Maharashtra. It upheld all the traditional academic teachings with an emphasis on sports such as cricket, boxing and table tennis. Mercury quickly discovered that he loathed cricket, but for a while he enjoyed boxing. Although he would later claim to have been brilliant at the sport, he wasn't really in his natural element. His whippet-like frame was better suited to the speed and dexterity of table tennis, a sport at which he later became school champion; equally he excelled in athletics.

Around the age of eight, Mercury began taking piano lessons at St Peter's. When his mother had taught him, he had practised his scales out of dutiful obedience. Now with professional tuition, he began to flourish, and the more his aptitude became apparent, the more he grew to enjoy playing the piano. He also looked forward to his trips home. His school friends had long since rechristened him Freddie – no longer Farrokh – and his family had adopted the name, too.

Religion was to play an important role in his early life. Parsees worship at fire temples, where sacred flames burn continually – some for over 2000 years – and before which prayers are said to pledge allegiance. Like other Parsee children, Mercury attended these temples, and, as was the custom, his formal induction occurred when he was eight in a Navjote ceremony conducted by a Magi priest. It was a ceremony steeped in the oldest tradition, and one that Mercury as a child engaged in with all the required solemnity.

As India's commercial and financial centre, Bombay boasted a huge urban population, and the city's vitality thrilled Mercury. Whenever he could, he pitched himself into its chaos. He adored all its aspects, from the glamour of the Malabar Hill district, overlooking the Arabian Sea, through the plush Victoria Gardens on Parel Road, to the bedlam of Bombay harbour, watching merchant ships put out to sea. He would wander the labyrinth of narrow streets lined with bazaars, where snake charmers sat cross-legged on the ground, piping eerily hypnotic tunes, and fakirs spread themselves on beds of nails. This exotic culture of Bombay conspired with its breathtaking architecture in a sense of grandeur, colour and flamboyance that began to inspire Mercury's emergent creativity.

As a young boy, Mercury was irresistibly drawn to these hectic marketplaces. Haggling with wily Arab street traders, with only a few rupees in his pocket, he had an eye for what he wanted and learnt to barter effectively. Years later, as a millionaire he would shop in the world's choicest establishments until those around him dropped from fatigue. Paying huge sums of money for collectable antiques and art treasures, he derived almost as much pleasure in the getting, as in the possessing.

In tune with its polyglot population, the music of Bombay was a kaleidoscope of genres, practically all strains of which were influential to Mercury's early development. His parents were cultured and preferred classical music and opera, which he himself would enjoy in later life. But the predominant local influences were rooted in the mystical rhythms of Indian music, and by the mid to late 1950s a trace of the new popular music craze, rock 'n' roll, seeped into Bombay.

Soon to attain Grade IV on the piano, in both theory and practical, Mercury was by this time mad about music. He had formed his own band, the Hectics, appropriately named to reflect Mercury's powerhouse of energy. He was enthusiastic about singing and desperate to perform publicly, something his school's archaic rules would not allow. Nevertheless, he already sang in the school choir and regularly participated in amateur dramatic productions. When he played these early gigs at school fetes and parties, the combination of his choirboy training and overblown sense of theatrics was obvious in the originality of his performances.

Although it was a tough regime, in many ways Mercury liked boarding-school life. The downside was that he didn't see much of his family – a fact, according to those who knew him well, he later grew to dwell on. During his adult years in Munich he would often visit the home of record producer Reinholdt Mack, where he saw a loving rapport between Mack and his children.

Mack has maintained that he once overheard Mercury privately tell his son how much he had missed out on the homely side of life because of the amount of time he was separated from his parents. Publicly Mercury would only admit, 'One thing boarding schools teach you is how to fend for yourself, and I did that from a very early age. It taught me to be independent and not to have to rely on anybody else.'

But despite this bravado, he was often very lonely. Because his father frequently travelled, at times Mercury had to spend school holidays with relatives; on occasions he even stayed at school when the other pupils had all gone home. This meant that during his formative years there wasn't as much opportunity as he would have liked to develop the best bond, right then, with his family. Hiding his feelings about this, he gradually built a protective shell around himself. As he grew older, this strengthened to the extent that if he wanted to, he could completely shut something out, effectively banishing it from his mind.

This insular attitude was not the only reason Freddie never

mentioned an important development that had taken place in his life by the time he had entered his teens. For what would turn out to be his last couple of years at St Peter's, two extra-curricular activities, both synonymous with English public school life, were to preoccupy him: bullying and homosexuality.

As far as any bullying was concerned, with his rudimentary boxing skills the young Freddie Mercury was capable of taking care of himself and this didn't seem to leave him with any residual problem. Homosexuality he viewed differently. Although he later became renowned for his camp and outrageous behaviour in public, Mercury was in fact an intensely private man. Considering his worldwide fame, he granted relatively few interviews, and when he did, he gave little away about either his upbringing or his homosexuality.

At St Peter's, it appears Mercury felt not so much confronted by the unorthodox sexual behaviour of his peers as just gradually more aware of it. He once confessed, 'I've had the odd schoolmate chasing me. It didn't shock me. There were times when I was young and green. It's a thing schoolboys go through. I'm not going to elaborate any further.'

He later privately admitted to his first homosexual encounter at St Peter's, but the matter-of-fact way in which he accepted the situation would suggest that he had no regrets, nor any particular resistance to it. It is in any case unlikely that he would have felt able to confide in his parents: the Zoroastrian faith considers homosexuality morally detestable.

Doubtless Mercury prided himself on his ability to handle his secret so well. In later life he would become fond of stressing the fierce sense of independence that school life had vested in him. That independence – which may have done nothing more than sow the seeds of an acute vulnerability – was soon to be put to the test. Due to the political unrest in India at the turn of the decade, his parents were among those who decided to leave the country. Packing up their household belongings, they moved to England, settling in Feltham, Middlesex.

Located not far from London's Heathrow Airport, Feltham must have been a culture shock for the highly charged Mercury, brimming with teenage energy and already bright and experienced beyond his years. In appearance, accent and temperament he must have felt different, and in his neighbourhood he was treated as such. From the start he suffered from ignorant bigotry – made the butt of constant ridicule and abuse. His first reaction was to retreat into a shell. But, recognising that he was there to stay, he realised it would be impractical for him to hide away. Applying his well-developed streak of self-discipline, he worked out a simple plan of attack.

Since his narrow-minded tormenters saw him as a funny foreigner, he played the Persian popinjay for them and parodied himself ruthlessly. This took the sting out of their tails, effectively robbing them of their fun. But, brazening it out took its toll, and at home he became unhappy and insecure, desperate to fit in and yet aware that he was different. Perhaps the insecurity and alienation Mercury experienced at this time fuelled a need in him to seek attention as a form of acceptance. But, the more extrovert his behaviour became, the more he inwardly developed a sensitivity and reserve.

On arriving in Middlesex, the Bulsaras had stayed initially with relatives, until they moved into a small semi-detached Victorian house near Feltham Park. Unknown to Mercury, less than five minutes walk away lived a couple, Harold and Ruth May, whose only child, Brian, was already a budding guitarist.

The move to Britain was a drastic change for everyone. Bomi Bulsara had exchanged his privileged diplomatic position for a mundane job in the accounts department of Forte's. It was effectively, he considered, a demotion. Gone were the servants to pamper them, gone, too, the glorious weather. Reality for

Mercury was a drab bus ride to his new grammar school in Isleworth, where the mickey-taking took on epic proportions. This is one period of his life that Freddie Mercury later refused ever to discuss.

Not surprisingly, this third home move in fourteen years – with the attendant unhappiness and disruption at a crucial time in his educational life – resulted in Mercury's school grades slipping. He managed to pass just three GCE O levels, in art, history and English. But this in itself wasn't much of a blow. For a long time Mercury had preferred music and art to purely academic subjects, for which he had never shown any pronounced aptitude. Besides he had no intention of pursuing a place at university.

He had no desire to work manually for a living either. At seventeen he held down a couple of summer jobs, one with the catering services at Heathrow and another handling crates in a local warehouse. At the warehouse Mercury was so workshy that his colleagues ended up taking on his share of the work on top of their own. His feeble excuse was that, as a musician, he couldn't possibly roughen his hands with toil.

At Isleworth Polytechnic one A level in art was all that Mercury needed to get into art school. His parents were reluctant to encourage this ambition, as they had nurtured different plans for their son. Mercury's need to gain acceptance in his new surroundings had not been shared by his parents, who had clung to their old culture, customs and beliefs. and consequently it hadn't taken long for a vast difference in outlook to divide the generations. Mercury, driven initially by his need to integrate himself into British life, now found that his parents' beliefs held little allure for him – and he couldn't see them playing a relevant role in his future. Concerned that the bohemian atmosphere of art school might further distance him from them, his family wished to dissuade him from going there. But by nature Mercury was a good manipulator. Years later Brian May reflected that the star was the most self-motivated man he'd ever known. In 1966 his sights were set on art college – and Mercury usually got what he wanted.

TWO

Mercury Rising

By 1965 Britain had really begun to swing. There was an explosion in the arts – photography, fashion, theatre and the rest – spearheaded by music, with the main battle for chart supremacy enacted between the Beatles and the Rolling Stones. Hardly a town in the country remained untouched by the new spirit of freedom, and London, which seemed the centre of the universe at the time, was definitely its hub.

More than ever rock stars were the new icons, and throughout the sixties Rolling Stones founder Brian Jones, the epitome of that glamorous era, would elevate dressing to an art form. His androgynous style: frock coats, fedora hats and Berber jewellery, became the prototype for later generations of pop stars. Out on the London scene that fired his imagination, Freddie Mercury recognised the importance of making a visual statement to complement the music. By the turn of the decade, having found an outlet for his flair for flamboyance, he would alarm other band members with his determination to encourage them to wear women's clothing on stage.

By the mid-sixties the American writer Ken Kesey introduced a new dimension to all the excitement and experimentation of the decade by holding Acid Test parties. A manmade drug so new that it hadn't yet been declared illegal, LSD, more commonly known as acid, was at the heart of it. Psychedelia with all its garish colours and complex patterns was beginning, and Freddie Mercury was drawn to it.

Just after his twentieth birthday in September 1966, Mercury won his parents round and enrolled at Ealing Technical College and School of Art in west London, on a graphic art and design course. He also subsequently moved into his own flat in London's Kensington. For many the option of art college was little more than a glorified doss, a front for hanging out with friends and indulging in the more important business of talking, preferably making, music. But by then successful chart-toppers John Lennon and Pete Townshend were both products of art school – Townshend was even a graduate of Ealing College itself. Art school was beginning to be considered the classic training-ground for sixties British rock stars, and Mercury saw its function clearly. 'Art schools', he said, 'teach you to be more fashion conscious, to be always one step ahead.' With his A grade pass in A level art he had arrived in style.

Grammar school, however, had made Mercury wary of college life, and he was quite timid for his first year or so at Ealing. Former tutors recall him as unassuming and in no way remarkable, except for his annoying, perhaps nervous, habit of giggling, sometimes uncontrollably. One ex-student later starkly referred to Freddie as having been a talentless drip, while another remembers with affection his considerate nature.

By 1967 with his raven-black hair now fashionably long, Mercury wore velvet jackets, skintight trousers and platform shoes, together with lots of silver jewellery. As this was the style of the times, he didn't stand out: indeed there were others who were far louder in their dress and behaviour than him, which with hindsight has baffled those who knew him then. Many would never have credited Mercury with the ability to fulfil his desire to become a rock star. Just as no one would have guessed at his sexual past. Since leaving Bombay it appears that there had been no more homosexual encounters, though he was not known to party with girls either. He kept himself aloof – but not out of touch.

Mercury's art and design course had a good reputation, and his year's intake of students turned out to be talented. He studied a variety of options, including ballet, which thrilled him then and later, when he would briefly become involved in dance. But it was music that anchored him, never more so than in the summer of 1967 when he fell under the spell of the dynamic American guitarist Jimi Hendrix.

Hendrix was by now living in London, thriving under the managerial guidance of Chas Chandler. Musically, Hendrix's arrival was important for lots of people, and Mercury was among them. The deafening, largely improvised, rock of 'Hey Joe' and 'Purple Haze', dominated by rapid electric lead guitar work, appealed to Mercury. Of mixed Cherokee Native American and Mexican descent, Hendrix's exotic gypsy style fascinated him, too, and he became a devotee. Plastering posters of his idol all over his walls, he dressed like Hendrix and constantly sketched him.

As time went by Mercury's obsession with Hendrix permeated his life, including his studies. After a session in the pub at lunchtime, Mercury needed scant encouragement to climb on to his desk and cavort about in a wild impersonation of Hendrix. Howling out the lyrics of his songs, he would pretend that the twelve-inch wooden ruler, dug suggestively into his groin, was a guitar. He was not alone in his passion for music, and by now had some like-minded friends. With Nigel Foster and Tim Staffell, he would occasionally practise three-part harmonies in the gents, where the acoustics were the best in the building.

Tim Staffell corroborates the view that Mercury's early Ealing days were unremarkable. He recalls how 'My first impressions of him were that he was quite straight culturally. That's to say, conservative – I didn't ever think about his sexuality. He was fairly reserved, and you wouldn't have described him as being at all "in your face", as they say. He also had a fair degree of humility.

'But Freddie's persona was developing rapidly, even then, linking his natural flamboyance with the confidence he'd later acquire from his singing. As far as being a star was concerned, I personally think he was already in the ascendant. People certainly responded to him.' Desperate to join a band, Mercury knew that Staffell played in one regularly and was delighted when he finally gained an introduction.

Tim Staffell introduced Freddie Mercury to the rest of Smile in early 1969. As ever with strangers, Mercury was initially reserved, weighing up the other band members from behind the safety of an invisible barrier. Roger Meddows Taylor, a dental student at the London Hospital Medical School, was the extrovert blond drummer. His musical leanings had drawn him first to the ukulele and then to the guitar, but in 1961 he was given his first drum kit and discovered that his talent lay in percussion. During his teenage years he had experimented in a couple of West Country bands, most successfully with Reaction.

Guitarist Brian May was tall and skinny with a studious manner and a shock of dark curly hair. Mercury discovered they had been near neighbours living just streets away from each other in Feltham. Like Mercury, May had started piano lessons young and also reached Grade IV. Taught the rudiments of playing the ukulele by his father, on his seventh birthday he was given his first steel-strung acoustic guitar. His first electric guitar was handmade by him and his father and christened the Red Special.

Staffell and May went back a long way, with Staffell having joined May's school band, as its singer, in 1964. In 1965 when Brian won an open scholarship in physics to London's Imperial College of Science and Technology, Staffell, too, was in

London, preparing to study graphics at Ealing Art College. When Brian May left his school band at the end of 1967, he kept in touch with Staffell, who stayed on for a while, before he, too, quit the group. The more time the pair spent together talking about music, the more they realised just how much they missed being in a band. Deciding to form a new group, they advertised in Imperial College for a MITCH MITCHELL/GINGER BAKER TYPE DRUMMER. They were swamped with applications, but when they auditioned Roger Taylor on the bongos he got the job virtually on the spot. 'We did hold a second proper audition with Roger, setting up our gear and playing for real, but it was obvious that he was dead right for us,' maintains Staffell.

In early autumn 1968 Smile began to rehearse with enormous dedication, perfecting their musical style, while May and Staffell also branched out into songwriting. Their nerve-racking first public appearance was in support of Pink Floyd at Imperial College on 26 October. From there, with Roger Taylor's contacts, they took bookings all over Cornwall. PJ's in Truro and the Flamingo Ballroom in Redruth became familiar haunts, but they preferred the London college circuit. Being based in the central Kensington area of the capital, it made more sense to play at venues in London. Besides, the gigs there were better paid.

Although they had work, May, Taylor and Staffell were increasingly ambitious for Smile. It was almost three months since they had backed Pink Floyd, yet apart from playing support to T-Rex and Family, nothing else was happening. However, on 27 February 1969, they took part in a concert organised by Imperial College at the Royal Albert Hall. The prestigious line-up included Free and Joe Cocker. Smile was amazed – and delighted – to feature above Free on the bill, and their anticipation of the event was immeasurable. As it turned out, the gig was most memorable for a couple of embarrassing mishaps, involving the wrong length of guitar lead for the stage, and Staffell, by playing in his stocking feet, ending up with splinters. But the occasion still left them reeling, and talking about it for days afterwards. It was in the midst of this high that Staffell introduced his Ealing College friend, Freddie Bulsara, to the rest of the band.

By the sixties Kensington itself, with its famous market and boutiques – Biba among them – had become the place to hang out; the arty cosmopolitan atmosphere suited Mercury well. Mercury first met the Smile band members in a popular pub called the Kensington. From that day on, they got on well. And, from the first moment of meeting, Mercury set his heart on getting into the band, even though he hadn't yet heard them play.

Later that evening he invited himself along to one of their rehearsals. Enthusiasm was one thing, but Mercury instantly became the bane of their lives at practice sessions. He loved the sound they were creating, but their presentation, in his opinion, left a lot to be desired. With the possibility of taking the trio in hand, he found it impossible to resist his endless ideas for jazzing them up.

Says Tim Staffell, 'We didn't take Freddie that seriously as a singer at first, as it took a few years for him to develop the quality and assurance he showed when he was into his stride.' Roger Taylor was amused but apparently immune to Mercury's vocal bombardment, and Brian May tolerated him with patience, ignoring the hints about joining the band.

But Mercury was relentless. Listening to Smile, his own urge to perform again became so desperate that when he attended their gigs, he would sometimes stand at the front of the audience and shout, criticising them for what he considered they were doing wrong. Cupping his hands round his mouth, in his frustration he'd yell, 'If I was your singer, I'd show you how it was done.' And still it had no effect. But Mercury was a planner.

As a full-frontal assault was clearly too abrasive, he decided to try another tack.

Mercury hung out with the band as much as possible and continued to attend their rehearsals. As well as showing them up in public, he also went to work on each band member, pandering to their individual weaknesses. In Brian May's case, Mercury played Hendrix records for him all evening on a small second-hand stereo. Already besotted by the rock guitarist, May's analytical brain was quick to absorb the extraordinary sound of Jimi Hendrix in stereo. All night Mercury paced obligingly from one speaker position to the other with May, ostensibly trying to figure out how the maestro produced such effects; in reality he was just trying to find a way to gain an ally.

Despite his best efforts, a place in Smile continued to elude him. This was particularly galling when it began to look as if the band were becoming successful. On 19 April they played at London's Revolution Club, after which they were approached by Lou Reizner, then involved with Mercury Records. The US label was about to break into the UK market, and Reizner had been favourably eyeing up Smile all evening. When he asked them if they would sign with Mercury, they said yes at once.

Freddie could only enjoy the band's excitement from the outside, when soon after having signed a contract in May 1969, Smile were booked into Trident Studios, Soho, to make a single with producer John Anthony. The A-side was 'Earth', a number written by Staffell, and backed by 'Step on Me'. Reminiscent of Barclay James Harvest in style, 'Earth' was the better single, with Staffell's melodic vocals and Taylor's strong drumming to anchor the track. There was no sign yet of Brian May's distinctive guitar work, and if the number had a weak spot, it was in the slight incoherence of the mid-track instrumental. Understandably, expectations were high as Mercury fixed its release date for August.

In the sweltering heatwave that summer, Mercury's hopes of joining a band took an unexpected turn with the arrival in London of a Liverpool group, Ibex. Like Smile, they were a three-piece outfit: drummer Mick 'Miffer' Smith, bassist John 'Tupp' Taylor and lead guitarist Mike Bersin. With their manager Ken Testi, they had headed south in a rusty old van to seek fortune and fame in London. 'My girlfriend Helen McConnell had a flat in Earls Court with her sister, Pat, so at least we had somewhere to crash,' Testi explains.

Testi remembers that they met Freddie Mercury almost on arrival. 'It was Pat's birthday, and we thought we'd take her out for a drink. She was adamant it had to be in Kensington. At that time there was very much a collegy subculture in the area, and there was quite a student thing going on – a substrata to the more opulent side of Kensington.

'Pat had seen Smile playing at Imperial College and knew that the Kensington was their boozer, so we went, and right enough the chaps were there. In no time at all the two bands got chatting. They had a friend with them who wasn't in Smile but clearly felt that he ought to be, and this was Freddie.'

Says Testi, 'Freddie was wearing a short fur jacket and had well-groomed shoulder-length hair. He looked the business. I suppose to him we must have appeared brusque northerners that night and not at all sophisticated, but you'd never have guessed it. On first acquaintance Freddie would be very quiet.

'After the pub shut we all ended up back at Pat's flat where Smile performed for us, and Fred kept throwing in harmonies as if he couldn't help himself. That night my focus centred on Brian's playing, and I felt that I was listening to something potentially special. But I noticed that Freddie was clearly extremely comfortable in that company.'

Like Ken Testi, Ibex guitarist Mike Bersin recalls that the person who made the most impact at that first meeting was Brian May: 'I was dead keen to hear him play but the big surprise for me ended up being that he used a sixpence coin instead of the usual plectrum,' an idiosyncrasy that still fascinates guitarists. But as both bands met up often after that night, it wasn't long before Mercury made his presence felt.

'That was an unforgettable summer,' he continues. 'Brian Jones died, and the Stones held that huge Hyde Park memorial to him, and the weather was stiflingly hot! What I remember most is everyone sitting outside the Kensington on the low window ledges drinking barley wine, because it was cheap. Although Freddie had been quiet at first, he quickly lost that.

'One evening we were all outside the pub discussing music as usual, and Freddie suddenly piped up, "What you guys need is a singer." We looked at each other and wondered how he could possibly know that because he hadn't heard us play. I guess it was a lucky opening line, but anyway he promptly offered to front us.'

Ken Testi watched Mercury moving in on his band with a knowing smile! 'Ibex had no designated singer, although Bersin was holding that down too, but we really could've done with one,' he says. 'It was obvious to us all that Freddie's heart was still set on joining Smile but that wasn't going to happen so that's why he'd turned his sights on Ibex.'

The ease with which Mercury, at least superficially, transferred his affections has stayed with Mike Bersin, who says, 'Well, he came to our rehearsals a couple of times in a basement flat but far from doing much singing, he really just talked his way into the band. We had no real resistance to the idea and that was it. He joined Ibex.'

Finally securing a place in a band was not the only success for Mercury at this time. For months he had haunted Barbara Hulanicki's trendy boutique, Biba, with an ulterior motive. Although it was one of the hippest places in town, the main attraction there lay in his developing friendship with one of Biba's sales assistants, Mary Austin. They had begun to date,

Mercury presumably choosing to suppress his homosexual tendencies. His feelings for the petite blonde, and hers for him, were strong enough for them to start living together in a tiny first-floor flat, close to Kensington market. It was the beginning of a lifetime's devotion to one another.

Mercury's involvement with Mary Austin was to offset any doubts among his friends about his sexuality. 'I'd no idea he was gay until long after I'd gone,' admits Tim Staffell. 'In those days it was fashionable to adopt campness as a kind of social passport, as if it implied artistic integrity or sensitivity.'

'Freddie had just started living with Mary when I met him,' says Mike Bersin, 'which I guess threw us off the scent, because in his behaviour in every other respect he was wonderfully camp in that beautifully English foppish way. In many ways, you know, Freddie almost wasn't real.'

What was real to Mercury was the perpetual shortage of cash. Although still averse to getting his hands dirty, he realised that independence meant he needed a paid job. But he was not only unwilling to spend time out of the Kensington area but was also only interested in music and art. His solution was to rent a stall in Kensington market. By August 1968 Roger Taylor had left medical school with only the first part of his dental degree. Seeing a golden opportunity to solidify his connection with Smile, Mercury asked Taylor to join him in business.

They rented a stall for £10 a week in an avenue that traders depressingly dubbed 'Death Row'. Years later, in early Queen publicity releases, it would be grandly elevated to the status of 'a gentlemen's outfitters', but, as Ken Testi confirms, their market stall was the size of a telephone box. Stocking it was easy, Mercury's art-school friends brought paintings and drawings to sell, and occasionally he displayed his own work. But sales were so slow that they switched to selling clothes and soon turned a small profit.

Tim Staffell recalls this time: 'I had a stall of my own for a couple of months trying to sell original artwork, mine and that of other Ealing-ites. It was some place. I particularly remember an extremely uncomfortable pair of calico trousers that some shyster sold me.

'Freddie and Roger worked part-time at their stall selling fashion items. There was a strong emphasis on personal adornment; naturally, I suppose, since that would be the motivation for wearing and selling the stuff. But there was an air of narcissistic coquettishness about the place that I loathed. I guess it was very influential in creating the sense of outrageousness that Freddie cultivated. But I didn't like it. It was all a little too deliberate for my liking.'

Kensington, however, became Mercury's stomping ground. Although it paled against the exoticism of Bombay's bazaars, he thrived on the activity of the market. Comfortable, too, with his new circle of friends and infected by the end-of-sixties buzz, Mercury's increasing flamboyance became an acceptably surreal part of everyday life. Mike Bersin remembers, 'We were all very conscious that Freddie always thought of himself as being special. With hindsight, I recognise the determination to succeed that he had in spades. He demanded to be treated as a star long before he was a star. His talent was his ambition really, and people reacted to it in different ways, but it wasn't an unpleasant thing.'

Doubtless Mercury's drive to succeed had received a boost, albeit at second-hand, as he watched the band he longed to be a part of preparing for the launch of their first single. Mercury Records released 'Earth/Step on Me' in August 1969, but the joy of rushing to the nearest record store to see it on display was denied them – it was released only in America. Weeks of anticipation turned sour, until their profound disappointment was diluted when Mercury invited the band back into the studio to record more tracks for an album.

Tim Staffell recalls that 'By now Brian and I had written a few songs and were looking forward to having the chance to record them properly. Our producer was Fritz Freyer and the tracks we cut for that album included "Polar Bear", "Earth" and "Step on Me", of course, as well as "Blag" and "April Lady", on which Brian sang lead. But although we were happy with the results, Mercury wouldn't release the album. It ended up surfacing years later in Japan.'

Disappointment set in yet again, and weighing it all up, Freddie Mercury was clear that this kind of thing was not going to happen to him. He had been denied the chance to jazz up Smile, but he had gained a foothold with Ibex and was determined to make an impression. The band played gigs wherever Ken Testi could book them, mainly at venues in the north of England. They worked in particular around the Liverpool area, where he had a lot of useful contacts.

Testi recalls, 'Ibex had been into progressive rock, very much influenced by bands like Wishbone Ash, Free and Jethro Tull. Then Freddie arrived and brought something else entirely to it. It was dramatic, but it worked. He also brought an injection of culture. He was already fashionable. Not quite the peacock he later became; of course money was tight. But he had an eye to being well turned out. Ibex had been into jeans and trench coats, whereas Freddie was more your satin-and-fur man.'

Mike Bersin agrees that 'As a front man, there wasn't a lot of difference then to when he became famous with Queen, except that later he wore louder clothes and had more space to strut around. But all the movements were there with Ibex, lots of poses, many of which I now recognise had been there right from the very start. I mean we were three guys from Widnes, all shoe-gazing bluesmen with minimal stage presence or movement and totally religious about our music. Then along came our new front man who was, to say the least, a culture shock. Freddie always worked extremely hard though, to instil

in us a sense of being something to look at, as well as to listen
to. And even in the cramped space available to pub bands he
would strut up and down wielding the mike stand and pretending to play guitar.

'Freddie always took stock of what was going on, but he
never copied another performer. Freddie was always Freddie,
very angular, very showbizzy about everything he did and
entirely his own creation.

'He was also continually concerned that he looked just right.
He was never scruffy and yet to my knowledge he only had to
his name one pair of boots, one T-shirt, one pair of trousers,
one belt and one jacket. Still, he remained immaculate. As to
the person inside? I would say non-stop in his life, both on and
off stage, Freddie put on a performance.'

When Ibex travelled north to play gigs, Smile would invariably join them for moral support, if they weren't engaged at
Imperial College. It wasn't always easy to find a reliable mode
of transport for both bands and their friends, and at times they
risked their lives driving up and down the motorway in vehi-
cles little better than deathtraps. But it was good fun – and
good experience.

Mercury's most memorable gigs with Ibex were probably
when they played at the Bolton Octagon Theatre in August
1969, followed by an appearance at an open-air festival the next
day in the city's Queen's Park. 'I brought along this guy I knew
called Steve Lake,' says Ken Testi, 'who was seriously into photography, experimenting with light shows and liquid slides,
which were very advanced for the time, and he took some
great shots of Freddie in this amphitheatre in the park. The
seating was like orange segments behind a pool, and there was
one memorable shot of Freddie in full flight striding the stage
totally *à la* Queen. It's an image that's stayed with me ever
since.'

The Bolton gigs proved to be a significant milestone in the

development of the band's image. Mike Bersin vividly recalls getting ready for the lunchtime gig. 'We had decided to go to town dressing up. I wore a gold lamé cloak, which, when the time came, I felt a twit wearing – but Freddie stood out a mile. He'd been backcombing his long hair to make it stand out more, and before going on he'd been twitching at himself in the mirror for ages. I eventually yelled at him, "For God's sake, stop messin' with your hair, Freddie!" To which he retorted, "But I'm a star, dear boy!" There's not a lot you can say to that.'

According to Bersin, it was hard to tell if Mercury suffered any pre-performance nerves. 'He would get more jokey than normal,' he recalls, 'which was maybe a form of psyching himself up, but the male society in bands then was definitely insult-based, and we'd all be slagging each other off. Freddie would take the piss out of people something rotten and, in turn, they took the piss out of him. He loved it.'

It was around this time that Ibex decided they were tired of the exhausting motorway shuttle back and forth between London and Liverpool. Disappointingly it didn't look like much was happening for them in the capital, even with the advent of their colourful new singer; so taking a vote, they agreed to stay for a while in Liverpool. Mercury didn't like this arrangement, but his desire to remain in the group meant he had to go along with it. Based up north, he managed to maintain his links with Smile because they would often hitch-hike to Liverpool to see him play, staying with him overnight at his digs.

His lodgings had been found through one of their friends, Geoff Higgins, whose mother was catering manageress at the Dovedale Towers Banqueting Halls, 60 Penny Lane. Higgins explains, 'At this time "Tupp" Taylor was heavily into Jethro Tull and was dying to learn the flute so that he could incorporate it into the band's repertoire, and he asked me if I could play bass for Ibex instead for a while, which I did.

'Initially my mum had been shocked when I came home at the way I was dressed but nothing fazed her for long. She liked all my London friends, but she just adored Freddie, thought he talked ever so posh, and he was wonderfully courteous to her. Behind and slightly to the left of the main tower at Dovedale there was an enormous flat on two floors, which was where I was living, and when Freddie was looking for digs, he had to look no further.'

Mercury may have missed Kensington and longed to return there, but he did enjoy Higgins's company: 'We all by now semi-suspected that Freddie's sexuality was different from ours,' Higgins recalls, 'but then again at that time Liverpudlians classed all Londoners as fucking fruits anyway, so you couldn't go by that. Freddie stayed with me at Penny Lane, but he never once came on to me.' Geoff Higgins admits that this was a huge relief, considering his vivid memory of the time they had first met.

'The first words I heard Freddie say,' he explains, 'was when Bersin had invited me some months before to kip on the chaise longue in his flat, when I was in London to do interviews for a few colleges I was hoping to get into.

'I was fast asleep one day when in walked these two blokes. It'd been howling a gale and raining, and one of them dashed to the big mirror over the fireplace and squealed, "Oh, my God! Have I been out looking like this?" and I thought, well, I'm not going near that one, that's for sure! It's strange that we went on to become such good mates.'

What surprised Higgins most was that for all Mercury's posturing antics he was, in reality, a very sensitive bloke. 'Fred was also a very good confidant,' he reveals. 'If I was feeling crap, he was good at noticing it – and drawing me out to talk about what was bothering me – and he'd always get me back on track. He was like that.

'He was a couple of years older than me, which seemed to

make all the difference, and it wasn't only with me either. He'd be there if anybody in the gang needed an ear, and, let's face it, at that age among blokes it's not often that someone notices, let alone cares. But Fred did, and he was very good at helping. He was a terrific listener.' As with much in Mercury's personality, this side of him mostly remained hidden, swamped in public by the outlandish clowning that he was allowing himself more freedom to express.

Mercury began to feel he had been in Ibex long enough to try to change something he considered important – the group's name. Mike Bersin recalls the way he went about it: 'He phoned me up one night saying that the others in the band weren't happy with the name Ibex, and, if I didn't object, the rest wanted it to be changed to Wreckage. I said that if that's what everyone else wanted, then it was fine by me. Two days later we met up at rehearsal and discovered that all our equipment had already been stencilled with the new name. It transpired we all got the same call that night! Having said that,' adds Mike, 'Wreckage was a good choice. It probably said more to people. Not many knew what an Ibex was and cared even less, I guess. But Freddie knew if a name sounded right.' What was interesting about Mercury's manoeuvrings was that he managed to give the illusion of democracy while neatly getting his own way and not upsetting anyone in the process.

While Smile frequently came to Liverpool to watch Ibex play – and to perform themselves, as Ken Testi would occasionally arrange gigs for them too – Mercury and the others returned equally often to London. Testi was frantically busy fixing up Wreckage with work, often at the last minute. 'This whole period was pretty hectic,' he recalls. 'I didn't know sometimes whether I was coming or going. Once we'd all been in London, and I'd hitched up to St Helen's because I'd decided to go to college there. I'd literally just got in the door when

Mike phoned to tell me that they'd had word that they were booked for the next day and asking if I could return to take them up in a van they'd borrowed. Nothing daunted, I grabbed a snack and started thumbing a lift back to London, arriving late that same day.

'Early next morning I hoofed it round to Imperial College, picking up Freddie en route, who was supposed to help me load the gear. It was a science college and not particularly set up for music, but they had a small rehearsal facility on the third floor of an obscure tower with a spiral staircase, and the gear was stashed at the top. Well, while I humped down a big bass cabinet on my back and all the other heavy gear, a trip at a time, in total Freddie managed three journeys; one carrying the maracas, the second with a tambourine, and the third time he took down a music stand that we didn't need. When I told him so, he replied with a gigantic sigh and a flick of his wrist, "Oh, could you possibly take it back up, then." He was bloody useless, but never mind he was there in spirit.'

All this effort was in aid of a gig at the Sink in Hardman Street, a basement club below the Rumbling Tum, which Geoff Higgins remembers well: 'The Sink was so small and clammy, it made the Cavern look like the Empire State Building. It wasn't licensed to sell alcohol, but they got around that by selling bottle tops at the door, which you then exchanged downstairs for ale. Anyway, that night Freddie was up to his usual tricks, cavorting about. We were always telling him, "For God's sake, man, stand still! It's really uncool to be poncing about the stage like that!" You just didn't do that in Liverpool, and we were forever telling him that he was embarrassing us, but Fred didn't take any notice. He was really into the look of things.'

It was just as well that he was concentrating on their image because, according to Higgins, the sound was way off. 'I taped that gig, and Wreckage were doing a Beatles number but giving it a mega over-the-top Wishbone Ash-type treatment, and Fred was lost. He was way off tune.'

There was to be, however, something very significant about this gig. Says Higgins, 'Smile had been playing the pre-dip ball at Liverpool Art College that same night, and afterwards they crashed in on our gig. No sooner had they arrived than they got up on stage with Wreckage, which meant that that gig, on 9 September 1969, was the first time that Freddie, Brian and Roger all played together on stage.'

Because Ken Testi was so worn out with all the travelling, he doesn't recall much about this gig, but he does remember the moment when Smile joined Wreckage: 'Freddie was really in his element when he guested on a few of Smile's numbers. He knew all their stuff by heart, you see.' Watching Mercury on stage, Testi maintains that apart from the odd occasion when he sang off key – Freddie was already rapidly developing as a performer: 'He had all the strong qualities that he would later bring to Queen; striding across in front of the band, using all those, now familiar, exaggerated gestures. He was bloody good.'

For all that, though, Liverpool was not where Freddie Mercury saw himself getting his big break. Soon after the Sink gig, he headed back to London with Mike Bersin and went on to graduate from Ealing Art College with a diploma in graphic art and design. He also teamed up again with Roger Taylor in Kensington market. Brian May was by now in his second year as a postgraduate student and still pursuing a career in astrophysics, having joined, as part of his PhD, a research team studying zodiacal light. The work involved long stretches away, building an observatory in Tenerife. Left alone more often with Roger Taylor, Mercury's relationship with the drummer developed into one of his strongest friendships.

Mercury's flat share with Mary Austin had ended while he was away in Liverpool, although she had often spent weekends with him in Merseyside. Once he was back in Kensington, they

didn't immediately start to live together again, and for a while
Mercury was homeless, part of a shifting galaxy of friends with
no fixed address. 'At this time no one really knew where
anyone was kipping,' Ken Testi says. 'I remember staying in one
mate's already overcrowded flat when there was a knock on the
door early one morning, and there was Roger clutching a mat-
tress, hoping to doss down.'

There was nothing grand about any of their accommodation
by late 1969. Most places they leased on a short-term basis, and
in any case they usually fell behind with the rent and were
evicted. Finally a few friends from Smile, Wreckage and other
bands found a flat in Ferry Road, Barnes. This was only supposed to house three people, however, and, according to Mike
Bersin, when the landlady came round for the rent, everyone
else would hide in the bedroom until she'd gone.

'The flat was ghastly,' Mike Bersin recalls. 'There were odd
chairs and a red vinyl sofa, which had burst at the seams in
places with ugly horsehair stuffing sprouting out. But we played
Led Zeppelin's first album all day, every day, on the old mono-
gram record player, until the needle wore out. At that age,
though, it was wonderful. Lager and lime was the big drink,
and you went about without shoes on your feet, which in dog-
shit covered pavements wasn't the best of ideas, but there was
just such an amazing buzz at the end of the sixties. It was post-
pill and pre-AIDS, and promiscuity felt mandatory rather than
optional. It was kind of romantic, too, jumping into a battered
old van and travelling miles to play gigs practically for free.'

Although fastidious by nature, Mercury wholeheartedly
shared in the chaos of the Ferry Road flat. He thrived, too, on
its atmosphere of camaraderie, and it was here that he seriously
began to write songs, as well as rehearsing harmonies with May
and Taylor. 'Freddie loved talking music, would burn with
enthusiasm when he was trying things out,' Mike Bersin says.
'He had endless patience, too, and would show you anything

you needed to learn on piano. On that level you could get close to him, but probably only on that level.

'Fred and I wrote a couple of songs together, which was quite an experience. If he thought there was a song in the offing in you, he drove you enthusiastically all the way until you got there.' In tribute, after Mercury's death, Roger Taylor spoke of how intensely he drove the others in Queen, forever determined to get the best out of them.

'That determination to succeed was an irresistible force in Freddie from the start,' maintains Mike Bersin. 'And it was like a moving train. Once it pulls away, you can't impede it by holding on to the door handle. You either jump on and go with it, or you step back and let go. And everyone around Freddie either went with it or they didn't. People were forever calling out jokingly as soon as he arrived on the scene, "Ah, here comes Freddie, the star!" but it was all good-natured.'

Of these crazy days, Tim Staffell recalls, 'I never lived there but was always visiting as Pat McConnell and I were close-ish at the time. I smoked my first joint there and was absolutely transfixed by Freddie's Frank Zappa album *Only In It for the Money*. The actress Sylvia Sims lived next door, I seem to recall.'

Geoff Higgins occasionally stayed at Ferry Road, too. 'There were at least three bedrooms,' he says. 'Freddie, Roger and another bloke shared the first one you came to on your right when you came in, and the two other bedrooms were at the end of a long corridor. People came out of them, but I never saw a soul go in! It was very strange. Then there was the breakfast room, where Freddie, Brian and Mike would write songs. "Son and Daughter" was definitely written there because they went over and over it one Sunday morning when I was recovering from a major hangover. They were driving me nuts trying to get it right.'

As well as penning songs at the breakfast table, Mercury had bought a cheap guitar, which wasn't actually of much musical value. Mike Bersin confirms: 'No, Freddie could strum a little bit, maybe play a couple of chords at a push, but that's it. Mind you, he wasn't above taking a guitar off of you, to show you how it would look better if you did this with it, or that. A guitar was a prop to Fred.' Mercury was soon to graduate to a better class of prop with a white Fender Telecaster electric guitar. He wasn't bothered with details such as plugging it in. He just loved to dangle it strategically low round his neck and make a nuisance of himself at the crack of dawn as a wandering minstrel. He would prowl the flat, stepping over the sleeping bodies and serenading them with his latest favourite chart hit, the Who's 'Pinball Wizard'.

Financial realities such as paying the rent and buying food were an unwelcome interruption to his dreams of stardom. But as his income from the stall wasn't enough to live on, Mercury had to take on an extra job; one that at least utilised his art-school training. 'Freddie sketched all the time to keep his hand in,' Mike Bersin says, 'and at some point drew us all. But one day I happened to look over his shoulder and saw that he was sketching a woman in her underwear, and I said, "OK, what's going on here then, Fred?" It turned out Freddie was making ends meet by doing fashion drawings for newspaper adverts.'

Mike Benin's momentary confusion about Mercury's sketches was not supported by any doubts about his sexual preferences. Geoff Higgins recalls, 'Freddie would ask me along to Kenny market saying, "Come and help me sell something today, for fuck sake," and when I was there some of his friends would turn up. They were all as effeminate as him, but at the time we mostly thought they were just larking about.'

While Ken Testi explains: 'In these touchy times it's hard to find the right words to describe Freddie without offending someone, but it was common then to see him behaving in a very affected manner. He certainly displayed all the qualities we attribute to gay people. But then again he and Mary had become a fixture in a relatively short space of time, so it was hard to tell. To be honest, no one took that much notice. There was too much else of more importance going on. Like having fun.'

Fun was always a high priority then, and Higgins reveals that 'At Kensington market we'd get a regular supply of marijuana which was mixed with jasmine tea, and once home we'd take turns to separate the grass from the tea. Years later Freddie was heavily into cocaine, but in those days he wouldn't go near dope of any kind. One day "Tupp" took home the tea but dumped it, still all mixed together, by the kettle and went straight out. Freddie came home and made himself a pot of tea. God! By the time we got in he was completely out of his head.

'His prized album was *Only In It for the Money*, and one track features a noise like a stylus scraping across the disc. He was freaking out to this album and busy wheeling about the flat waving his arms around when he heard the scraping noise and dashed straight to the record to examine it, thinking somebody had scratched his precious LP. He was well gone that day.'

When Mercury later found out what had happened to him, he thought it was a great joke that he couldn't wait to play on someone else as equally unsuspecting as himself. His chance came when two policemen arrived at the flat one night to break up a particularly rowdy party. Playing the accommodating host, he offered the officers tea and cakes – baked with marijuana – which they promptly accepted.

That Mercury had no interest in drugs then is confirmed by Ken Testi: 'To my knowledge Freddie had no involvement with drugs of any kind at this point, and even his alcohol consumption was limited. He wasn't particularly into excesses of any kind. Part of the reason for that, of course, again came down to money. He didn't have much of it to splash about on booze and getting Freddie to let someone buy him a drink was a bit of an uphill struggle, too, but if he did agree, you can bet he wouldn't have a beer. He'd say, "A port and lemon then, if you insist, my dear. For the voice, you know.'"

For Mercury, the chance to use his voice wasn't frequent enough with Wreckage, and he had begun to show an interest in the possibility of joining another band. Scanning the music press for singers-wanted ads, he sent out several applications, receiving only one reply. Taking Roger Taylor with him for moral support, Mercury went to Leatherhead for the audition, armed with his precious personal Schure microphone and numerous ideas on how to win them over.

The band, with the unlikely name of Sour Milk Sea, comprised Paul Milne, Rob Tyrell, Jeremy Gallop and Chris Chesney. They were, as planned, knocked out by Mercury's panache and promptly gave him the job. But his reign with this band was brief, playing almost as few gigs as rehearsal sessions, nearly all in Oxford. At seventeen, Chris Chesney was six years younger than Mercury, but the two quickly became close friends, and Chris moved into the Ferry Road flat for a time. Unhappy with the guitarist's sudden allegiance to their new lead singer, the other members of Sour Milk Sea grew disgruntled, and the band folded within weeks. Soon afterwards, Chesney left Barnes and returned to Oxford.

The year 1969 had proved to be a good one for Mercury. Probably for the first time since his family had moved to Britain, he felt truly among friends; some of them would be with him for life. And in his private life, although the future held complications, for now he had found a unique and loving bond with a woman who was devoted to him. Professionally, however, he was dissatisfied. Despite the brief interlude with Sour Milk Sea, he remained lead singer with Wreckage, but their prospects were dim. The same could be said of Smile. A recent showcase gig at the prestigious Marquee Club in London's Wardour Street had been a disaster, and the band's relationship with Mercury Records was beginning to turn stale.

There was a general despondency, but, like Mercury himself, Brian May and Roger Taylor were still ambitious for success in the rock world. Tim Staffell, a songwriter showing increasing signs of seeking his own direction, seemed restless. Within Smile, the scent of change was in the air. Always on the alert, Mercury was poised and ready, just waiting in the wings.

THREE

What's In a Name?

At the beginning of the seventies, Mercury conceded defeat. Wreckage were never going to be famous, and rather than prolong the agony, he made a clear-cut decision to leave the band. By day he still worked the Kensington market stall, his income now supplemented with freelance commissions for the Austin Knight commercial art agency. The rest of the time he spent deep in discussion with Brian May, Roger Taylor and Tim Staffell – who were all aware, too, that Smile's days were numbered.

'Like most student bands, we suffered from a lack of finance,' says Staffell. 'We'd played some notable gigs and backed some great names, and we'd had a good time doing it, but for me now was the time to move on.' In late February 1970 he decided to quit. 'I was tired of playing rock full blast,' he explains. 'So I went to see Colin Petersen, ex-drummer with the Bee Gees, to audition for his band.' Staffell wasn't sure that he was making the right move, but he felt strongly that he was now searching for a quieter style than Smile's. 'I left for my own reasons, but in a sense I was moving out of the way, and the birth of Queen was an inevitable outcome of that,' he adds.

With Staffell's departure Mercury Records, not unexpectedly, parted company with May and Taylor. It was no particular loss on either side. Relations had been cool for some time, and with their contract fulfilled, there was nowhere else to go. Convinced it was simply a watershed moment in their careers, May and Taylor remained undaunted, and with Staffell out of the frame, Mercury lost no time muscling in on the act. After their resistance to letting him join Smile, it now seemed only natural to team up with the live-wire singer. As friends there had been plenty of time to recognise each other's talent and common ambition: to take the rock world by storm.

In April 1970 Freddie Mercury, Brian May and Roger Taylor formed a new band. Their immediate task was to find a bass player, and Taylor suggested Mike Grose. A former member of Reaction, Grose was also co-owner of PJ's in Truro; just a few weeks before, when Smile had played there, he had helped out the band at the last moment, so they knew he was a good musician.

'When Roger rang and asked me to join the band it was good timing because PJ's was under a demolition order,' says Mike Grose. 'They hadn't actually named themselves Queen at this stage, but it was the three of them plus a bass player, which I agreed would be me.' Grose accepted their offer of a flat share in Earls Court and packing up vital equipment – his guitar and a huge, much-needed Marshall amplifier – he left Cornwall for London in his Volkswagen van; another valuable asset he would be bringing to the band.

In the past when Smile had played PJ's, Mike Grose had sometimes witnessed friction between Roger Taylor and Tim Staffell. Once in London it didn't take him long to discover that this time Taylor and Mercury were often at odds. 'It was a cramped flat,' he explains, 'with four guys sharing one bedroom. Two girls were there as well who had the other room along the passage and that was it. There was a garden, but it could get very claustrophobic, and Roger and Freddie used to squabble a lot. If it got too much for Brian, he would go home to his parents for a while.'

Sometimes the squabbling arose from discussions over the band's direction, but there was little doubt about who won here. 'Both Roger and Brian had plenty to say,' stresses Mike Grose, 'and even I had input. But Freddie was the ideas man. He had great plans. They were pretty intense about practising, too, and twice a week we went to a room at Imperial College that Brian had got permission for us to use.'

As well as this, all four band members would often sit outside in the garden, bouncing suggestions around, in imaginative brainstorming sessions that drove Mercury and May to write some new material. 'What would turn out to be their first single "Keep Yourself Alive" and also "Seven Seas of Rhye" came out of sessions like that,' reveals Mike Grose. 'Even ones like "Killer Queen", which came a good bit later, were rumbling around in those days.'

According to Grose, what to call the band occupied much of their thoughts: 'I clearly recall that the name Queen came up for the first time one day while we were all in the garden. It was Freddie's suggestion, of course, and he also wanted to design a very rude logo based around the letter Q, but the others downed that right away.'

Having waited a year for the chance to form a band with May and Taylor, Mercury was keen to go. To him, everything they'd been involved in so far was just a precursor of better things to come. He saw this as his chance to find fame – but to make the band into something special it was vital that they presented themselves with a professional polish that left nothing to chance. Mercury's ambitions for Queen were on a grand scale so it's possible that his indecent proposal for the logo was no more than a distraction. He had cleverly engineered the change from Ibex to Wreckage, so perhaps he decided that, by giving May and Taylor the satisfaction of dismissing his outrageous idea for the logo, they would be more likely to allow him to have his own way with the name,

Queen. This was a change that he considered crucial to his plans.

Mercury put his case strongly. Queen was short and therefore memorable. It was a universal concept, with a majestic ring that undoubtedly appealed. It was perhaps the latter quality that eventually sealed it, but still there was one drawback – there was no way of avoiding the camp overtones of the name, something Mercury himself acknowledged. 'It was open to all sorts of interpretation. I was certainly aware of the gay connotations.' This was presumably satisfactory for Mercury, who, as Geoff Higgins puts it, had been 'poncing about' for a long time now, but the other band members had to decide whether they wanted to promote themselves with an image like that. Rock was, after all, a very macho, male-dominated world.

Brian May ran the idea past Ken Reay, his tutor at Imperial College, who, acquainted with Mercury, had no need to ask who was behind the suggestion. 'I wouldn't say Brian had much trouble with it though,' admits Reay. 'Certainly he recognised it would be risqué, but that seemed to amuse him more than anything. The bottom line was, he saw it as being a very good move to call themselves Queen.' In no time the vote was unanimous, and once again Mercury had got what he wanted without anyone else noticing that they had been steam-rollered into it.

Watching all this debate over the band's name at the time, with hindsight Mike Grose feels that it ought to have told him something: 'Freddie was a super guy. We went out drinking together a lot, and I didn't have a clue that he was gay.' It wasn't that Mercury obviously enjoyed the company of women and, unlike some gay men, liked them around him in his life, nor that he had a steady girlfriend. As others would later attest, Mercury's homosexuality was not something he generally flaunted when out socialising.

With Grose as their new bassist, the band looked forward to

their first gig. It was again in Truro, this time at the City Hall on 27 June 1970, but after all Mercury's efforts to adopt the name Queen, they were billed as Smile. 'It was a long-standing booking,' explains Mike Grose. 'I suppose we could've notified them that the band was different, but we didn't bother.'

The gig was a charity performance, organised by the Cornish branch of the British Red Cross, and although the hall held 800 people, only a fraction turned up, which, according to Grose, was a stroke of luck. 'We were a bit rough at the edges that night,' he admits. 'We had practised, but playing live is different to rehearsing in a college classroom. We also got a bit lost with one of us remembering a different arrangement on a song to the rest. We did our best to hide the gaffes but, let's put it this way, we didn't expect to be asked back.'

Collective gaffes aside, Mercury was unhappy with his personal performance. Not even the generous £50 fee, which they were relieved to receive at the end of the night, eradicated his self-recriminations – how unpolished he'd been – and for days he dissected the gig, analysing precisely where he had gone wrong. There was a plus side, however, for they had undoubtedly left a strong visual impression. The statutory stage wear of current bands such as Free and Black Sabbath was faded denims and T-shirts, but Mercury's vision for Queen from the outset was to stand out from the crowd. When they took the stage at Truro's City Hall, they were dressed stylishly in black silk, and weighed down with gaudy junk jewellery.

The strength of their visual impact was some consolation to Mercury, but he was still frustrated that the band had not yet performed officially as Queen. Keen for them to start promoting themselves properly, he would insist this never happened again. And he was equally adamant about the decision he had now reached to change his own name. Countless performers had done this as a matter of course, but Mercury's reasons seem fairly deep-rooted.

The name Bulsara tied him too firmly to his Persian ancestry, and as Queen's first PR man, Tony Brainsby, confirms, Mercury was always careful during interviews to avoid any reference to his Asian background. His parents' religion and culture represented a world from which he had been distancing himself for some time. Although his name change was not intended as a slight to his family, he preferred to close the door on Farrokh Bulsara and reinvent himself as someone else – someone synonymous with glamour, fame and strength. For this he delved into Roman mythology and chose Mercury, the messenger of the gods. As of July 1970, Queen's lead singer was to be known as Freddie Mercury.

Friends accepted the change easily, but for Ken Testi, with whom Mercury had stayed in touch after leaving Wreckage, the new band name came as a shock: 'Since no one stayed in a flat with a phone, we kept in touch by using the public call box at the end of the aisle at Kensington market, where Fred and Roger worked. Freddie wanted me to help get the band bookings, and one day he rang me at St Helens, urging me to fix them up with some gigs as soon as possible. I asked him what they were calling themselves now, and Fred said, "Queen". Well, I guess that was a giveaway when you think about it, but anyway I gasped, "Freddie! You can't get away with that!" To which he replied airily, "But of course we can, my dear."'

But behind the cavalier façade lay a calculating brain. Although they had been formed for only a few weeks, Queen's lack of progress was wearing them down. Playing local gigs was all very well – though even then bookings didn't just drop out of the sky – but their horizons went far beyond that. They wanted the band to attract the interest of record companies. Apart from Smile's brief liaison with Mercury Records, none of them could boast any real experience of how to do this. But they refused to be deterred, and Mercury had already put the first phase of his attack into operation.

In those days, Kensington High Street thronged each weekend with people who could be helpful to an aspiring band. Fully aware of this, Mercury made a point of being there. His apparently effortless display, mincing up and down the street, draped in velvet and fur, with feather boas tossed casually around his neck, concealed a determined attempt to catch the eye of the media, preferably someone useful from the record industry. Ken Testi confirms that 'This was an every Saturday occurrence. He'd go on the prowl up and down Ken High Street. Sure there was a bonus – he could cruise, and it was very important to Freddie to go on the promenade – but he never lost sight of the fact that he was there for a more important reason, and it was a case of, you never know your luck.'

Queen were counting on a showcase gig they had arranged for mid-July at Imperial College. The audience would include their friends, who could be depended upon to clap enthusiastically, but the bulk of the audience, they hoped, would consist of the music executives whom they had personally invited. It didn't turn out to be their night, though. Some executives did turn up, and the band's friends did their best to make the gig swing, but absolutely nothing came of it.

Having to content himself with the knowledge that at least their performance was improving, Mercury shelved his disappointment and concentrated instead on a gig just over a week away, on 25 July, at PJ's in Truro. They would be publicly billed here as Queen for the first time, but this gig turned out to be the last for Mike Grose. 'Basically, I'd had enough of never earning decent money and of living in squalor,' reveals Grose. 'I thought, to hell with it. There wasn't any animosity, and in fact Roger rang me up a fortnight later to ask me back, but I didn't want to.'

When Mike Grose left that August, he had an uneasy feeling that he was walking away from something special. But, at twenty-three, having played already for six years, he was ready to quit. By contrast, Mercury, at much the same age, was driven all the more to succeed. Time was not running out for the band, but by their mid-twenties most rock stars were established. Queen remained in its infancy, and was now short of a bass player.

There was some urgency to fill the vacancy left by Mike Grose, for in less than three weeks' time they had a booking at Imperial College. For a second time Roger Taylor's West Country connections proved useful, when Barry Mitchell heard in Cornwall that a London band were in desperate need of a bass player. 'I was given a number to ring,' says Mitchell, 'and Roger invited me to meet them. I went to the flat they were sharing around the corner from Imperial College, and from there we walked to a lecture theatre for my audition. We did a couple of bluesy numbers then returned to the flat for a chat, when it was kind of generally agreed that I'd passed and was in.'

Fresh-faced with long blond hair, Barry Mitchell looked the part as well as being good on bass. But he never felt that he quite fitted in. May later called Queen an 'efficient little machine', clearly resistant to outsiders, and Mercury, May and Taylor were established as something of a clique. Nevertheless, Mitchell looked forward to the new challenge. His first impressions of Mercury were clear: 'Outside band business Freddie was very deep, and you never knew quite what to make of him. But professionally it was obvious right from the start that he was the driving force in the band. His ideas to be flamboyant, to wear women's clothes on stage and so on were, without doubt, all very much part of his plan to grab as much attention as possible. It's the same as him naming the group Queen. He knew exactly what he was doing.'

Mitchell's debut with Queen took place on 23 August. Performing again in front of an invited audience, it was hoped this show would be their springboard to fame. By now

Mercury's anticipation had reached fever pitch, and he'd asked a dressmaker friend to make him a couple of special stage outfits, based upon his own rough sketches. He saw himself in a slinky black one-piece of sensuous material, so figure-hugging that it left little to the imagination. Slashed dramatically to the waist to expose his hairy chest, with a quilted wing effect at the wrists and ankles, he called it his 'Mercury suit' and commissioned a replica in white. Getting ready for that gig, Freddie Mercury was to take their new bass player by surprise in other ways, too.

'I walked into the flat and stopped dead at the sight of Freddie not only in this outfit, but with great big curlers in his hair,' says Mitchell. 'I thought, Wait a minute! What's this? I came from long-haired, greasy blues bands, and I wasn't getting into any of this lark.' Unperturbed by Mitchell's dismay, Mercury continued meticulously painting his fingernails black and making the finishing touches to his hair with a set of heated curling tongs that he wielded like a pro.

But it wasn't only Mercury's stage clothes that were different. There was also the extraordinary trouble the band was prepared to take to please their audience. Mitchell recalls that 'Earlier that same day, I'd been round at the flat to help them get things ready. We were making our own popcorn and orange juice, which was being laid on free of charge. It sounds corny nowadays, but it was a heck of a lot more than other bands did.' There was no return on their hospitality, however, and they reverted to scraping together as many gigs as possible. Mitchell admits, 'Queen were busier than any band I'd been used to. We played another gig at a private school in London not long after that night, but it was the Liverpool scene that was special then, and it was clear they [Queen] had good local connections.'

Those Merseyside connections continued to be made through Ken Testi. By now social secretary at St Helen's College of Technology, part of his job involved booking bands for college dances, and as such, he was invaluable to Queen. Even so, at the beginning of September, bookings dried up when May's academic studies required another trip to Tenerife, leaving Mercury, Taylor and Barry Mitchell to content themselves with rehearsals. One practice session, in particular, remains vivid in Mitchell's memory.

'It was on 18 September,' he says. 'I arrived at the flat to meet the others and had just walked in when Freddie, very pale-faced, asked, "Have you heard? Jimi Hendrix is dead." God, the stunned feeling was immense. He'd been our idol, and we were all absolutely shattered. Freddie and Roger closed their stall that day as a mark of respect, but by night we were still in a state of shock, so at rehearsal, as our own tribute, we played nothing but Hendrix songs the whole session.'

Hendrix's death had genuinely shaken Mercury. The American guitarist, singer and songwriter was one of a handful of artistes whose influence played a tangible role in shaping his own musical taste, which as Ken Testi reveals, was difficult to define: 'Freddie's album collection in those days struggled to get into double figures, and those he did have he kept flat in a drawer. He had Liza Minnelli's *Cabaret*, *The Beatles* (*White Album*) and *Sgt. Pepper*, Led Zeppelin's first album, because he loved all the power chords, the Who's *Tommy* and one by the Pretty Things called *SF Sorrow*, which Freddie considered to be the first rock opera.'

Mercury himself cited his two major influences as Minnelli and Hendrix, an odd cocktail which perhaps helps to explain the showbiz flair that formed such an integral part of his own performing style. It is often said that you can tell a lot about a person from their record collection, but this ragbag selection of Mercury's was only confusing. He was right, however, about *SF Sorrow* – it was the first rock opera.

The Pretty Things had deserted their early R&B roots and were involved in London's psychedelic underground scene.

When *SF Sorrow* was released back in December 1968, it was
critically acclaimed several weeks before the appearance of the
Who's now much-vaunted *Tommy*. The band's lead guitarist,
Dick Taylor, formerly an original member of the Rolling
Stones, confirms, 'We recorded our album before *Tommy*, and
in fact, there's a track on it which sounds extremely like
"Pinball Wizard". Phil [May] had concocted a story, and we all
wrote songs around that. It was kind of surreal and poetic and
quite complex, about someone's life and death. To tell you the
truth, I don't think I've ever really understood it myself, but the
thing is, it was certainly pre-*Tommy*. But the Who got their
album out in the States first, and that was all it took for *SF
Sorrow* to get sidelined, and *Tommy* hailed as the first rock
opera.'

Dick Taylor and his then wife, Melissa, were friends with
Mercury and Mary Austin. 'Melissa worked at Biba, when
Mary worked at reception, and it was through their friendship
that I got to know Freddie,' says Dick Taylor. 'We met up
often, and I never knew he felt that way about our album, but
it doesn't surprise me. He really was very quiet in private. He
didn't say much at all to many people, at any time. He invited
us to some of their gigs when he was newly starting out, and I
was very impressed with how hard he was working at it. When
I saw him with Queen later on the telly I thought, Blimey,
that's a bit over the top.'

Mary Austin's increasing significance in Mercury's life continued to deflect any doubts about his sexuality. 'Although ours
was very much a business arrangement,' says Barry Mitchell, 'I'd
often head off to the market to see Freddie and Roger, just to
knock about. Freddie was always full of wild gestures, hands
flying around, and would be very demonstrative when he
greeted you. Don't get me wrong, he was great fun, and we all
got used to him, but all this limp wrist stuff – I was sure it was
all part of the act. I already knew what he was up to with the

band's image, and I assumed this caper was just an extension of that. I never wondered seriously about him being gay, because there was no sign of anything other than a heterosexual relationship with Mary.

'As a couple, what came across most was that they were very good friends. There was a solidity there, even then. Freddie trusted Mary ever so much. She was someone he could confide in.'

For Ken Testi, now effectively Queen's manager, Mary Austin was something of an enigma: 'She was good-looking, quiet, caring and ever so sweet but difficult to really get to know. I think later on, when stardom came along, that Freddie developed in similar vein. And the thing is people who do get close to a star tend to protect their own closeness by excluding others from getting to the star, and as such it creates a huge, impenetrable cladding around that person, which becomes highly exclusive to outside influences. By the time this happened with Freddie he might very well have wanted it that way, but personally I'm not so sure.'

The rarefied exclusivity to which Ken Testi refers was years away then, and in 1970 Mercury was only too glad of Testi's help in securing bookings for Queen, which still tended to focus to a large extent on the Liverpool area. 'Every time I booked them for a gig up north I tried to make it worth their while by booking another one for the next night,' Testi explains. In those days Testi's mother ran the Market Hotel in St Helens, which was where Queen stayed on these weekend trips.

'There were only ten letting rooms,' he goes on, 'but whenever the band came up my mum would give them beds if she had any to spare. If not, they'd sleep on my bedroom floor. But she always made sure they all got a cooked breakfast in the morning. Freddie, without fail, made sure they gave her a big box of chocolates for her trouble.'

One weekend at the end of October 1970 still stands out as memorable for Geoff Higgins and Barry Mitchell. As usual, St Helen's Tech featured on the first night, and Higgins was there. He remembers Mercury being more obsessed than usual with his looks that night and recalls, 'Queen were using the college kitchen as a dressing room, and Freddie had poured himself into the tightest velvet trousers I'd seen. There was a seam up the back of each leg, like in ladies' nylons, and he was going berserk trying to get them to lie straight. Eventually he asked Ken to get him a big mirror, so he nipped off to the fashion department and returned with a full-length one. Well, Fred started writhing and twisting furiously, struggling to straighten these seams, and he flatly refused to go on stage until he got them right, no matter if it made the band very late.'

When they did finally prise Mercury away from the cheval-glass to perform, it had all been hardly worth it: 'London progressive rock, which is what they were playing, was just a no-no in Liverpool, and they were flogging a dead horse trying to serve up that music that night,' Higgins reveals.

They were to perform the same set the following evening, but the excitement of the venue overrode any doubts left over from the night before. 'Freddie was a huge Beatles fan, and so when I fixed up this Halloween gig at the Cavern he was thrilled,' recalls Ken Testi. But the omens were not good. Mitchell's amp chose that night to die, and when he plugged in his guitar to another band's equipment, it promptly exploded.

'The Cavern itself, though, was quite an amazing place,' maintains Mitchell. 'For all its reputation, it was nothing but a dingy basement, with so many people squeezed inside it that it became a cauldron, with their sweat making condensation run down the brick walls. Yet undeniably it had something.'

What the night didn't have was a front man singing in tune. Just as Higgins revealed that Mercury often sang off-key when fronting Wreckage, so Mitchell confirms continuing problems with the fledgling Queen: 'And it wasn't just the Cavern night either. I didn't rate Freddie's voice at all in those days. He didn't always hold the note very well. There wasn't a lot of depth to his voice, which was, to be blunt, pretty thin.

'Years later he was absolutely amazing and could hit and hold practically any note in creation. I've often wondered, in fact, if he took voice training on the quiet, although that's always been hotly denied.'

With Mercury's intermittently unreliable singing voice, Queen played a shaky handful of bookings in the next couple of months, only to end the year on a sour note. 'We had a New Year's Eve gig in one of the Imperial College refectories,' recalls Barry Mitchell, 'but we got stopped after only half an hour. They asked us to pack up, so that they could put on the disco. They said we were too loud and gave this and that excuse, but it was obvious they just didn't like us. Freddie was completely disgusted. He argued with the bloke, saying, "You've got live music here, man! And you want to put on records?!" He was thoroughly cheesed off about it.'

Following that gig, Barry Mitchell decided to leave Queen: 'I didn't feel that they were going anywhere,' he explains, 'and not just because Freddie was often flat. Plus I didn't like where they were headed musically. Freddie, in particular, although he liked rock 'n' roll, was into the sort of music I wasn't used to. He forever wanted to make it more intricate and much more melodic. The band was playing hard-rock stuff, but Freddie's influences were definitely very tuneful.

'They were getting heavily into performing all their own compositions, too, which I personally didn't like. Queen's first two albums contained what I felt was a lot of pretentious stuff, although they found their hard-rock base eventually.'

Mitchell honoured the immediate two dates of 1971, the first of which, on 8 January, marked Queen's debut at the

Marquee. His final gig with the band came the next night, at Ewell Technical College, Surrey, when, with Genesis, they played support to Kevin Ayres and the Whole World Band. What Barry Mitchell remembers best about that night is Peter Gabriel's persistent attempts to talk Roger Taylor into joining Genesis. But unlike Mitchell, Taylor elected to stay with Queen.

Mitchell had lasted longer than Grose, yet still Queen had got through two bass players in ten months. They had six weeks before their next gig, and surveying the available musicians, they called on the services of someone else on the session circuit temporarily to fill the gap. Within the space of two gigs, this was a decision they came to regret. The excitable bassist cavorted about the stage like a lunatic; with Mercury's increasingly bold stage act, there was room for only one flamboyant focus. The musician was not invited back after a gig at Kingston Polytechnic on 20 February.

That last gig was in support of Yes and Wishbone Ash. Wishbone's lead guitarist, Andy Powell, confirms that Queen's music was still based in progressive rock: 'What they were playing then was similar to us, although having said that you could certainly detect an edge to them that was a bit more mainstream, and it wasn't long after that that they became a glam band.'

A former Kingston Polytechnic student, Tony Blackman, recalls that night, too: 'Two things have stuck in my memory. The first is that although Queen, whom nobody really knew at this time, were supporting Yes and Wishbone, they amazingly didn't come over in any way as second rate. And also their image stood out. Dressed completely in black, their clothes were skintight, and there was no doubt about the fact that they were going out of their way, particularly the singer, to project an effeminate image. That kind of thing just wasn't done in those days, but he was flaunting it.'

Queen's on-stage confidence was undermined by their frustration at the lack of a bass player. They made a huge effort to see other bands, in the hope of finding the right person to replace Barry Mitchell. This paid off when May and Taylor attended a dance held at the Maria Assumpta Teacher Training College, Kensington, where Brian May's by then steady girlfriend, Christine Mullen, was studying. Here, they were to meet John Richard Deacon, a student too, and one who played bass guitar.

Since childhood, John Deacon had played guitar and, gripped by Beatlemania, had formed his first band by 1966. Leaving school three years later, he had enrolled at Chelsea College in London to study electronics. He retained his love of music and attended various shows, including an earlier Queen gig. He had been less than impressed at the time. Four months later it was a different story when he heard that Queen was looking for a bass player. His flatmate Peter Stoddart knew May and Taylor, and it was through Stoddart that he met them that night, with the express purpose of offering them his services.

Neither Taylor nor May could believe their luck, and they invited Deacon to audition for Queen at Imperial College a few days later. Two things impressed them about him, apart from his obvious musical skill: his knowledge of electronics, which with experience of faulty equipment in the past was no small consideration, and his placid manner. Similar in temperament to Brian May, and opposite to the vibrancy of Freddie Mercury and Roger Taylor, he seemed to promise to balance the band. John Deacon joined Queen in late February 1971. He was to be the final piece in their line-up.

Months of intensive rehearsal followed, so that by the summer they were able to accept bookings. For much of this time Brian May was absent, once again committed to his PhD studies in the Canaries. But the band was thriving, and confident that they were finally on the right track. Mercury threw himself enthusiastically into their practice sessions. He was determined to learn from past mistakes – and doubtless to work on his voice. He couldn't wait to get started with what, at last, felt instinctively like the complete Queen.

FOUR

Blind Faith

John Deacon played his first gig with Queen at a Surrey college on 2 July 1971, followed just over a week later by his initial appearance at Imperial College. In the late sixties, Smile had been known as 'the Imperial College band'; Brian May himself was an IC student, and Freddie Mercury for a long time had been part of that crowd. Deacon felt an outsider, and he wasn't sure what reaction he'd get. It turned out to be potentially a special night when record producer John Anthony, with whom Smile had worked two years before, was spotted in the audience. As he left, he gave the band encouragement and said casually that he would be in touch.

Mercury wasn't too hopeful. He had witnessed Smile's excitement at Lou Reizner's earlier interest, but remembered all too well how that had worked out. With Queen, Mercury was looking for something more substantial than the hint of a promise. It was a wise attitude to take because there was no immediate phone call from John Anthony. Instead, what preoccupied everyone was simply how to survive.

Roger Taylor registered for a biology degree course, for which he would be eligible for a grant. In July 1971 he enrolled at the North London Polytechnic to study plant and animal biology. Brian May had been giving tutorials at Imperial for a small fee, and Freddie Mercury, in an attempt to shore up the often non-existent takings at the market stall, continued to seek commissions with commercial art agencies but hardly anyone responded to his efforts.

In these early days, bookings were as essential for the money as for the work experience and exposure. Their four-month rehearsal period, to integrate John Deacon into the band, meant that although the year was half over, they had only played a total of six gigs. But Roger Taylor's Cornish connections came to the rescue again when he managed to arrange a West Country tour, this time involving almost as many gigs as they had played during the whole of 1970.

Kicking off on 17 July at the Garden in Penzance, the tour could hardly be classed as uneventful. Gigging through Wadebridge, Hayle and St Agnes, nightly rows with pub landlords over the volume at which they insisted on playing became a standard occurrence. The band had learnt to make sure they were paid before a gig, for fear of being deprived of their fee at the end of the evening. Their unconventional stage image – in particular Mercury's penchant for ambiguously sidling up to May as he played on guitar – combined with their long hair provoked heated reactions from some locals, including servicemen from nearby RAF Culdrose. On occasions they had to make a swift getaway.

Being pursued by a car full of drunks psyched up for a fight was a hair-raising experience, while the buzz of outwitting them on the road could also provide an amusing anecdote later. None of this squared with Mercury's vision for the future. That still lay in trying to persuade the music moguls that Queen was worth signing. When the tour ended with a gig at the Carnon Downs Festival, Truro, in late August, Mercury couldn't wait to get back to London. There, May's IC contacts remained good, and there were plans for another private show, in early October, this time to an invited audience from a selection of London booking agencies. So far, their gigs had been mostly in town halls, colleges and pubs, even young farmers' clubs. Their goal was a foothold in the major venues, and that meant wooing the right people.

Mercury's return to London brought a welcome change in his personal life. He and Mary Austin had been sharing a poky flat together again, close to Kensington market, but they had had plans to move on for some time. Tired of the nomadic existence of the past few years, living in varying degrees of discomfort, Mercury had decided to move upmarket, as much as he could afford. He still wished to stay in Kensington and had found somewhere he liked, as Ken Testi recalls.

'Freddie went on to own some fabulous homes, but the first place he really coveted was a ground-floor flat at 100 Holland Park Road. It was more spacious than he'd known to date, but what he thought was bloody marvellous was the ritzy sound of the address. He loved that. It was very important to him, and he also recognised the benefits of having a good address.

'There was a substantial front room, which thrilled him because it was the first place any of them had had where you could fit all the members of the band sitting down at the same time. As a result, a lot of discussion as to their musical future took place there.' According to Testi, the new apartment also featured in small ways then in Mercury's songwriting: 'The opening lyric in "Killer Queen", which speaks of a woman keeping Moet & Chandon in a pretty cabinet, referred to a beautiful cabinet Freddie was particularly proud of at that time,' he claims.

A future connoisseur of the good things in life, exquisite furniture and art were always important to Mercury, even in the days when they were financially out of reach. But even then, in small ways, he managed to indulge his sense of refinement, as Testi recalls: 'I remember being round for a meal one day, and Mary reverently brought out a few beautiful plates they'd bought from Barkers, and it may sound twee in this day and age but there was something very special in the care both of them took to make their flat a home. It had a sense of care and charm.'

Of their relationship at this time, he adds, 'They were nice together, very much a couple. Somehow one always felt that them being together was appropriate. When Freddie later ended up with a helluva profile internationally, I always felt for Mary and still, she went with him to award ceremonies, and was always a foil for all the talk when Freddie himself was into denial.'

Mercury was now concentrating once more on the band's progress. Their showcase gig was a month away, but he guarded against raising his hopes too high. A recent development, though, held much more promise. It involved Terry Yeadon, a friend of May's, who was to provide Queen with their first real break.

In the autumn of 1971 Terry Yeadon was involved in setting up De Lane Lea, a recording studio in Engineers Way, Wembley. He had known Brian May from his Smile days, and in 1969, as maintenance engineer at Pye Studios in London's Marble Arch, he had worked informally with the band, recording a couple of acetates of 'Step on Me' and 'Polar Bear'. After that they'd all lost touch for a couple of years.

'By this time Geoff Calvar, a disc-cutting engineer, and I were putting together this new complex in Wembley,' says Yeadon. 'There were three studios, and we had a problem with isolation between them. We were carrying out tests like firing pistols in one studio, while taping in the next to see if it picked up the noise. And we'd just come to the conclusion that we really needed a rock band to play loud, when out of the blue Brian appeared saying that he was in a new band with a new singer and a full-time bassist. Like when he wanted me to record Smile back in the sixties, this time he was hoping that I could record Queen. This was right up my street, so we made a deal. They played as we tested, and all the while they had a few demos cut!'

Mercury was ecstatic. It was the perfect opportunity – not only to record using state-of-the-art hardware free of charge, but also to audition informally through their continual live testing sessions at the studio. It was an informal platform for introductions to the moguls of the music business. Record producers and engineers were invited along daily to De Lane Lea to view the new facilities.

Producer Louie Austin was in charge of their sessions, and although they had to work around lots of hitches, in the end it proved worthwhile to listen to their first professional demo of four of their own compositions, 'Liar', 'Jesus', 'Keep Yourself Alive' and 'The Night Comes Down'; the first two of which were Mercury's work.

Of these sessions, Terry Yeadon particularly remembers Mercury's impact: 'Even then Freddie struck me as being larger than life. He obviously thought of himself as the leader of the band but wasn't big-headed about it. He was just such a personality that in a short space of time he kind of bowled you over. He knew exactly what he wanted career/music-wise and was equally determined to get it. Ultra confident in what they were doing would about sum him up, and the thing I couldn't help being aware of was that his confidence spread to the rest of the band. Queen were *so* sure that it was going to happen for them, which was unusual in my experience.

'Of course age-wise they weren't so young compared to other bands, certainly if you compare them to bands nowadays, and that was bound to factor into it too.'

Let loose in a professional recording studio, Mercury was in his element and not discouraged by all the technical teething problems. 'There are always problems with new studios, and we'd often have to do it all over again but that was never a problem with Freddie,' says Yeadon. 'He had remarkable patience for our troubles. He'd say, "It's OK, we'll just do it again." In fact I'd go as far as to say that I think he revelled in it because it gave him the chance to perform again.'

Yeadon's choice of the word 'perform' was significant: 'That was the thing about Freddie. A studio is a cold, almost sterile environment, in which people usually just get on with it. There's no audience, and the crew are too busy working to give you any feedback, so it's not a place to put on an act. But still, Freddie performed. It was almost as if he literally couldn't sing a song if he didn't do all the actions to go with it. He was very much a showman even in these circumstances.

'They were a little rough at the edges, but that was to be expected, yet Queen was very much there and had been already there before Freddie joined them, with Brian's guitar playing and Roger's drumming to a large degree responsible for the sound, but Freddie unquestionably put the cream on it.

'A lot of bands came through De Lane Lea, and I guess there were bigger-named bands who should've impressed me more, but I don't know, there was always that something about Queen. They appeared as a unit right from the start. They'd been through their changes and were absolutely set, and you knew it.'

Unfortunately Yeadon's belief in Queen's prospects wasn't shared by the booking agents who attended their showcase gig at Imperial College on 6 October. Fired up by their sessions at De Lane Lea, Queen performed well, but once again no bookings came of it. Ken Testi, who was still working on their behalf, experienced the same negativity when he approached two professional acquaintances: 'I knew two bookers who worked for separate agencies and I used to pester them to death to book Queen. One was Lindsay Brown and the other was Paul Conroy who I shared a flat with for a time. Principally, they worked for their agencies but when the occasional support slot became available they did indulge me a few times, which meant a lot to Queen' He goes on: 'One day I took a Queen demo tape to let Paul and Lindsay listen to it. Afterwards, they went off to a bedroom for ten minutes to discuss it privately. When they returned, I said: "What do you think, then? Great, huh?" For the life of me, I couldn't imagine anyone thinking anything else, but Paul's reply was: "The last thing the music world needs right now is another Led Zeppelin." He added as he handed me back the tape: "I don't think they're going anywhere. Sorry."'

Ken Testi did not give up, and in addition to Queen's work at De Lane Lea he encouraged them to record other material to give him more to work with: 'I was very frustrated that they were going nowhere fast,' he says. 'A friend of Roger's had a reel-to-reel facility, and, as he was going away for a while, he told Roger that they could use his flat to record themselves. Which they did. The only thing was because it was done this way we didn't have anything on which to play it ourselves, but this is the tape we took round the record companies.' According to Testi, much of their first album release was on that tape, although clearly later rerecorded. When Ken Testi went knocking on doors, Freddie Mercury often went with him.

Despite the discouragement, Mercury was still so determined to break into the rock world that he had time for little else. Next door to De Lane Lea was Wembley Stadium. Although staging regular rock gigs in outdoor sports arenas was a long way off, his urge to perform in such a venue before crowds of fee-paying fans was growing stronger. The other band members felt the same, to the extent that Brian May viewed his trips to Tenerife with less enthusiasm, and Roger Taylor gave up the market stall. Freddie Mercury drifted into a collaboration with Alan Mair, whose boot stall was on the corner of their aisle. This had its perks, as Ken Testi and Geoff Higgins both recall.

'Besides boots,' Ken Testi says, 'Alan also sold canvas trousers which were tight, slightly flared and very popular. I remember Freddie beating a terrific discount out of him for a pair on the grounds that he worked the stall too.' His days studying the Bombay traders had obviously not been wasted.

Geoff Higgins has a different tale to tell: 'On his first morning at the new stall Fred discovered that by shifting the till a fraction, he could see directly into the ladies' changing room of the shop opposite. He'd spend all day spying on women undressing and trying on clothes and not a soul suspected a thing.'

By the end of 1971 the major triumph was that Queen still had the run of De Lane Lea studios. Several producers and engineers had looked over the recording facilities, but nothing had come of it. Working on the theory that the next man through the door could be the one to give them their break, Mercury considered their continued presence there as a vital key to their success. His faith proved justified in late December when John Anthony and Roy Thomas Baker came to see what facilities the recording studio had to offer.

Record producer Anthony had, of course, promised to call them months before, while Baker was then staff engineer at the influential Trident Studios. Distracted by Queen's performance, they found themselves mesmerised by Mercury and when the session was over spent time chatting to the band. To Queen's delight they took away a demo tape to play to their boss, Norman Sheffield, who was co-owner of Trident with his brother, Barry. Sheffield, however, wasn't sufficiently impressed to give more than an expression of interest. This was naturally deflating, and as Brian May recalls, 'Once again we heard only a deafening silence.'

Perennially optimistic, Ken Testi focused on doing the rounds of record company A&R departments, although it often wasn't easy to get past the front desk. Testi admits, 'I tried making appointments over the phone first, but I'm talking severely crude method here, and I largely got the brush-off. But we kept at it, and eventually some did agree to see us.' Testi's detailed diary for this period stands as a record of the companies he contacted: Polydor, MCA, Decca, CBS, Island, A&M among others. 'It was a thankless task,' he recalls. 'I've a list of the names of those people who told me Queen were no good.' But not everyone in the industry thought so, and early into the new year one label declared an interest.

Tony Stratton-Smith was head of Charisma Records, and after listening to the demo, he decided he liked what he heard. Almost at once he offered to sign Queen, but astonishingly they turned him down. 'Charisma wanted Queen,' Ken Testi confirms, 'but they were a small outfit, and the funds on offer were not great. I think it was that, more than anything. The band felt they could benefit from having big muscle behind them, and although they thought Tony was a nice guy, he didn't have the resources available to the major labels. Also, Stratton-Smith's one big involvement was with Genesis, and Queen feared they would always play second fiddle.

'They were still confident, even when turning Tony down, that it would happen for them. That was one of the things I found so attractive about them. They were waiting for the right pieces to fall into place, and it was just a question of time.'

On 10 March, Queen were to play a one-hour support session at King's College Hospital Medical School in Denmark Hill, south London, a gig that had surprisingly come courtesy of Paul Conroy. 'That's something I've never forgotten,' Ken Testi explains. 'Although Paul had said he had no confidence in Queen, he and Lindsay were still good enough to toss work their way when they could. It was Paul who helped me get them the King's College gig, which, funnily enough, was the one that showed Queen off to the record companies properly.'

Planning ahead for this show, on a page torn from a memo

pad, Mercury drew up a playlist of eleven songs, the last two of which, 'Jailhouse Rock' and 'Bamalama', reflected his continuing affection for rock 'n' roll. On the reverse he had asked Testi to draw him a map of how to get there. With a pathological distaste for using public transport, he hoped to cadge a lift in a car rather than spend money on a taxi; the fee for the night was only £25, split among the four of them.

Representatives from several record companies turned up, and this time a handful of them showed interest. According to Testi, however, the night was marred by the arrival of Tony Stratton-Smith: 'Even though Queen had turned him down, I think Tony thought he was still set with them. Whatever it was, unfortunately there was a row between them.' The murmurs of encouragement were an improvement on previous showcase gigs, but there was still nothing definite.

The first six songs that featured on Mercury's playlist that night would end up on Queen's debut album more than a year later. Thoughts of cutting that first album now occupied much of Mercury's time. Trident's tentative expression of interest was tantalising, but before committing himself, Norman Sheffield wanted to see the band perform live. Queen had one solitary gig ahead of them, coming up soon at London's Forest Hill Hospital, and Roy Thomas Baker promised that he would urge one of the Sheffield brothers to attend. In the end it was Barry Sheffield who was persuaded to come, and although it must have been a nerve-racking night for the band – their first real chance of a break – Queen gave it everything they had.

Mercury had been working at strengthening his interaction with an audience. As Terry Yeadon had observed, in a studio setting with no soundboard, he still had to perform. With the crowd just feet away from him, the desire to attract their attention, and hopefully their appreciation, had been an overriding factor for Mercury from the start. It would continue to form an integral part of his stagecraft all his life.

That night, for once, everything fell into place. Ironically, at recent showcase gigs at IC, they had primed their friends to give them a rapturous reception, and nothing had come of it. At Forest Hill, while a core of their acquaintances came to support them, the audience was not a bunch of hand-picked conspirators – and this was the crowd that brought the house down. Barry Sheffield was so impressed that he offered Queen a contract with Trident Audio Productions.

Remembering their experience with Mercury Records, Brian May and Roger Taylor felt that they ought to seek a bigger say in matters and Freddie Mercury and John Deacon saw the wisdom of this, too. After discussion among themselves, Queen therefore came to Trident's negotiating table with specific stipulations about the terms of any agreement. They wanted three separate contracts, individually covering recording, publishing rights and management. Trident had probably never experienced such a reaction from an unknown band before and it is perhaps indicative of their strong desire to sign Queen that they eventually agreed to draw up documents to encompass this new deal structure. A seven-month delay would stretch between Trident's offer to sign Queen and the contracts being finalised.

Trident, meanwhile, got to work on the band, providing them with new equipment and instruments – except for Brian May, who would not part with his Red Special. Although Ken Testi's help had been invaluable to their career so far, the Sheffields brought in a full-time manager to handle their day-to-day affairs. American Jack Nelson had recently been advising Trident on how to set up their own production company, and he was allotted the task of securing Queen that Holy Grail of the music industry – a recording contract with a major record label.

Armed with a package that included a twenty-four-track Queen demo, a folder of photographs, mini-biography and specimen lyrics, Nelson began the rounds of the record labels. Ex-Yes keyboard player Rick Wakeman controversially said a band that is hunting for a deal isn't good enough to have one: 'If you're good enough to have one, *you're* hunted.' But, practically every band, from the Stones and Beatles onwards, had to find themselves a deal.

Self-belief is essential in the search for success, and neither Queen nor Jack Nelson lacked that. Encouragingly, Nelson got a rapid response from EMI, one of the British giants, then about to set up a new heavy rock label. But there was a problem. On Trident's instruction Nelson had presented Queen as a package with Mark Ashton and Eugene Wallace. Stalemate set in when EMI turned down Ashton and Wallace. But for Trident it was all or nothing.

According to Ken Testi, Mercury and the others were fully aware of this arrangement: 'Queen knew that Trident were trying to sell them to EMI as three acts *en bloc* and were up for it.' EMI, unfortunately, wouldn't reconsider and reluctantly pulled out. Acutely conscious of the band's disappointment, Trident encouraged them to work on their debut album. But here, too, disillusionment was not far away.

FIVE

Smoke and Mirrors

When Queen turned up to record at Trident, as an unknown band they fell foul of the practice of allocating newcomers what's called downtime. They would be allowed the use of the studio only when no other artiste required it. This resulted in long stretches of time waiting for the chance to record when the established stars had left. Some days it had a demoralising effect on Mercury, but he knew they were in no position to complain.

But at least they were one step nearer their goal of recording their first album, which was enough to keep them all content. For Mercury being so close to a studio without having the chance to perform was tantalising. Pacing up and down chain-smoking, he concentrated on his plan of attack, which occasionally led him spontaneously to burst into song. Producer Robin Cable, working in an adjoining studio, overheard him one day and decided he could put his talents to good use. He was interested in rerecording 'I Can Hear Music', which had been a top ten hit in 1969 for the Beach Boys, and invited Mercury to do the vocals on it. On its release the following year, it was Mercury's first solo recording and would become a collector's item.

The word solo is not quite accurate here, because once in Cable's studio Mercury requested both May and Taylor's input. The producer was experimenting with Phil Spector's famous

'wall of sound'; Taylor's drumming and heavy tambourine presence forms the constant backdrop, while May's guitar was not
at all distinguishable because of the song's style.

It was Mercury's voice that formed the crystal-clear centre-
piece, to remarkable effect. In the mid-eighties, when he
embarked seriously on producing solo material, his penchant
was for ballads. He enjoyed imitating the fifties' overblown
crooner sound with his cover version of 'The Great Pretender'.
With 'I Can Hear Music', he proved that his range could
encompass the sixties too. For the B-side he recorded the
Goffin and King Dusty Springfield hit 'Going Back'. Both
numbers were different from the material he was in the slow
process of recording with Queen, and they proved a welcome
distraction to the frustration of waiting. Cable was undecided
about what to do with the record. But he promised that were
he ever to release it, he would let Mercury know.

By September 1972 John Deacon had his degree in elec-
tronic engineering, and Roger Taylor had also recently
graduated in biology. Brian May had given up his PhD course.
Freddie Mercury turned his art diploma to good use by design-
ing a special logo for Queen, which, unlike his first crude
suggestion, had all the qualities of a royal crest.

Despite Trident's best efforts on Queen's behalf, no contract
had yet been signed. This state of affairs was hardly conducive
to a sense of security, yet, despite this, individually all four band
members put pressure on Trident to start paying them a weekly
wage. In the end £20 each was agreed; less than Mercury had
hoped for, but better than nothing.

On 1 November Queen finally signed with Trident Audio
Productions. The deal was that they would record for Trident
and Trident, in turn, would secure a good recording and distribution deal with a major record label. Trident was taking a
chance here. No other independent production company had
yet assumed complete responsibility for a rock band.

Trident booked Queen into the Pheasantry, a club in Chelsea. Five days later they invited all the usual A&R representatives, who lead busy working lives and are notorious for not turning up. Queen were veterans of the showcase gig and familiar, too, with nothing ever coming of it. Feeling this time ought to be different, the band rehearsed diligently, only to encounter technical problems at the club with the PA. John Deacon saved the day with his electronics expertise but, unnerved by the bad beginning, Queen were unsettled all evening.

For weeks back in the studio, recording continued on their first album. It was a time that impressed Trident's Dave Thomas. Echoing Terry Yeadon's earlier thoughts on first encountering Mercury at De Lane Lea, Thomas later recalled, 'When the band walked into the room you knew they were a class act. They were just a bunch of students, but they exuded this amazing charismatic energy, particularly Freddie. He was totally awe-inspiring.'

Less than awe-inspiring was what purported to be the finished album at the end of November. Its sporadic recording history perhaps accounted for the mistakes, but the band was far from happy with the mixes. It also transpired that one track had been overdubbed on to the wrong backing tape. Along with Roy Thomas Baker, they held out for more time to rectify this and fought for more control over the overall sound.

In January 1973 with the album at last ready, the pressure increased for Jack Nelson to sign Queen to a record company. By now he was working with Feldman Music Company executive Ronnie Beck, who proved crucial in his role of introducing the band to top EMI executive Roy Featherstone.

Attending an annual music festival in the south of France, Featherstone was weary of the endless demos from hopeful bands. When Beck offered him the Queen tape, he played it more in hope than with faith, and he was unexpectedly impressed. Bluffing, Beck told Featherstone that a couple of other labels were circling Queen, which was enough for Featherstone to telex Trident at once to declare EMI's interest.

This time the gods were smiling on Queen, for 5 February had marked their first recording session with Radio One's *Sounds of the Seventies*. Recorded at the BBC's Maida Vale Studios with producer Bernie Andrews, it was transmitted ten days later and elicited such a positive audience response that EMI were immediately prepared to talk terms.

Trident could have cost Queen dear at this stage when yet again they tried to insist that the label should accept Queen as part of a package. The record company was still only interested in Queen, and this became a sticking-point. Mercury prided himself on the deal they had struck with Trident, in a bid to have more control over their future. Yet it soon became obvious that they remained at the mercy of others. Anxiety took hold enough to cut through Mercury's usual posturings. 'I remember bus journeys with Freddie to Trident's offices,' recalls Brian May – presumably Mercury was willing to slum it in the quest to impress upon the Sheffield brothers that this was their big chance. It took weeks of deliberation, but in March 1973 Queen were formally signed to EMI.

With the UK/European deal in place, attention turned to the US market. EMI fixed up Queen's first gig of the year at the Marquee Club in London on 9 April in order to impress the managing director of the giant US label Elektra Records. Jack Holtzman was briefly stopping over in London en route to New York. In principle having expressed an interest in Queen, EMI promised him a live performance, guaranteed to make up his mind. The flawless display that night sent Holtzman home happy, their contract assured.

In the early seventies the British music scene was a kaleidoscope of conflicting styles. The progressive rock and psychedelia of the late sixties had given way to folk rock and teen heart-throbs; hard rock was mutating into heavy metal. By 1973, however, glam or bubblegum rock had gathered momentum with the likes of David Essex, Wizzard and Slade dominating the charts.

To cash in on this trend, Robin Cable decided to release 'I Can Hear Music'. EMI's interests lay with Queen's forthcoming debut album, and they were concerned by the lightweight nature of this cover version. Although EMI had been persuaded to release the single, they wanted no link whatsoever between the two works. As a result EMI vetoed any hint of releasing it under the name Freddie Mercury and insisted on the use of a pseudonym. At this time the acknowledged king of glam rock was Gary Glitter, famous for his outrageous stage outfits. Although Mercury's vocals on the Beach Boys number sounded nothing like Glitter, with no malice intended it was decided to release the disc under the jokey name of Larry Lurex. Mercury wasn't consulted on the choice and had no control over its release. All he had was a small session fee, and Robin Cable, along with Trident, owned the record. It was they who decided to put it out. By then it was of little importance to Mercury, who was only concerned with Queen's album.

The joke, however, seriously backfired. Although now disgraced, at this time, Gary Glitter was hugely popular in music and, upset by what was seen as a satirical poke from a bunch of upstarts, people refused to buy the single, DJs wouldn't play it, and it was a dismal flop. But if some Glitter fans chose to be affronted, the star himself took no offence: 'I thought it was great! Let's face it, it's the highest honour for any performer to have people copying you. It's a form of flattery, and it was only meant in fun. Anyway what does it matter? After Elvis Presley, it's all parody, isn't it? Queen are probably the only band I know with such a diverse amount of material.'

Keen to try out their material on the public, Mercury had

organised a selection of photographs for the album cover. At this point his flat was the most appropriate location for a shoot, so their photographer friend Doug Puddifoot went there to take a few group shots. Between them they had lots of ideas, but in the end they agreed to a Victorian look with sepia tinting against a maroon oval background. For the back cover, they found some old snaps, tentatively considering a collage. It proved a tiresome exercise, though, because Mercury stamped on anything that he felt didn't flatter him. Some would call it pure vanity; later, with the cushion of his fame, others reflected fondly on his sheer professionalism. But eventually they submitted all their ideas to EMI for consideration.

For Queen's debut single, EMI selected two songs by Brian May: 'Keep Yourself Alive', backed by 'Son and Daughter'. Released in the UK on 6 July 1973, it drew mixed reviews from the music press. To a band eager for a favourable reaction, it wasn't as big a blow as being ignored by radio. Clearly the lifeblood of any record, radio play was all but denied them. The single was sent to every local and regional station, but only Radio Luxembourg included it on its playlist. The culprit here was BBC's Radio One. Licensed commercial radio stations had yet to surface, and the broadcasting corporation enjoyed a virtual monopoly of the pop airwaves. The fact that they rejected 'Keep Yourself Alive' five times was enough to strangle it at birth.

Their eponymous debut album followed on 13 July, and given the way the single had vanished, it was vital now to secure national exposure. EMI circulated the usual white labels – early pressings of an album in a plain paper sleeve, which carry no band name or record label – with the usual publicity release. One of the most popular rock programmes on British TV at this time was the BBC's *The Old Grey Whistle Test*, and EMI sent out the album to them, unfortunately without any explanatory PR material. Had it not caught the attention of the programme's producer, Michael Appleton, it too could have slipped into oblivion.

'We used to get sent loads of white labels,' recalls Michael Appleton. 'They're highly prized nowadays and were actually of top class cut. One day this white label arrived on my desk but with absolutely no indication as to who it was, or where it had come from. I listened to it and liked it so much that myself and Bob Harris decided to use it on that night's show. In those days we played tracks accompanied by our own visualisation. We chose "Keep Yourself Alive" and played it along with a cartoon of the President Roosevelt Whistle Stop tour.

'We said on air that this was a really good track from a really good album, but we'd no idea where it came from and that same night, I think during the transmission, someone from EMI furiously got in touch and told us it was their white label of the debut album of a band called Queen.'

Whistle Test presenter Bob Harris vividly recalls first listening to *Queen*. 'I absolutely loved it,' he says. 'I especially thought "Keep Yourself Alive" was wonderful. Personally I was very enthusiastic about them.' The band's association with *OGWT* and Harris, in particular, became a strong one, spanning several important years and providing them with valuable exposure.

'*Whistle Test* concentrated on sound first and foremost rather than vision,' explains Michael Appleton, 'which was peculiar to us in broadcasting in those days, and I think Queen appreciated that and in turn reciprocated by being very professional to work with.'

Throughout Queen's career, although it would later start to level out, Mercury dominated the band's songwriting. Half of each of the first four albums were his compositions, and of the seventeen tracks on Queen's *Greatest Hits* album, ten were by Mercury. This first album would feature five of his songs, which had been around for at least a year. Two were follow-up singles, both of which would do substantially better than 'Keep Yourself Alive'.

The enthusiasm of the *OGWT* team was a boost to the band's morale, but the general public didn't share it, and initial sales were disappointing. Trident, though, kept their nerve and booked them into Shepperton Studios, Middlesex, to make their first promotional film, for what they hoped would be worldwide distribution. They also enlisted the PR services of Tony Brainsby, one of Britain's top publicists. Brainsby, with Paul McCartney, Steve Harley and Chris de Burgh at one time among his clients, had worked with numerous EMI artistes. He first met Queen in mid-1973, when Mercury in particular made his mark.

'My first impressions of Freddie were that he was strong-willed, gregarious, very ambitious, charming and striking,' says Brainsby. 'He was also such a raving poofter, I couldn't believe my eyes! He wore red velvet skintight trousers, had black varnish on his fingernails and long hair, and of course all those teeth. God, was he touchy about his teeth! He never allowed himself to be photographed smiling and would automatically cover his mouth whenever he burst out laughing.'

According to Brainsby, in addition to Mercury's naked ambition, there was an unusual quality to the entire band: 'Of all the groups I've handled, I'd say only two made an instant impression on me. One was Thin Lizzy, and Queen was the other. They knew what they wanted and knew they'd be big – it was just a question of finding the way. In my experience that's not normal, but it's a huge advantage for a PR consultant when a group has that depth of belief in themselves. It's also that edge that was going to make them stars.'

Catching one of Queen's live gigs at a London polytechnic only confirmed his professional instincts about the band and marked the start of a profitable working relationship between them. Although Mercury invariably stood out from the others, he looked for no special preference. 'Freddie never lorded it as the star of Queen,' states Brainsby. 'It was always a group, and from the start we were all made very conscious of the importance of treating them equally. Of course, with Brian's guitar sound and Roger's high falsetto voice, each one had a Queen sound to add.'

But there was one aspect that he feels did relate specifically to Mercury: 'When I first knew Freddie he was inwardly a very aggressive and angry man. He knew he should be a star, and he wasn't, yet. To Freddie stardom was his by rights, and he could get extremely frustrated at the time it seemed to be taking other people to recognise this. He didn't like too many people to see it, but he had an incredible need for acceptance, and in my view he was very much the fight in the band.'

Brainsby's task to get them as much exposure as possible was greatly aided at the outset by the story behind Brian May's homemade guitar: 'It was a heaven-sent introduction into all the music magazines, because it became a huge talking-point, which started to get them noticed,' he recalls.

They were already being noticed in other ways that mattered. When they set to work on their second album, downtime was a thing of the past. Then, on 4 September, *Queen* received its US release on Elektra Records. The album attracted enough radio play to enter Billboard's Top 100 Chart; an achievement for a new British band. But once again the single 'Keep Yourself Alive' failed to ignite interest.

It became clear to Jack Nelson that Queen needed to be seen on tour. They were not yet headlining material but securing a good support slot was vital. Nelson knew Bob Hirschman, manager of Mott the Hoople, and through him he secured for Queen the job of backing them on their forthcoming UK tour. Initially this wasn't straightforward, as matching support bands to headliners isn't easy. An established band often won't risk being upstaged by too good a support act, and it's equally undesirable to be backed by a dull performance that leaves the audience restless. Hirschman hadn't heard Queen play and it was proving a difficult sell. A £3000 contribution to sound and lights helped to ease his qualms and give Queen the job.

Queen hadn't played live for several weeks, so Nelson organised half a dozen gigs for practice. Starting off at Golders Green Hippodrome on 13 September, the band had dates abroad in Germany and Luxembourg, before returning home for three London venue performances. The last two of these were in early November with a return to Imperial College. A former fellow student recalled that Queen were the loudest band on the planet that night, and journalist Rosemary Horide gave them a glowing review.

The twenty-three-date Mott the Hoople tour, which stretched from Edinburgh to Bournemouth, began on 12 November at Leeds Town Hall. It was Queen's first real taste of life on the road, playing every night in a different city, and proved an invigorating experience. For Mercury the adrenaline was still pumping when the first gig was over. Instead of getting some sleep before heading to Blackburn the next day, he sought out a bit of nightlife, as one now famous nightclub owner, Peter Stringfellow, recalls:

'I first met Freddie when he came into my Cinderella Rockerfella club in Leeds, and I thought he was a really nice bloke, obviously not a mega star yet and so he had no entourage surrounding him. He sat at my table, and we had a laugh and a few drinks. I had a Polaroid camera and asked if I could take his photo. As I say, Freddie wasn't a star, but what a performance it turned out to be! I thought to myself, "This guy is certainly different!"

'I went through two packs of film before Freddie decided that one shot was all right to keep. He promptly insisted on destroying the others. His vanity was out of all proportion, but the way he scrutinised each photo and discarded it until one came out just right I suppose, with hindsight, was a lesson in professionalism. Apart from that we had a good night.

'I had absolutely no idea that Freddie was gay then. There was nothing in his behaviour to remotely suggest it. But I'd say that was the first and last time I had a truly enjoyable evening with him. Later on he was always completely mobbed.'

At this point the only crowds Mercury saw were those that turned up for Mott the Hoople. But with each gig his confidence was building. There were no passengers in Queen, though it is true to say that with Roger Taylor hemmed in behind his drums, and John Deacon and Brian May being naturally retiring, the onus was heavily on Freddie Mercury to electrify each performance. It is something he perfected to a fine art in later life, but even in these early days Queen were beginning to draw their own reaction, as Tony Brainsby confirms: 'I also handled Hoople, and both bands had met for the first time in my office when it transpired they were to go on the road together. That tour was one helluva experience. You came out of gigs just breathless with it all.'

Someone else who recalls Mercury at this time is his ex-Ibex friend Mike Bersin. Queen were appearing at the Stadium in Liverpool, and Bersin had gone to see him for old times' sake: 'I went backstage to the dressing room,' he says, 'and found Freddie pacing up and down muttering. "What can I say? Give me something to say!" I wasn't sure what to make of it, then someone handed him a copy of the *Liverpool Echo*, which he flicked through while he was still pacing. Suddenly he stopped, peered at an article and snapped the newspaper shut, saying, "OK. Got it."

'I went out front to watch, and Freddie walked up to the mike and said, "Good evening, Liverpool," adding, "Nice one, Kevin!" – which was a reference to Kevin Keegan, who'd scored a vital goal for Liverpool Football Club. Nobody had been sure of him at first, with the way he was dressed and that, but suddenly the place erupted, and they were all completely on his side. *That* was typically Freddie. It's that amount of attention to detail which made him different.'

The tour ended on 14 December with two gigs at London's Hammersmith Odeon. Elated by the experience and at having established a strong rapport with Hoople, Queen's performances were exceptional enough to leave their audiences wanting more. The six-week tour had proved a success, something unfortunately not echoed in the music press. The media either criticised the band or, worse still, ignored them. Tony Brainsby is blunt about this and says: 'They accused Queen of being a hype band, when in reality they resented that their management put a lot of money behind them, and I was successful in getting them plenty of exposure. They chose to overlook the fact that Queen had a big following before their first single. When a band is receiving fan mail that early, then you've obviously got something special on your hands. And Freddie was an easy target for any journalist out to make a name for himself.'

For all Mercury's antics, which grew wilder the more journalists went for him, Brainsby confirms that for as long as he knew him, the star never admitted that he was gay. 'He never said, "I'm gay." In the early days, in fact, he'd make a point of telling people that he had a girlfriend called Mary. But their love lasted throughout his entire life, which was quite surprising in the circumstances. It must've been very hard when Freddie later became overtly gay. I mean he was always obviously campy and had that iffyness about him. But that was different to being gay, and he only ever referred to being bisexual. But he and Mary had an unusually strong bond, and, I'd say, the way it lasted showed that Freddie had a true depth to him that wasn't perhaps obvious to many. Later he flitted from one gay relationship to another, but Mary was always the rock.'

Shutting out the critics, Mercury focused instead on Radio One recording sessions that Queen had booked with Bob Harris; sessions that still stand out in Harris's memory: 'Freddie was so special. He always gave 100 per cent. To give an example: one Monday morning early – and hard after probably the busiest time of their lives right then, when they might've been forgiven for perhaps coasting a bit – I was watching from the control room, and there was this pin spotlight on Freddie. And there he was, giving so much to his performance that the veins were literally standing out on his temples and neck. I thought, how much more can you give?'

As to why Queen elicited such a poor response from the music press, Harris suggests that: 'It possibly stemmed from their inability to label Queen and because of their own inadequacy they took it out on the band. When Queen were huge, and they still attacked them, it was the same old thing. The British press love to build 'em up and knock 'em down. They just don't or can't recognise achievement and leave it at that. You sometimes get the feeling that they feel duty-bound to smash holes in people. Part of it, of course, stems from a worry that they could be accused of sycophancy if they constantly admire anyone's work.'

After the stint with Hoople, Queen played four more gigs to the year's end; the final performance of 1973 taking place on 28 December at Liverpool's Top Rank Club in support of 10cc. It was the last show Ken Testi was to book for Queen: 'By then I was working in a shop in Widnes,' he recalls. 'Brian had phoned to ask if I wanted to become their personal manager. Naturally I was thrilled, and I asked what the money would be like. I hated having to ask because for myself, I wouldn't have cared but I had a mortgage to meet. Queen were now getting £30 a week each, and I was offered £25, which I thought was good, but I had to say no.

'It was everything that my life had been leading up to, and I had to turn round and refuse. But on that money I couldn't make the payments on the house, and I also had to look after my mother and sister. One can't live on what-might-have-beens but I've regretted it to this day.' Queen's final link with the man who had done so much for them came at the Top

Rank Club, when they featured on a bill that included a local band, Great Day, in whose line-up was Ken Testi.

For Mercury, although they had released a single and album in Britain and the States, it was still only the beginning. It was too far from the eternal spotlight he craved more than ever. The Liverpool show ended their most successful year yet, and on the strength of the UK tour, Mott the Hoople invited them as support on their tour of America. The music press had enjoyed dubbing Queen, 'Britain's Biggest Unknowns'. If Mercury had his way, they would soon be proved wrong.

SIX

One of a Kind

Queen's drive to reach the top shifted up a gear in 1974. The band played twice as many gigs as in the previous twelve months and by autumn had reached the number two slot in Britain with their single 'Killer Queen'. But the way up proved to be something of a minefield. The band was booked to headline in January at the open-air Sunbury Music Festival in Melbourne, but Brian May had unfortunately been taken ill. After inoculations for travel to Australia, his arm had swelled up and become gangrenous from a dirty needle. Rehearsals for their first headlining foreign tour suffered as a result, but it was not to be the only disruption.

Since his days fronting Ibex, Mercury had harboured a passion for dramatic stage lighting, an interest shared by the other three members of the band. Now that resources were less tight, they could indulge this to better effect. Proud of their new and specially designed lighting rig, they had had it transported, along with the rest of their equipment, to Melbourne. Because the apparatus was complicated to use, they also took over their own crew to operate it, something that, unfortunately, upset the local technicians. On arrival Queen had sensed a general air of resentment that an unknown British band had been chosen to headline in preference to their own Aussie groups, and this grievance was aggravated by the imported lighting-rig operators.

Already concerned that May's arm would be too weak to last a performance, Mercury himself developed an ear infection. The antibiotics prescribed him were so strong that he began to feel increasingly drowsy as the day progressed. As they waited for darkness to begin to fall, so that the light show would be most effective, he found it hard to psyche himself up for the show. Out front the audience began a slow handclap, and as Queen prepared to go on, the show's compère didn't help when he introduced Queen as 'stuck-up pommies'. As soon as Mercury launched into the first number, he was immediately disoriented when he realised his ear infection made it impossible to hear himself sing. Conscious of the huge disappointment this show was becoming, the rig gave out just when it was dark enough for the lights to be seen at their best. Sabotage was suspected.

Far from buckling under the strain, Mercury pushed himself to the limits to perform. Brian May battled valiantly with an extremely painful arm, and John Deacon and Roger Taylor focused on the music. By the end of the performance their effort had paid off, as the crowd's hostility evaporated, and they demanded an encore. Queen were more than happy to oblige, until the compère took the stage and manipulated the audience into calling instead for the return of one of their own bands.

Furious at the humiliation, their ordeal continued the next day when the press got in on the act and slated them. By now Mercury's ear infection had worsened, and he was also running a temperature. For these reasons alone, even without the worry of May's gangrenous arm, Queen pulled out of the second night's performance. With the promoters' wrath ringing in their ears, they boarded a flight for England and went home.

It had been a costly exercise. Not only had they paid the return air fares to Australia themselves, but the tour had turned into a damaging fiasco. So early in their career, this was bound to have been demoralising. Yet Brian May vehemently denies this, insisting that none of them thought it disastrous. Clearly, though, they could have done without bad relations with the Australian press adding to the hostility from the British media.

As individual music-press journalists disparaged them, the music magazines themselves published annual polls that showed the strength of Queen's popularity on the street. In February, for example, *NME* readers placed Queen second to Leo Sayer as the Most Promising Newcomer.

February saw the US release of Mercury's first Queen single 'Liar', which sank without trace. Undaunted, he anticipated EMI's next release, again one of his own compositions, which was planned for a couple of weeks later. Although Queen hadn't proved big earners for the record label yet, they had acquired an ally in Ronnie Fowler, EMI's head of promotions. Impressed with their sound from the first spin of a white label, Fowler plugged Queen everywhere he went.

Every new group's ambition was to appear on BBC One's prestigious Thursday night *Top of the Pops*. Fowler received a call from its producer Robin Nash one Tuesday evening. David Bowie's promo clip for 'The Jean Genie' hadn't arrived in time for the show, he said; did Fowler have any ideas for a replacement? Fowler, of course, suggested Queen. Unfamiliar with the band's work, Nash asked to hear a demo, which he fortunately liked. But, as artistes in those days mimed to special backing tracks, the demo was useless. EMI and Queen seized their chance, when that night Fowler persuaded Who guitarist Pete Townshend to relinquish some studio time and allow Queen to record the necessary tape. At the BBC studios the next day they prerecorded their slot for transmission the following night.

Mercury and the band stared at the bank of televisions in an electrical shop window, all four glued to the glass. It was 21 February 1974 as they watched themselves perform 'Seven Seas of Rhye', a single not yet released. The song showcased Mercury's weakness for swirling crescendos and fantasy lyrics. It fades incongruously at the end into a sing-a-long of the very English ditty, 'Oh, I Do Like to be Beside the Seaside', which Ken Testi recalls recording back in 1973: 'I joined in on the reprise at the end of "Seven Seas of Rhye". So did Pat McConnell and a whole bunch of us. I seem to recall an awful lot of reverb, and Brian played the stylophone on it. But it was done in one day, and we were all totally pissed at the time.'

Keen to capitalise on Queen's appearance on the show, Ronnie Fowler and Jack Nelson blitzed the radio stations next day with white labels. When EMI rush-released the single on 23 February, the combination of the TV exposure and subsequent airplay secured Queen their first hit. By the second week of March, it had reached number ten. Their follow-up album *Queen II* should have been in the shops by now and could have benefited from the single's success, but a spelling mistake on the sleeve had delayed its release. Britain was limping along on a three-day working week, crippled worse by an oil crisis, and the government had imposed restrictions on the use of electricity. All of this delayed sorting out this minor printing error.

Basking in the first flush of success, Freddie Mercury hailed it as the beginning of something big. Even so, he had no idea of how huge they'd become. He was certainly ambitious, but so were scores of others. He once prophesied that Queen would survive for five years, which in the days of disposable pop equalled for ever. Towards the end of their forthcoming first headlining UK tour, he declared: 'I've always thought of us as a top group.'

Preparing to go out on the road with this top group for their vital tour, Mercury felt it was inappropriate to buy his stage wear from Kensington market or to use a helpful but amateur seamstress. Persuading Brian May to join him, he approached fashion designer Zandra Rhodes. 'Freddie had loved the tops I did for Marc Bolan, and what I was doing with a variety of fabrics right then, and he came to me knowing very much what he wanted,' says Rhodes. 'My workshop then was an absolute deathtrap in a brownstone building in Paddington, which had a winding rickety staircase with a low ceiling leading to it, and I vividly recall Brian stooping forward with Freddie just behind him as they tramped up to see me.'

After the embarrassment of stripping off before a roomful of machinists to try out various styles, Mercury opted for two particular outfits. One, in white satin with a glorious pleated-wing effect, would become world famous. But although he had arrived fired up with his own ideas, he was happy to be guided by the professional: 'Even if someone has had wonderful artistic training, it doesn't always follow that they know best, and Freddie was always extremely appreciative of what I did, which was lovely,' says Rhodes. 'Queen's look was very much part of their success and has always been important to their whole make-up in conjunction with the music. I think, in fact, that they only toned it down when Freddie became ill and started trying to look straight.'

Excited by his two sumptuous Rhodes creations, Mercury felt vibrant as their first headlining UK tour commenced on 1 March 1974 at the Winter Gardens in Blackpool. It was hard work, especially for Brian May. One month after the Sunbury Music Festival, his arm was still sore, something initially aggravated by the fact that Queen were playing alone, with no support band. By the time they reached Plymouth's Guild Hall, they were touring with Nutz, a Liverpool band who remained on the bill as support for the rest of the dates. This tour saw the birth of the audience's curious habit of singing 'God Save The Queen', while awaiting the band's arrival on stage. Later, Queen closed their shows with the national anthem.

With the success of 'Seven Seas of Rhye', everyone fixed on the launch on 8 March of *Queen II*. Its most distinguished physical feature was its innovatory white and black sides instead of the traditional A and B. The original material on it clearly appealed too. As they toured the country, the band discovered that the audience were often word-perfect with the lyrics. Within a fortnight *Queen II* had reached the top forty in the album charts.

From previous experience, no one seriously anticipated glowing reviews. But neither did they expect the music press to savage them. One reviewer described their debut album as 'a bucket of stale urine', and it was hard to imagine going further down than that. They were slated as lacking depth and feeling, even denounced as 'the dregs of glam rock'. Fortunately, the critics were once more out of step with the public, who were nightly enjoying the gigs. At the critical point of live contact between band and audience, Queen were thriving, which was essentially what mattered most.

Keeping this in mind, Queen concentrated on perfecting their art. Each member of the band worked on his individual performance, carving out his own particular niche, though it was clear that Mercury was the band's dynamo. He dominated the stage, a hugely flamboyant and captivating front man.

The band was never known as Freddie Mercury and Queen. Tony Brainsby says that Mercury never tried to lord it over the rest of the band, and in interviews Mercury himself would correct any slip of the tongue and talk of how he enjoyed singing *'our* songs'. Nevertheless, on stage, as he paraded and pirouetted in an electrifying performance before an audience that came to number hundreds of thousands, he must have felt uniquely potent.

Those who knew Mercury are unanimous that he was quiet and reserved in private and among strangers. This didn't stop his alter ego from giving free rein to his increasingly mercurial moods, both on stage and at after-gig celebrations. Queen were halfway through their tour when, at Stirling University, one of only two gigs they played in Scotland, a riot broke out. The pitched battle in the hall resulted in four people being hospitalised, two with stab wounds.

With the press already tagging them with lurid headlines, they performed further south on the Isle of Man at the Palace Lido, where they courted controversy again. In Douglas a party spun out of control, and, it was said, a hotel room was wrecked. Their subdued return to the mainland the next day was brightened by the news that their new album had got to number seven. Furthermore *Queen*, which had so far disappointingly underperformed, benefited from *Queen II*'s popularity and enjoyed a passable number forty-seven in the top hundred albums.

Although press accusations of inciting riots were unwelcome, there is no doubt that the coverage helped to publicise the band's existence. By the tour's end, their shows were regularly sold out, and fans were becoming vocal in their adulation. Queen were now keen to play the bigger venues, and the prestigious Rainbow Theatre in London certainly fell into this category. Their gig there on 31 March was special, even though it was marred earlier on in the day.

Perhaps it was fatigue setting in at the end of a hectic tour or his first taste of fan adulation going to his head, but in the afternoon Mercury began behaving like a prima donna during the sound check. It was enough to goad the normally patient Brian May into calling him an old tart. Mercury responded by stalking off and staying away just long enough to make everyone anxious. Calls from May over the mike got Mercury back on stage, peeved but prepared to return to work. It wouldn't be the last time tensions emerged among the four, but it appears that Mercury would usually emerge as the peace broker.

Their Rainbow gig, before a capacity crowd, turned out to be one of their most memorable. Sound engineer John Harris experimented to brilliant effect with the hall's acoustics, while Roger Taylor poured beer on top of one of his drums, so that each time he struck it, it sent up a frothy spray. Freddie Mercury, in the Zandra Rhodes creation he called his 'eagle suit', shone that night. At every opportunity he spun round, swirling his arms to show off the mass of silky knife pleats that splayed out behind him. The sheer panache of the performance was enough to silence many of their critics in the music press and elicited a second good review from Rosemary Horide.

Elated by the experience, the news that *Queen II*, newly released in the States, had struggled to reach number eighty-three was in no way deflating. Mercury was confident that his stage triumphs would be repeated in America, where they were touring as support to Mott the Hoople. The US tour was due to kick off in under a week. Apart from the odd European gig and their recent trip to Australia, they hadn't had much opportunity to win over an overseas audience. The American market was massive, and it was vital for Queen to make their mark. It sounded like fun, especially with the bonus that they got on so well with Hoople. But they must have been aware that after their album's slack performance, they had a lot to prove from Elektra's point of view.

Flying out on the 12th, the tour started four days later. They travelled from Denver to Kansas City, St Louis to Memphis, initially with a muted reception at each gig. Because Queen records had done nothing in America so far, it wasn't surprising that the crowds didn't recognise the songs. Their stage image, too, was not what American audiences expected, and Freddie Mercury, pouting and posing in clingy costumes, did not fit the stereotype of heterosexual rock. The crowds took quickly to Queen's music, though, and what began as diffident acceptance grew warmer as each night progressed.

Life on the road was tougher than they'd been used to. The distances covered by travelling between cities were much greater than in Britain, and, once there, things didn't necessarily go smoothly. At the Farm Arena in Harrisburg, Pennsylvania, for example, an argument erupted between Queen and the American band Aerosmith. They had both been booked to play support that night, and bickered about who was entitled to go on stage first. With professional pride at stake, neither side wanted to budge. But, essentially, such vanity was of little consequence.

Then something occurred unexpectedly to blight their entire trip. Three weeks into the tour they played New York City, with six consecutive nights at the Uris Theatre. Halfway through, Brian May began to feel unwell, and after the final gig on 12 May he collapsed. Attributing this to fatigue, he was advised to rest before their next performance in Boston. But the first morning he awoke in the city's Parker House Hotel, it became clear his condition was more serious.

May turned out to have hepatitis, which came as a bomb-shell to Mercury. Besides his natural concern for May, he had been worried that they might need to pull out of a couple of their imminent gigs. On discovering it was a potentially dangerous, certainly contagious, illness, he realised that their first assault on the American public was over.

Dispatched back to Britain, May was hospitalised, while all those with whom he had been in contact were immunised against the virus. Mercury refused to see developments as having ruined their chances in America, maintaining, 'We did what we had to do. Sure, a whole tour would have helped us more, but there's no such thing as, "We lost our chance."' Encouraged by the write-ups they went on to receive, he was convinced that their time there would come again. Reassuring May that he had not let them down, the other three band members started to write some new material.

To put these ideas into practice, work began at Rockfield Studios in Monmouthshire, early in June, by which time Brian May had decided he was fit to join them. He spent most days, however, being sick and was visibly weak. When recording began on their third album at four different studios the following month, his fragility culminated in collapse. Rushed to

King's College Hospital, he underwent emergency surgery for a duodenal ulcer. Because of his need to convalesce, Queen's planned return to the States had to be abandoned.

Mercury was aware of how inveterate a worrier May was, and guessed correctly that while they were busy in the studio with producer Roy Thomas Baker, he was convincing himself in hospital that the band would consider replacing him. So again he visited him there to put his mind at rest.

Superficially jokey and quick to clown, privately Mercury saw himself as mothering the band. For years he had proved to be a trusted confidant to friends, and he could as effectively heal a row within Queen as much as cause one. When it came to health, he was acutely conscious of May's needs. In response to press queries about the band's reaction to their abortive US tour, Freddie said, 'Brian has got to look after himself in the future. We all want to make sure something like that never happens again. So he'll have to eat the right things and steer clear of hamburgers. I tend to worry about him a lot because he'll never ask for anything if he's not feeling well.'

While they put the finishing touches to their new album at Sarm Studios, *Queen II* earned the band a silver disc. It had sold in excess of 100,000 copies during the first six months. This heralded an upsurge in media interest: interest that they greeted with caution, considering the journalistic treatment meted out to them so far. Brian admits: 'I still had the naive belief that if you opened your heart to the press, they'd be fair to you.'

It had also been over six months since their only hit single, and a decision had to be made about which of the intended thirteen new album tracks should be extracted first. As on the previous albums, Roger Taylor had contributed a track; John Deacon made his songwriting debut with 'Misfire'; and 'Stone Cold Crazy' was the first number to be credited collectively to all four members. Brian May made his regulation four contributions, while the rest were Mercury's, and it was one of his songs that became their autumn single release. A fortnight later, on 26 October 1974, 'Killer Queen' raced up the charts to number two, only blocked by the David Essex hit 'Gonna Make You a Star'.

David Essex later considered Queen the best British band to have come out of the seventies: 'Freddie's voice was absolutely unique. Image quickly took over from music, but with Queen their musical ability obviously had the staying power, where others vanished.'

'Killer Queen', in particular, is Essex's favourite Queen record: 'With their stacked-up voices and guitar work, it was extremely well produced and very clever.'

This is a view endorsed by Oscar-winning lyricist Sir Tim Rice, who a decade later would become personal friends with Freddie Mercury: 'I hadn't particularly liked "Seven Seas of Rhye" at first, although I got to like it better when I knew the band, but it was "Killer Queen" which really turned me on to Queen. The composition of its lyrics was quite sophisticated, particularly for its time. I have absolutely no doubt about Freddie's immense talent as a songwriter.'

Mercury was proud of what he dubbed the 'bowler hat, black suspender belt number'. 'People are used to hard rock, energy music from Queen,' he declared. 'Yet with this single you almost expect Noël Coward to sing it.' With a number two hit to their credit, the public assumed that Queen had reached the big time. But although 'Killer Queen' was a turning point in their career, they were still impoverished, as the state of some of their living accommodation proved. But the illusion of success had to be maintained, and for this Mercury's gift for exaggeration came in useful. Without a scrap of modesty, he would say proudly, 'The reason we're so successful, darling? My overall charisma of course!' Years later the tables turned when, genuinely wealthy, Mercury annoyed the rest of the band with boasts that they were all 'simply dripping with money'.

As Zandra Rhodes reflected, a large part of Queen's initial success lay in their look. But it was a visually challenging time, with each act adopting a gimmick – be it Leo Sayer dressing up as the French pantomime character Pierrot, or Mud in their zoot suits and brothel creepers. At a college dance one night Mercury was struggling with an ancient microphone stand when its heavy base suddenly fell off. Left with only the top half of the chrome shaft, he realised it wasn't only much lighter to manoeuvre, but easier to move suggestively over his body and face. By the time he sang 'Killer Queen' on *Top of the Pops*, twisting the shiny rod skywards, his fingertips groping their way sensually up its length, this had become as much his hallmark as his long black feathercut hair and scoop-neck leotards.

Mercury's stage act was a polished extension of his image on the college-band circuit, when his performance was heavy with homosexual overtones. A lead singer usually has his strongest on-stage affinity with the band's lead guitarist, and Mercury was fond of sliding his shoulder up against Brian May's right side, apparently deriving an ambiguous pleasure in the process. At the height of the glam era, he wasn't the only one perpetuating a bisexual image, but whereas Sweet, for example, were taken to be joking, Mercury's intentions were less clear.

He wanted to reinforce this image when Queen embarked on a European tour at the end of October. From Manchester to Barcelona, the trip had been arranged to replace their abortive return to America. Undeterred by their experience in Australia, the performance included an impressive light show, with an experimental fireworks display. Fans loved it, but music-press critics were quick to dismiss it as pure theatrics.

Pure showbiz probably most accurately describes Mercury's approach to performance, and he would have stormed the Edwardian music halls. He saw no reason to apologise for his enthusiasm for expression. At times, especially during the punishing US tours, that enthusiasm would be tested, but performing came as naturally to Freddie Mercury as breathing. His desire to draw the very last ounce of response from his audience drove him to establish a unique emotional bond with the fans, sometimes to a dangerous extent.

Nine days into the tour, fans at Glasgow's Apollo Theatre were chanting and waving, just below the footlights. In a second's mistiming, Mercury got too close, and in a flash, a sea of hands had pulled him off stage and into the hysterical mob. Security guards plunged after him and retrieved him, breathless and frightened, but unharmed. Learning that Mercury was in their midst, however, fans at the back had surged forward in a stampede that turned ugly. With Mercury rescued, frustrations erupted, and fights broke out, resulting in a few bruises, and damage to several rows of seats.

That same day, 8 November, saw the release of Queen's third album, *Sheer Heart Attack*. Four days later it went on sale in the States. Then the following week they returned to London's Rainbow Theatre. Originally just one gig had been planned, but the huge demand for tickets had ensured a second consecutive date, and it was also decided to film, as well as record, them. If nothing else, this could provide a live album later.

Queen left for Gothenburg soon afterwards to commence the European leg of their tour, playing sell-out gigs and reaping the rewards with rising album sales. Although it was difficult to deny their increasing popularity – voted by *Sun* readers as Britain's Best Live Act of 1974 – their old adversaries continued to confront them. It got to be a no-win situation. Given their track record, all four band members were wary of talking to journalists they felt were ready to trap them. The press in turn took this lack of compliance as further proof of Queen's conceit. And Mercury, in particular, with his provocative posturing and pronouncements, remained their biggest target. He was close to refusing interviews, which was a problem for Tony Brainsby.

'Over the years a myth has grown around Freddie, that from the start he rarely gave interviews,' says Brainsby. 'That's not true. In the very early days, of course he did them. Any aspiring pop star has to, otherwise they don't get their name known. Freddie, for example, did tons of stuff for *Jackie* and the teenybop magazines. He'd wave and throw around a few "my dears" and really give out his great fruity laugh. One of the things I remember most about Freddie is his rich resonant laugh.

'There were no set preconditions, but every time Freddie was asked about his background he'd toss back an answer, without really answering. For a long time no one in the press had a clue even what his real name was. Freddie avoided at all costs mentioning Zanzibar, I think because he thought it might make him look a bit too Asian. It wasn't meant in a prejudicial way. He just didn't think it fitted the image. He desperately didn't want to be thought of, or seen as, an unlikely rock star.'

As 1974 drew to a close, on the band's return to Britain, they became involved in another round of frustrating talks with Trident. There had been salary disagreements for some time, and with a third album out and their popularity growing, Queen's horizons were higher than ever.

Mercury and Mary Austin were still living together in Kensington in reasonable comfort. Home for Brian May was a dingy room in the basement of a rambling old house, while John Deacon had become engaged to his longtime sweetheart, Veronica Tetzlaff. They hoped to start married life in something more salubrious than Deacon's current home.

The band was also concerned about mounting debts for lighting and sound services. This was not peculiar to Queen, and indeed it became no better for many later bands. Queen had no intention of standing still, however, and when the Sheffields proved impervious to their pressure, they hired music-business lawyer Jim Beach to examine their contracts for a way out of their association.

Glad to escape this tense predicament, Mercury anticipated the new year ahead. He had recently declared the need for a break but added, 'You've got to push yourself. We're at a stage in our careers, my dear, where it's just got to be done. I shall be resting on my laurels soon.'

On 17 January 1975 their fourth single, 'Now I'm Here', written by May while recovering from his operation, was released. In early February, at last, Queen's first headlining tour of America and Canada began, followed closely by their first tour of Japan. They were set to kick off on 5 February with a gig at the Agora Theater in Columbus, and Tony Brainsby fully understood why they felt nervous.

'Queen's effect on America had been slow,' he admits. 'But this happened with most bands. It goes back to the sixties, when US bands couldn't get arrested in their own country. Only British bands counted, and, I think, come the seventies, that it was simply a backlash of this; that Americans, in simplistic terms, got their own back by being downright cool to any English band.'

Steeped in hard-rock machismo, US audience reaction to Mercury's foppishness, too, was hard to gauge. Certainly one bemused TV presenter declared Mercury, 'One of life's originals!' adding, as a camera trailed him sashaying through a deserted shopping mall, casually flicking a bull whip, 'So far Freddie Mercury shows no signs of succumbing to conservatism!'

'Killer Queen' had reached number five in the US charts, and this success was mirrored by demand for tickets at each scheduled gig, with extra dates being squeezed in to accommodate the band. Yet many rock critics compared them unfavourably to Led Zeppelin. But, according to Brian May, this wasn't the whole picture. He claims that what he calls 'the Anglophile element and the new A&R generation' had already made them heroes, adding that on the whole it was the only place they got good reviews.

Although delighted at the demand for extra dates, by the end of the first month, on four separate occasions Queen had been required to play twice on the same day. It was double work for all, but the burden was greatest for Mercury, who not surprisingly developed voice problems. Coming off stage at the end of the second day's performance at the Erlinger Theatre in Philadelphia, he was in such pain that a throat specialist was brought over from a nearby hospital to examine him.

He was clearly suffering from voice strain, but the doctor suspected that he was also developing nodules on his vocal cords. His recommendation was for the star not to sing, but it was advice Mercury rashly ignored: 'I'll sing until my throat is like a vulture's crotch,' he vowed.

So saying, he appeared the next evening at the Kennedy Center, Washington, and promptly paid for his folly. He tried to excel as usual, but it was obvious that he was struggling. When the performance was over, he was in agony again. A Washington consultant had little patience, knowing that Mercury had ignored his Philadelphia colleague's advice. Unimpressed with his sense of duty to his fans, he diagnosed him as suffering from severe laryngitis and ordered him to rest. This time Mercury had no option and gave in; the next six gigs were cancelled.

Impatient at the delay, Mercury was heartened by news from England that Queen had just been voted Band of the Year by *Melody Maker*. He was convinced that this was to be their time in America and could hardly wait for the tour to resume. When it did, though, the rest proved to have been too short, as he discovered on launching into his first number at the Mary E. Sawyer Auditorium in La Crosse. Yet more cancellations were necessary, and the last four weeks operated on this stop-start pattern, with the final date in Portland on 7 April having to be cancelled at the last moment. Because of the tour's erratic nature, it was hard for Mercury to assess its impact.

The news about Trident, too, was still not encouraging. Among the people with whom they had come into contact during the trip was the colourful showbusiness manager Don Arden. Impressed by Queen, he headhunted them with promises of lucrative deals if he could be their manager. Before they left America he had got all four band members to sign letters of authorisation for him to act on their behalf and deal directly with the Sheffields.

This experience of the States seems to have affected Mercury in different ways. Contact with a cosmopolitan cross section of people was something he had always loved, and such opportunities were numerous on tour. It appears likely that although in his private life he still enjoyed a heterosexual relationship with Mary Austin, while abroad he had started to indulge his homosexual desires. On his later trips to America, he certainly enjoyed such encounters, but, according to one close friend, by 1975 Mercury had realised he was gay.

By mid-April Mercury was relaxing with the others on a brief holiday in Hawaii, before tackling their debut tour of Japan; a country and culture that would play a huge part in his life. All the optimism in the world could not have prepared them for the reception they would receive on their first visit to Tokyo. Pandemonium broke out among the 3000-strong crowd of teenagers cramming the airport to greet them, as they screamed themselves hoarse under the uncomprehending gaze of the airport security guards.

The first gig was at the Budokan Martial Arts Hall. Prior to going on stage, the promoter had warned them that the audience would be very quiet at first, but they were not to worry. As it turned out, the show was the start of something new in Japan, and the experience, in various ways, remained with Queen for ever.

The night itself was certainly one to remember. Transferring the blind hysteria from the airport to the hall, the fans lost themselves in a sea of delirium, drowning out the music with their screams and working themselves into such a frenzy that finally they lost control and stampeded the stage. Alarmed as much for the fans' safety as their own, Mercury stopped the show and appealed for calm. That night, this eventually worked – but Queenmania spread to Nagoya, Okayama, the ancient city of Kobe and beyond.

Japan was the first country to recognise Queen as a major force in music. Off stage their hosts, with an excess of polished decorum, treated the band with enormous deference, showering them with expensive gifts. Queen reciprocated in the best way they could – by appearing on stage for the encore on their final night, again at the Budokan, dressed in traditional kimonos. The audience went berserk, but certainly in Mercury's case, he was paying more than lip service. His fascination with this country was to grow, and in time he became respected as an expert in Japanese art. When they returned to Britain at the beginning of May, both 'Killer Queen' and *Sheer Heart Attack* topped the Japanese charts. The album was also a hit in the States.

Back home the stalemate with Trident was sobering, but as summer wore on, Mercury was more interested in working on their fourth album. They had all benefited from their foreign tours, the adulation fuelling an increased sense of self-confidence. The fresh material they were putting together in the studio felt the most exciting yet, and Mercury in particular would discover a new dimension in creativity – later securing him legendary status.

By autumn, Queen were working hard in six different studios. Equally intensive were the attempts to release them from Trident. In August severance agreements were drawn up for signature. EMI would assume more direct control of recording and publishing, and the band were at liberty to find themselves new management. Glad to be free, there was a payment of £100,000 in severance fees to Trident, as well as the rights to

1 per cent of album royalties. In effect Queen had to trade in their income from the first three albums so far for their future.

They were broke again. The planned American tour had been called off, due to the upheavals. And, with such discord around, rumours circulated that Queen were about to disband. But nothing could have been further from the truth. They were, however, in urgent need of new management, and as Don Arden's offer had fallen through, the band had to think again.

They drew up a shortlist of three names, which included 10cc's manager, and Peter Grant, who handled Led Zeppelin, but for different reasons both possibilities were discounted. This left John Reid, who looked after the affairs of Elton John. Reid's initial reaction was not encouraging, but he agreed to a meeting. Apart from Queen's conviction that they'd be superstars, on paper the reality was that they were simply an impressive live act with a couple of hits and healthy album sales to their credit. As such they were better than many and not as successful as others. But something inspired Reid, for by the end of September 1975 he had become Queen's new manager.

Mercury's view on parting from Trident was characteristically blunt: 'As far as Queen are concerned,' he announced, 'our old management is deceased. They cease to exist in any capacity with us whatsoever. One leaves them behind, like one leaves excreta. We feel so relieved!'

His reaction to John Reid, according to Queen's new personal manager, Pete Brown, was rather different: 'I can vividly remember Freddie saying, "I decided John Reid was the right man for the job of our manager the moment he fluttered his eyelashes at me!" Freddie was always kidding around.' Brown had previously worked with Reid who had asked him, on signing Queen, if he would return and take the job as their personal manager. 'From that moment,' says Brown, 'I was with them every day for the next seven years.'

Developments moved fast under Reid. With Jim Beach he addressed the problem of where to find the huge sum owing to Trident. Before the November deadline expired, he had persuaded EMI to provide it as an advance against future royalties. Having secured this, he then threw a party at the London Coliseum. Here, amid a blaze of publicity, Queen received a barrowload of gold and silver discs in honour of record-breaking sales of 'Killer Queen' and their first three albums.

Mercury had also become involved for the first time in producing a record for singer/songwriter Eddie Howell, whose manager, David Minns, knew John Reid. Through this connection, Mercury had seen Howell perform 'Man From Manhattan' in a Kensington club. He was so impressed that he kept asking Howell if he would let him produce it. It was an unusual step for Mercury. In time he would produce for a handpicked few outside of Queen, but only among his friends.

He listened first to an acoustic four-track demo of 'Man From Manhattan', then a few days later invited Howell to Sarm East Studio, where part of Queen's album was in the making. Already familiar with the song, Mercury played it straight through on the piano for Howell, who was delighted that he had sensed the precise feel of the song.

Watching Mercury take control in the studio – and amazed at the amount of pre-production work he had already put into the song's arrangement – Howell was struck most by the meticulous way in which he incorporated the harmony. Sitting at a table, a pencil in his hand, he worked incessantly until he felt he had it just right. Unfortunately, he invited Brian May to the recording session, and the combination of May and Mercury felt to Howell too much like a Queen takeover. He was careful to ensure that Taylor and Deacon weren't also involved.

Recording the song took an age, but Mercury was an unusual producer. Whereas Howell and the others came to work in everyday clothes, Mercury treated the occasion as a performance. He arrived as flamboyantly dressed as if he were about to step on stage. But the way he worked could not have been more serious, and if he couldn't spontaneously achieve the effect he was looking for, he would abruptly adjourn the session.

Howell later remarked, 'Freddie had generosity of spirit but was a little volatile underneath.' When the single was released the following year, Warner Brothers made mileage of its Queen connection. But, just as it seemed set to chart, a bureaucratic hitch forced its withdrawal. It never saw the light of day again for almost twenty years.

The time had come to choose an album track to release as Queen's next single. After missing the top slot with 'Killer Queen', 'Now I'm Here' had peaked at number ten, and they were determined to improve on that. It was a bold decision, but by October the band unanimously agreed to opt for another Mercury composition, 'Bohemian Rhapsody'.

The boldness of the choice was not so much about the lyrics – instead of the usual boy-meets-girl love song, it tells of a murderer full of remorse for the consequences of his act – rather, the fact that in its uncut state it was an unheard-of seven minutes long, and distinctly operatic. Not surprisingly Pete Brown was shocked, and actively tried to dissuade them: 'I tried to make Freddie see that they were quite mad proposing "Bohemian Rhapsody" as their next single. I personally thought it spelt the kiss of death, and actually John Deacon privately agreed with me. But Freddie, Brian and Roger all felt strongly that they needed to establish their credibility and were stubborn about the whole thing.'

Someone who corroborates this intransigence was record producer Gary Langhan: 'My connection with Queen goes back to mixing the track "Now I'm Here" in 1974 for their album *Sheer Heart Attack*. By the following year I was tape operator and assistant at Sarm Studios, where they were finishing off their new album, and I vividly recall being at the back of the control room when "Bohemian Rhapsody" was nearing completion. I just knew I was hearing the greatest piece of music I was ever likely to. There's two feelings you get about a record. One's in your head, and that can often fool you. But then there's the sensation you get in the pit of your stomach when you know. That time, I felt it in my gut. They felt it too.

'As far as arguments over the song's length were concerned, they just dug in their heels. There *was* a touch of arrogance, I suppose, but it was more like sheer belief in the number, and their attitude was, well, if it's twice the usual time slot allocated to each record on radio, they'll just have to play one less record a day. And if they play "Bohemian Rhapsody" three times, that's just three less records they can play that day.'

John Reid might admire Queen's determination to defend their professional integrity, but as the band's manager it was his job to anticipate, and try to avert, possible disaster. No one in his position could have felt anything but anxiety in the circumstances. Initially he tried to persuade Mercury to edit the song down. Getting nowhere, he soon realised the depth of their collective faith in the number. With his blessing, the record went to press.

No one has ever admitted that Mercury had any inner doubt that he'd made the right decision. However, it is possible that he did, unconsciously, feel slightly anxious. In the autumn of 1975 Queen were not superstars and in no position to demand special treatment. They needed airplay, just like any other artiste.

With an advance copy of the single, Mercury went to see his friend DJ Kenny Everett. On discovering how long it was, privately Everett doubted that any station would respond well to it. But he said nothing to Mercury as he placed 'Bohemian Rhapsody' on the turntable. 'Forget it! It could be half an hour long,' he enthused when he'd heard it. 'It's going to be number one for centuries!' Mercury knew what he was doing when he left Everett with the leaked copy of the yet to be released record. Capital Radio hadn't officially accepted it, but Everett was a law unto himself. Pete Brown recalls, 'Kenny was great. He'd yabber about this record he had but couldn't play, then say, "Oops, my finger must've slipped," and on it would come.' Everett accidentally played 'Bohemian Rhapsody' so often that Capital's switchboard was blocked with callers. They wanted to know one thing: when could they expect the new single to be released?

Everett's agent, Jo Gurnett, confirms: 'Kenny was hugely instrumental in getting Queen airplay for "Bohemian Rhapsody". He was incredibly enthusiastic about the record and played it all the time at home too.'

And Tony Brainsby recalls how 'Everybody now says what a great record, but Kenny Everett was the only person brave enough to play it at first. It was the kind of record that would either go to number one and make Queen, or it'd die a death and be their epitaph. My first reaction was, Hey, good number, but who the hell is going to play it? It's ridiculously long, and what on earth is Freddie playing at with this opera bit in the middle? I mean, let's face it, it just wasn't what was going on at the time.

'Freddie realised it was a risky move, but underneath it all he was astute enough to take a chance with it. Other records were nice and safe and regulation length. This was stunning and a whole EP on its own. But we were sure radio would block it.'

On 31 October 'Bohemian Rhapsody', sporting a picture cover, went on sale. It knocked the music industry sideways. Already 1975 had spawned an odd mix of musical styles, but no one was ready for this. From its ballad beginning, the song segued into complicated multi-tracking harmonic operatics, which had involved almost 200 vocal overdubs, before exploding into gut-busting hard rock. Incomparable to anything else around, its impact on the music scene resembled that of the Beatles' 1967 watershed album *Sgt. Pepper's Lonely Hearts Club Band*.

'Bohemian Rhapsody' was Mercury's most positive creative statement and remained so until the day he died. Future Mercury solo and Queen compositions forever strived to match it, but despite their subsequent success, this never happened. Mercury's response to queries about the inspiration behind it always varied. It had a touch of fantasy about it, he said, and gently scoffed that people should be taking it so seriously. But at the first hint of criticism, he would bristle, 'Who can you compare it to? Name one group who've done an operatic single!' He would grow irritable and snap that it hadn't been plucked from thin air. But he refused repeatedly to go into any detail. The grandiose pomp of the song squares with Mercury's love of drama and passion, but it is worth considering if there were other forces at work.

In 1969 when he innocently made himself that tea laced with marijuana, friends testified to Mercury's total avoidance of drugs. Six years on his horizons had broadened through travelling and meeting new people on tour. His exposure to drugs and drug-taking must have also increased. Before long he was known to be using cocaine, which had to have started sometime around the mid-seventies. Is it possible that his early experiments with cocaine coincided with writing this song? He would not have been the first or last performer to believe that drugs unlocked the mind and released his best work.

Whatever influenced 'Bohemian Rhapsody', its effect on the public was polarised. A decade later, one Midlands radio station poll revealed that the single topped both the Best Ever Record and the Worst Ever Record categories. This was typical of the extreme reaction Freddie Mercury, as a person and performer, elicited all his life. In 1975 reviewers were split in their response, but what did prove unfounded was the fear that radio would not play the single in its entirety. Demand for it was so great that it received massive exposure on the airwaves.

'Bohemian Rhapsody's' phenomenal impact had journalists clamouring for interviews. This time, to tackle Mercury's resistance to talking to the media, Tony Brainsby adopted a new strategy: 'By the time Queen started to get themselves a name, then Freddie began doing just the major interviews. He became a commodity only to be brought out when the big guns were around, like national newspapers, *NME* front cover, that sort of thing. When they were interested, then I could talk him into doing interviews. Later, Brian and the others became cover material, but in those days it was very much Freddie who was the focus.

'Their fame came quickly by comparison to some and with "Bo Rhap", as it became known, Fred was suddenly a star. Even so we didn't have to use him all the time. We simply wouldn't have dreamt of asking him to do something that wasn't considered big enough so we worked around it.

'In this business you must maintain the mystique, and you just can't do that by trotting someone out at the drop of a hat. The fact that this was right up Freddie's street was a bonus, I guess. When Fred did do an interview, mind you, it wasn't that the people got close to him, because he treated these sessions the same as performing. He'd put on a big show for the journalists and photographers, and be wonderfully colourful and camp.'

As it happened there wasn't a lot of time to fend off the media, for Queen had a lengthy UK tour lined up for mid-November. Before that there was other work to do. 'Bo Rhap' had entered the charts at number forty-seven and was rising fast. *Top of the Pops* was the obvious next step, but the song's highly technical make-up ruled out live performance. Director Bruce Gowers, who had previously filmed Queen at the Rainbow

Theatre, was approached to make a promotional video.

The concept of pop promos had hardly moved on from when bands like the Stones played on a beach and people off-camera lobbed boulders down a hill behind them. What Mercury and the others had in mind was different. Having already booked time at Elstree Studios for pre-tour rehearsals, on the morning of 10 November 1975 they put their ideas into practice. What they produced took four hours to shoot, cost £4500 and required one day to edit. The result was semi-psychedelic and eerily dramatic, the prototype hard-rock video promo, which, when premiered on *Top of the Pops* ten days later, was to change the face of pop-music marketing for ever.

Already captivated by the single, the public reacted well, and sales rocketed. 'Bohemian Rhapsody' would go platinum, selling in excess of 1.25 million copies in Britain alone. But amid the gasps, sighs and envy in the music world, there were the odd dissenters. DJ John Peel admired Queen at the outset but had grown to dislike what he felt was their bombastic style. Having made fun of them one night on *TOTP*, he recalls that soon afterwards Mercury had told reporters he intended punching Peel out next time they met. Far from concurring with the rest of the world that 'Bo Rhap' was the making of Queen, in Peel's opinion it was the end of the band. Brian May has subsequently suggested that it was Peel himself who was too bombastic – and that what Queen actually became was too successful. 'It's a problem to do too well in Britain,' May says.

Someone else who had a mixed reaction to 'Bohemian Rhapsody' was Dick Taylor, Pretty Things' lead guitarist and a friend of Mercury's: 'I think it's great now. I mean it's a classic. You can't argue with it. But, at the time, I kind of fell in and out of love with it. The first time I heard it, I thought, Blimey! That's a bit OTT! But that was Freddie, and he was so bloody good at it.'

The TV première took place one week into Queen's tour.

The next day the single's album, *A Night at the Opera*, was released. For the first time Mercury was responsible for the cover concept. Four days later 'Bohemian Rhapsody' hit the number one spot in the charts.

It might have been that success had gone to his head, or just that he felt Queen were not receiving the respect they deserved, but Mercury began to show signs of excessive self-importance. Tony Brainsby was an independent PR consultant, which for him had advantages: 'It's good to handle other people, because it proves beneficial to everyone. If someone phoned me up for a Freddie Mercury quote that I couldn't deliver, I might have to say, Well, no-can-do, but I can get you an interview with so-and-so; it equally worked the other way round. I was always talking to people about Queen and had often got them attention when someone had rung up looking for another band entirely.

'The only problem I had with Freddie occurred during this tour. At this point I also represented Wings, and they were touring the UK at the same time as Queen. As a rule I didn't go on the road with any band, but this was, after all, Paul McCartney and on something like only his second tour of Britain in a long time. The media, of course, went mad, and the national newspapers were giving Wings daily coverage. But although I went on that tour, I was still dealing with all my other business by phone, and neglecting no one, but Freddie got jealous that McCartney was getting loads of attention.

'Queen were basking in all their "Bohemian Rhapsody" glory, but they weren't yet superstars. But, anyway, I got this imperious summons from Freddie to come to Manchester to see him, and that's the only time we had – well, I hesitate to call it a falling out as such, but let's say he tried to give me a right bollocking. We met in a hotel room, and Freddie paced angrily about demanding, "What's going on? Why are you not on the road with us? And why is McCartney getting all this coverage?"

'Well, what could I say? I told Fred I was getting Queen as much attention as there was to get, and that there was nothing more to do. He still went on about it, so in the end I told him straight that I was talking incessantly to people about Queen, but they were queuing round the block to talk to McCartney, and that was that. Freddie just wouldn't accept it.

'Harvey Goldsmith was the promoter for both tours, and he was getting it in the neck from Freddie then too. My final word to him on the matter was that I couldn't be in two places at the same time and left to rejoin McCartney.'

The fracas with Brainsby over, the Queen tour trundled on through four Hammersmith Odeon gigs, before heading north. Here they were to run into trouble, as personal manager Pete Brown recalls: 'They'd played Newcastle and were heading for a few gigs in Scotland when our coach was stopped on the motorway by police waiting for us. The police mounted roadblocks, sealing off every exit route, which must've cost them an absolute fortune . . . Nobody had anything, but I remember the silent anxiety that some silly sod in the entourage might have something, however small, on him. But no one had.

'Still, we all got dragged to the cop shop, and my main concern was that the delay might mean cancelling a show. The police thought they had the scoop of the year and were furiously rifling through the bus, even sticking their noses in the ashtrays. When they couldn't come up with so much as a joint, their disappointment was almost laughable.'

On the whole they were treated well, particularly when the police began to realise that they'd been hoaxed by someone who had told them that Queen were all high on drugs. Eventually they were released in the early hours of the morning, which left Brown worrying whether they would reach Dundee in time for their date at the City Hall.

The furthest north Queen ever played in Britain was a gig on 14 December at the Capitol in Aberdeen. By this time it looked as if 'Bohemian Rhapsody', still at the top, would hold on long enough to be that year's Christmas number one; a distinction much fought over. Towards the end of the tour, the band had a few days off, and Pete Brown recalls going to Brighton with them to see a gig: 'We'd all gone to the Dome to see Hot Chocolate. They had a terrific number just out, called "You Sexy Thing", and it was a good night. Later, back at our hotel, suddenly the restaurant door flew open, and Errol Brown (Hot Chocolate's lead singer) burst in. He headed straight for Freddie, shouting, "You bastards! My main shot at a Christmas number one! You bastards!" God, it was so funny!'

On Christmas Eve 1975, Queen returned to the Hammersmith Odeon for a performance that was to be televised live by *The Old Grey Whistle Test* and picked up for simultaneous broadcast on Radio One. Three weeks before, *A Night at the Opera* had been released in America, while in Britain it had already gone platinum. The day after Boxing Day, it, too, hit the top slot in the UK album charts. This was Queen's most successful year to date. For Mercury personally it had been a period of great change, something that would, in crucial ways, cause trouble ahead. But right then, the future meant tomorrow, and wider horizons were at last visible. Mercury had always known that he had been born to live life to the fullest; all he had so far lacked was the opportunity. He had a feeling that was about to change.

SEVEN

Excess of Ego

By mid-January 1976 'Bohemian Rhapsody' had reigned over the UK singles chart for nine consecutive weeks. This matched a twenty-year-old record set by the American singer Slim Whitman with 'Rose Marie' and secured Mercury and Queen innumerable accolades at the annual music-press poll awards. With the confidence, too, that *A Night at the Opera* had already topped the half-million sales, rehearsals were in progress for the next stage.

In March they hoped to repeat their triumph in the Far East with their second tour of Japan. This was to be followed immediately with what would be, in effect, their first tour of Australia – baling out after one gig at the Melbourne Festival two years earlier hardly counted. And before all this, there was an extensive tour of North America and Canada. In contrast to the previous whistle-stop itinerary, this time they played at fewer venues but often stayed four consecutive nights in the same city, which cut down on the punishing travel schedule. As they flew out of Britain on 20 January, Mercury was pleased to be working with Gerry Stickells. As ex-tour manager for Jimi Hendrix, no doubt he quizzed him for reminiscences of his late idol.

Queen opened to a rapturous reception at the Palace Theater, Waterbury, a week after their arrival. Their response there augured well for the rest of the tour. Like true rock stars, everywhere they went now fans mobbed them, the more ingenious among them tracking the band's whereabouts, on the trail of anything from an autograph to a kiss. A growing army of groupies had even begun bribing their way into hotel rooms, in the hope of making their celebrity conquest for the night.

Despite Mercury's increasingly bisexual reputation, on stage his style, especially in America, had become more macho. With his slinky build, luxurious dark hair and lively wicked eyes, women found him incredibly sexy. They could prove determined in their pursuit of him, too, as Freddie learnt the hard way. One day in New York, as he stepped on to the kerb into a frantic gaggle of girls, the scarf around his neck was grabbed at both ends and pulled tight. He could have been choked to death had it not been for the swift intervention of his companions. What amused them most about the incident was Mercury's subsequent rage at the damage done to his precious silk scarf.

In New York he teamed up with his old Mott the Hoople mate Ian Hunter at the famous Electric Ladyland Studios, which had been founded by Hendrix. Hunter was working on a solo album *All American Alien Boy*, with producer Roy Thomas Baker, when he discovered that Queen were in town. He invited his friends along to a recording session, and May and Taylor, accompanied by Mercury, ended up singing backing vocals on 'You Nearly Done Me In.'

Mercury adored New York. It was a city he would often roam, exploring especially its seedier sides. He also enjoyed visiting the numerous gay clubs and bars, and loved to cruise the streets at night in a darkened limousine. From the car he surveyed the parade of street life, sipping on his favourite iced vodka. He was living the rock dream as he saw it.

Queen were going from strength to strength, as news from

England revealed an unprecedented four albums in the UK top thirty at the same time; with even *Queen* reaching number twenty-four, two years after its release. Inspired by this proof of their popularity, at gigs Mercury took to toasting his loyal subjects with brimming flutes of champagne. He drank in the audience adulation, as much as the pale tawny wine in his glass. But behind the scenes it wasn't all moonlight and roses. Personal manager Pete Brown has his own memories of this tour, particularly of Chicago.

'Wherever we went, when the time came to move on it was my job to settle the hotel bills. We'd been two days in Chicago and were heading to St Louis, but when I tried to use the Queen credit card they said it was overextended. What made it worse was that it was a Sunday with no banks open, and I still had to organise their luggage and transport to the airport. Getting anxious, I argued with the desk clerk, insisting he'd just have to take it now and sort it out later, but he wasn't having it. I didn't know what to do and started to turn away when suddenly the guy pulled a gun on me. I can't remember if I actually threw my hands up, but I certainly froze and said, "Easy, mate! I've got all the time in the world."'

In the end Pete Brown persuaded the local promoter to come and settle the bill in cash, but by then he faced another problem. 'We'd missed the flight,' he explains, 'and I was scared stiff that they'd not be able to make the next gig. Hours had already slipped by, and my nerves were in shreds. I was convinced I'd be sacked, but I just did what I could to rustle up a string of station wagons to get them on the road.'

Nothing else major happened to upset Brown for the remainder of this particular tour. But trouble of a different kind lay in wait for him, when, having quit America mid-March for a short but rewarding return to Japan, their globe-trotting took them to the Antipodes.

This first tour of Australia, kicking off at the Entertainments

Centre in Perth, was important to Queen. Wary of their reception this time around, they were also exhausted. They had been on tour for nine weeks already, and Mercury in particular was feeling stressed. When they reached Sydney to play the Horden Pavilion, events turned ugly.

'It was all because when we arrived we discovered that to get to the theatre it meant going through a huge fairground,' Pete Brown explains. 'Well, from one look at the set-up, it was obvious that there was no way you could drive through the crowds of people, so I asked the band to get out of their respective cars and walk. Freddie's immediate response was, "My dear, I can't possibly walk anywhere!" and he point-blank refused to leave the limo. We had to drive through at a snail's pace so as not to injure anyone, and Freddie acted up with the champagne all the way. Needless to say, your average male Oz didn't much care for this, and the catcalls started – shouts like "pommie pussies" and worse. They lunged angrily at the windows, sticking two fingers up at those inside, and banged with clenched fists on the passing cars.'

When the cavalcade reached the Pavilion safely, despite the fact that his own arrogance had caused much of the trouble, Mercury took his temper out on Brown. 'When Freddie wanted to be, he was very tough,' he reveals. 'He often made me cry during the years I worked for him. This time, when we got inside he was in such a cold rage that he picked up a big mirror and literally smashed it over my head. Then he ordered me to find a brush to sweep up the glass.'

Mercury once blamed the pressures of fame for his temperament. His growing reputation for throwing things at people was, he stressed, very unlike him. Certainly Pete Brown must have known other, better sides of Mercury, for he held no grudge against the star for this latest abuse, maintaining, 'You see it was the humiliation he'd suffered. He just had to take it out on someone, and that time it was me. I understood.'

By their final gig at Brisbane's Festival Hall on 22 April, there was good reason to celebrate. The tour had been a great success. This time when their Quantas Air flight took off for London, both their single and album topped the Australian charts, marking their first major breakthrough there.

Queen arrived home to yet more good news. Bruce Gowers's *Queen at the Rainbow* was screening in UK cinemas, in support of *Hustle*, starring Burt Reynolds (the American actor about whom Mercury later confessed often to fantasise). As a result of their recent tour to America, 'Bohemian Rhapsody' had reached number nine in the US singles charts. In addition, the single won the Best Selling British Record category at the twenty-first annual Ivor Novello Awards held that year at London's Dorchester Hotel.

Days later Brian May married Christine Mullen at a Roman Catholic church in Barnes. John Deacon was already wed to Veronica Tetzlaff, and Roger Taylor, still the committed bachelor, remained content to play the field. Freddie Mercury, although still close to Mary Austin, was grappling with some serious choices; inner battles he would continue to fight for several more months.

According to Mercury, the first real financial return he began to see from his music came with Queen's fourth album *A Night at the Opera*. Some of that money he was now using to finance his growing use of cocaine. Perhaps his drug abuse partly accounted for the mood swings that had resulted in his assaulting a loyal employee. But, within himself, Mercury must have realised that his life was changing. As is often the case, it was the band who gave Mercury a sense of continuity – Roger Taylor would later refer to it as 'like coming home to mother' – and here something had changed too. Queen's first five singles had been written by either Mercury or May, but on this occasion John Deacon came up with a beautifully melodic ballad.

'You're My Best Friend' was released on 18 June and gave Queen a number seven hit. By this time Queen had reverted to what they called 'routine time', when each band member wrote songs that they would then argue about in the studio. Mercury was stubborn, but he wasn't alone, and these sessions were frequently a lively and spirited debate about the quality of material on offer. Working at The Manor, Wessex Studios, and Sarm East Studios, Mercury also found time to design the future album sleeve.

The urge to perform live, however, was never dormant for long, and around this time Sir Richard Branson, now the multi-millionaire founder of the Virgin Group, had come up with an exciting proposition. 'I'd had the idea to try to stage a free open-air gig in Hyde Park, which would promote a few bands at the same time,' says Branson. 'The problem was, I wasn't in a position then to finance something like that, so as I already knew Roger Taylor, I approached him thinking that Queen might go for it.' Remembering the impact that the Stones 1969 Hyde Park concert had made on him, Branson believed that Queen could really break in Britain with the same sort of exposure.

Queen agreed and were eager to arrange the gig that next month – which was hardly feasible. But Branson worked through the many stipulations laid down by the Metropolitan Police and the London Parks Committee, gradually pulling the pieces together. 'When I had all the necessary clearance,' he says, 'and the project was a goer, I handed it over to the Queen management to take from there.'

The date was set for 18 September, which worked out well with Queen's arrangements to play two gigs earlier in the month. The first show took place during the annual Edinburgh Festival at the Playhouse Theatre, when they were supported by Supercharge. And the second was in Wales, at Cardiff Castle. Billed QUEEN AT THE CASTLE, the outdoor gig came at the end of the worst drought in Britain for years. Rivers and reservoirs had dried up, and in some places the street standpipes were back in operation.

But, as the 12,000-plus crowd assembled that night, the rains started, pouring down as support acts Frankie Miller's Full House, Manfred Mann's Earthband and Andy Fairweather Low played their sets. By the time Queen appeared, the ground was a bog, and the crowd were soaking wet.

The compère in Cardiff had been Radio One presenter Bob Harris, who was on duty again eight days later at Hyde Park, when more than ten times the Cardiff crowd converged on the area. Capital Radio was covering the event live, with commentary from Kenny Everett and Nicky Horne. This night, too, was the first time Freddie Mercury met sixties' pop star Dave Clark, who would become one of his closest friends.

Besides his professional association with Queen, Harris had developed a close friendship with the band and already held them in high regard: 'They were very bright, and their overview was always keen,' says Harris. 'They were never an exploitative band either.' Referring to another stylish group at the time, he recalls, 'I remember being in a production meeting with the members of this group, and it was, "What do the punters want?" said in a very dismissive and blasé way. Queen were never guilty of that, and, in fact, genuinely cared very much for their fans.'

The support acts at Hyde Park included Steve Hillage, Supercharge and Kiki Dee. Having lately enjoyed a number one hit with Elton John with 'Don't Go Breaking My Heart', Dee had hoped to persuade John to appear with her. But, in the end, she settled for dueting with a cardboard cut-out of the star instead.

'Queen came on just as it was getting dark,' recalls Bob Harris. 'People had been amassing since midday, and, by mid-afternoon, when you stood on the stage, you could see the crowd literally stretching to the horizon line. The mass of humanity was an incredible sight.'

Greeting this mass of humanity with the words 'Welcome to our picnic by the Serpentine', Mercury, in a black leotard scooped to the navel and with ballet pumps on his feet, launched into a high-energy rendition of 'Keep Yourself Alive'.

'It was a brilliant event,' says Harris, 'and Queen were very special that day.'

The roar for an encore was deafening, making Mercury desperate to return on stage, as much for himself as for his fans. At Queen concerts, he often taunted an audience with the battle cry, 'This is what you want? This is what you're gonna get!' Only that day the police saw to it that no one was getting anything more. Prior to the event they had laid down a strict set of dos and don'ts, and as the schedule had already overrun by thirty minutes they threatened Mercury with instant arrest if he dared place a foot back on the stage. To prove their point, they pulled the plug on the power supply, momentarily plunging the park into pitch darkness.

Sir Richard Branson recalls, 'It was a vitally important gig for Queen – and a turning point in their career.' The band put this to best use in the weeks ahead, while working on their new album. *A Day at the Races* was released during the second week in December, when, despite music-press criticism that it lacked inspiration, it was a resounding success for them.

Almost exactly a month earlier, Mercury's love song 'Somebody to Love' had been chosen as Queen's next single. Kenny Everett once more bombarded his Capital Radio listeners with the number, to the extent that it topped the station's own chart, Hitline. When it was officially released on 12 November, however, it stopped just short of giving Mercury the satisfaction of a second national number one.

By now, in a deeply personal way, physical and emotional fulfilment was a serious issue for Mercury. He had battled with himself for a long time, but by the end of 1976, he felt he had to sacrifice his relationship with Mary Austin for stronger desires. That Mercury deeply loved Austin has never been disputed. That he felt compelled to redefine their life together did not mean he was less devoted to her, nor, time would prove, she to him. His decision led to an unusual coexistence. While Mercury pursued the gay life he craved, Mary Austin went on to make other relationships, from which she had children. She was pregnant with her second child when Mercury died. But she remained involved with him throughout his life. And Mercury's abiding love for the woman he had met when he was unknown and penniless always overshadowed his closest relationships with male lovers.

The break with Austin was a huge relief to Mercury, and 1977 began a period of promiscuity that lasted for at least five years. He boasted that his enormous sex drive led him to bed hundreds; not an unusual claim in rock, though the bragging usually refers to female groupies. After an evening's partying on the gay scene, Mercury would select whoever took his fancy. He wanted sex with no strings and would leave for home around dawn with his conquest in tow. It appears that he wasn't fussy, and for someone whose artistic sensibilities were becoming increasingly refined, he could go extremely downmarket. This period also saw a marked increase in Mercury's use of cocaine.

His diet of sex and drugs was indulged by Queen's hectic life on the road, especially during the two- or three-month US/Canadian tours. The most extensive of these was due to begin on 13 January, and Queen arrived in Milwaukee to find the country experiencing the lowest temperatures of the century. Joining them on the bill was Thin Lizzy, fronted by Phil Lynott and featuring lead guitarist Scott Gorham. The raucous rock band, which derived its name from Tin Lizzy, a comic-strip robot, had recently notched up two top ten UK hits.

Their manager Chris O'Donnell remembers getting this support slot:

'Thin Lizzy had been due to tour America on their own, when Brian Robertson got involved in a fight at the Speakeasy Club. Some guy had tried to smash a bottle over Frankie Miller's head, and Brian put his arm up to stop the bottle, which shattered and badly cut his hand. The injury was so nasty that he couldn't play the guitar. I went straight to America to see if I could find a way of keeping Lizzy's new album alive, and when I was there I got a phone call, out of the blue, from Queen's US agent then, Howard Rose. Rose told me that Queen were big fans of Thin Lizzy and wondered if they would like to support them on their States tour.'

Returning to Britain and substituting guitarist Gary Moore for the injured Robertson, O'Donnell set about negotiating terms on the band's behalf. 'I was a young manager then in partnership with Chris Morrison, and basically we couldn't believe our luck,' he admits. 'I heard myself saying we can't do this, or yes, we will do that, but at first it was very strange.' Controlling his delight, however, O'Donnell was less impressed in other ways.

'I'd gone to the Reid offices to discuss the tour,' he recalls, 'and at that time "Somebody To Love" had entered the charts, and Queen were hoping to do *Top of the Pops*. But the thing is, it had been at number two, and news had just come through that it'd quickly dropped back to five. Well, there was a girl there screaming down the phone to someone at the BBC that they just *had* to get on the show. The whole premise of *TOTP* was that it only featured bands whose records were rising up the charts, but this girl's whole attitude spelt out, "But we're Queen! We're apart from all that."'

Independent-minded himself, O'Donnell says that Thin Lizzy, unusually, did not pay to support Queen. It was a personal thing: 'I just don't agree with the practice. In the business it's called tour support money, and basically a band sells the slot to help defray the cost of sound and lights, with the payback for the support band supposedly being the exposure which could lead to them being big. I'm very sceptical about that so, no, Lizzy didn't pay to support Queen.'

According to O'Donnell, Queen's first couple of US dates were little more than warm-up gigs, and the tour only started properly once Thin Lizzy joined them. The trip was a revelation for him: 'There were definitely times when Thin Lizzy played Queen off the stage. I felt that, good as they were, Queen were now so stylised that the slightest thing going wrong threw the whole perfect balance right off. Whereas Lizzy were so hungry and raw that by contrast they had this unpredictable energy on stage, and it showed. Having said that, they were a great package.'

For someone who had started out in awe of Queen, reality proved disillusioning, especially with regard to Mercury's personality and behaviour: 'To me Queen were one of the greatest rock bands ever but not all America is New York and Los Angeles – you play an awful lot of gigs in between. We turned up at one airport and headed as usual for the cars which had been laid on to pick us up. Midwest towns would have a 20,000 capacity sports stadium, but beyond that the facilities were not great.

'This particular day we arrived and found that three shiny black saloon cars had been hired for us from the local funeral parlour; they were the best cars they had. Well, Freddie threw a major wobbly and went into a huge sulk because there was no limousine and flatly refused to get into the car. Now, I know for a fact that he had been told, well in advance, that in these places there would be no point expecting any stretch limos and yet he still had to make a big noisy issue about it.'

Unwittingly reinforcing Pete Brown's theory about the cause of some of Mercury's prima donna antics, O'Donnell adds, 'Of course, this kind of carry-on manifested itself in tantrums when they really stemmed from other, deeper problems.'

But that petulant display wasn't an isolated incident. O'Donnell generally found Mercury a difficult person. 'He was in a spiral of the lifestyle he led, as happens in many cases,' he explains, 'and it just isn't a real situation. He gathered this great court around himself. Pete Brown was on that trip, as were his personal assistants Paul Prenter and Joe Fanelli, but there were several others. He had an American hairdresser, for example, who accompanied him everywhere, a personal masseur and a dresser, and it was all, "Freddie darling, this" and "Certainly, Freddie darling, that." On stage he was the consummate professional and very driven by fame, but he had to live the whole thing off stage, too, and, of course, in one way he ended up paying the price.'

'In his Kensington market days he had been an entirely different person. Now he'd lost that. It's easily done. In management you become fully aware that it's a period of escalation – that's what you work towards in the first place. But it becomes very hard to control, and it's like holding the reins of a runaway horse – eventually you're scared to let go, and you wonder where it's taking you.'

Quite early on in the tour, one particular incident left its mark on O'Donnell. Having completed two Canadian dates, Queen returned to America for a gig at the Stadium in Chicago, when he recalls, 'The weather was atrocious – snow, ice and horrendously bitter – and the equipment trucks had been delayed travelling down from Montreal because of the conditions. Well, at the theatre the kids were queuing round the block, huddling and blowing on their hands to keep warm, and the promoter was *pleading* with Freddie to be allowed to open the doors and let them in.

'Queen were very late anyway, and he eventually told Freddie that many of the fans were actually turning blue outside. His only response was, "Darling, we haven't had a sound check yet. We can't possibly let them hear Queen until then." And what's more, I watched him deliberately set about delaying the whole process, just to make his point.'

Disgusted by this behaviour, O'Donnell continues: 'Freddie very much had a vision of where they were going, where he himself was going. He was totally professional in terms of how he was going to get it, too. And you can't take away from the fact that he wrote all those songs. During the tour, I'd stand in the wings and be amazed at Queen's performance and, particularly, Freddie's. As a showman, there was no one to touch him. He was brilliant, and I'd been such a fan of his songwriting. But, oh, close up, he irked me a lot. It was such a disappointment.'

That all four band members had different natures was, O'Donnell believes, the catalyst that made them a great band. 'But it was not at all relaxing to be around Freddie,' he goes on, 'for the simple reason that everything had to be about him and his performance. In fact, at times signs of jealousy crept in because of it, when, afterwards, they would sit around and dissect a show.'

After-gig dinners were also something of a performance: 'I'd never seen tour catering like it,' recalls O'Donnell. 'Not for Queen the obligatory backstage grub. They went for the four-course gourmet routine, complete with candelabra. What started to happen, though, was that Brian and Roger, who were the real rockers of the band, would slip away with Phil and Scott to hang out at some club in town, leaving Freddie and John behind. Then John gradually started leaving, too, and Freddie would go off to prowl the gay clubs, but even then I felt there was no room for spontaneity, everything always seemed rigidly planned.'

As the tour progressed, aspects of Mercury's grandiose behaviour, so alien to O'Donnell, began to rub off on Phil

Lynott. Other Thin Lizzy members, and some of their road crew, couldn't help but notice that the Dublin-born singer was hugely impressed by the way Mercury never carried his own luggage on arrival at an airport. Instead he would sweep ahead regally to the car, leaving his 'bag man' to do the labouring. How, once at the hotel, he would inspect the quality of accommodation on offer before agreeing to stay. Influenced, too, by Jimi Hendrix and decidedly flash himself, Phil Lynott clearly had an affinity with Mercury. He soon began to get difficult, complaining that his room wasn't big enough or the hotel not grand enough.

Lead guitarist Scott Gorham has own recollections of the tour. Born in Santa Monica, with his laid-back Californian outlook, he remembers Mercury with affection: 'Yeah, well, Fred was a real different kinda guy for me. Thin Lizzy were 100 per cent a politically incorrect band, and, I mean, all down the road, y'know? For a start, we were all completely homophobic, and, like, we didn't know how to treat this Freddie Mercury, until we met him and discovered that he was a lovely guy. He wasn't at all how we'd imagined, especially with our ready-made prejudices. But, you know, Fred had a strong personality, strong enough to win just about anybody over, and that's what he did with Thin Lizzy.'

Touching on the homophobia, Chris O'Donnell says that 'Despite having a name like Queen and their front man being the way Freddie was, it was very much a boys' band. The gay element on stage just wasn't there now. They played hard rock, and Freddie never came away with any of those familiar effeminate gestures. Off stage was another matter, and, I suppose, it was one of the hardest aspects for Freddie to be living one lifestyle on stage, which was so much at odds with his private life.'

The two worlds, however, were not always so distinct, something for which Scott Gorham can vouch. 'Hell, no!' he declares. 'We played one gig at the massive Winterland in Frisco, which is a city kinda known as having a big gay community. We were first up, and, OK, so I'm blastin' away and rushing about the left-hand side of the stage, thinking I'll go and mess with the audience on the right. The spotlight all the time is chasin' me, and I get over there and look up, and there's like five hundred of the gayest guys I've ever seen, man! They were wearing sequinned hot pants, satin jumpsuits, huge floppy hats with waving ostrich feathers, and they're jumpin' off their seats chuckin' feather boas in the air. As soon as I arrived at their side, they all started lunging at me shoutin', "Yeah! Shake it, boy!" Geez, man! I'm thinkin', Whoa there, buddy. I'm not real ready for that kinda contact! And I'm already makin' a beeline to the farthest left I can find!

'And that followed the tour around. But the funny thing is, the more you meet these people, the less weird they seem, and you accept that they've just got a few flamboyancies that you've to get used to. Most of them are real nice. I realised then that you've gotta open up your head about life.

'But if you could've seen Fred on that tour! He was just kickin', man. When Queen weren't going down particularly well, he worked his ass off to ensure they still ended up with two or three encores.'

During an arduous gig, in the midst of an equally strenuous tour, Mercury would gain the stimulus to keep going from sources other than his own adrenaline. It wasn't uncommon during a guitar solo for him to go backstage for a snort of cocaine. Of this tour, Gorham says, 'I never actually saw him doing drugs that trip. He wasn't throwing it about and making it a problem. He was very discreet.'

But it had been a different story before the tour began. Gorham recalls: 'I was recording at Olympic Studios at the same time as Queen, and I met Freddie in the lobby, and he had had a few hits. He said, "Hey, Scott, can you do me a favour?" I replied, "Well, yeah." Freddie asked, "Can you come up and check out what we're doing upstairs. I really want you to listen to Brian's guitar sound. I think it's great, but he doesn't like it. Come on up and give us your opinion." By this time I'm saying, "Well, I'd rather not. I mean the world's full of crit-ics – who needs another?" But Freddie just had that persuasive thing, so I went, and it sounded great.

'Anyway, by this time Fred had had a few more snorts and was really goin' at it. In fact that was the first time I saw him take coke. I guess that's what was making him buzz the way he was, cos he started saying to Brian about me, "Hey, isn't this a handsome guy? Couldn't he have a great career on his own without playin' the guitar – just on his looks alone? Hey, Brian, don't ya think?!" And he kept on and on, and I'm winking at Brian, taking it all as a joke. But Fred was real loose and pes-tering Brian bad now, so to please him, he finally agreed.

'Happy, Freddie swung on me and starts telling me how he had been his school's ping-pong champion. I'd played it my whole life, and Fred, buzzin' worse, was goin' at me to take him on. Eventually I said, "All right, pal. Let's go," and Fred shoots off to the table downstairs. By the time I joined him he was deadly serious. I mean, this guy wants to win bad, and all these rules come flyin' out – how many games we're to play, the scoring, the lot. After too much of this I shout, "Hey cut it, man, get on with it."

'By this time I wanna beat him bad, and that was us, our recording sessions forgotten as for like two solid hours all you heard from the basement was "Shit!" or "Aw, good shot!" or "God dammit!" In the end I won and became the Olympic Studio ping-pong champ!' It was just a game, but despite his coke-induced high, the hugely competitive Mercury was not a happy man.

For Gorham, Mercury was unlike any other star he'd worked with: 'There were times during that tour when he wasn't being outrageous and in fact was quite sedate. He was an intelligent guy and not your basic rock slob. He had refinement. You could sit down with the bloke and talk to him, and he talked to you. He was also a good listener. He had the knack of making you open up. He certainly wasn't the kind whose ambition in life is to get pissed and go out and cause some problems.'

Mercury did most things to excess, and he often had a lot of fun doing them, as Trip Khalaf, the sound man assigned to tour with Queen in the States, once recalled: 'What a strange person Freddie was! I mean, he was a lovely person, but he wasn't one of us. He was a fascinating creature. On one hand he was completely ridiculous, but he *knew* he was completely ridiculous, and he enjoyed being ridiculous.'

What Mercury didn't enjoy was any problem with his health, but with such a punishing tour schedule in America, it was not unlikely that his throat condition would surface again. Immediately after that San Francisco gig, his throat problem re-emerged, resulting in the cancellation of two gigs to allow him to rest. With the unexpected time off, he went sightseeing in Hollywood, soaking up its glitz and glamour, before meeting up again with the others for the Canadian leg of their tour.

When Queen returned home in mid-March, it was to discover that their latest single 'Tie Your Mother Down', a typical hard rocker of Brian May's, hadn't broken into even the top 30. With the advent of the punk movement, bands such as the Clash, the Damned, X-Ray Spex and the Sex Pistols ruled the charts. The Pistols are in particular universally considered to have single-handedly launched New Wave music in Britain, punk roots having been laid some years before in America. The movement itself would die out in something like eighteen months, but its influence would be long-lasting.

The music press had been quick to latch on to punk, to the

exclusion of established bands such as Queen. Perhaps particularly Queen, since they were the extreme antithesis of the punk philosophy. But, Freddie Mercury remained unconcerned about New Wave and almost seemed to go out of his way to offset its grosser aspects.

He was even more showy on stage than ever. When Queen opened their European tour in Sweden on 8 May, he appeared at Stockholm's Ice Stadium sheathed in a replica of an almost diaphanous costume once worn by the dancer Nijinsky. And not content with the impact that made, he took the final encore in a silver skintight leotard, so heavily sequinned that it blinded the audience as he shimmied under the huge array of spotlights.

Throughout Denmark, Germany, Holland and Switzerland, there were continual gigs and parties. In Holland they were presented with no less than thirty-eight awards, a tribute to their huge popularity in the Netherlands. On their return to Britain, the UK leg of the tour began in Bristol, ending on 7 June at London's Earls Court. But, just before that, they played two dates in Liverpool, as Mercury's first manager, Ken Testi, recalls.

'By this time I had a famous club in Liverpool, called Erics, on Mathew Street, on the opposite side to where the Cavern had been. The Sex Pistols, the Clash, Nick Lowe, Dave Edmunds etc., all played there. I gave Holly Johnson his first break at Erics, and around 1977 it was a hot venue. Anyway, during Queen's tour they played two nights at the Empire, and while they were here they looked me up. Freddie, John and Roger arrived grandly at the club in three separate limousines, and it was great to share an hour or two with Freddie again.'

But Ken Testi was conscious of a barrier between them, which now he concedes was inevitable but regrettable and attributed to others. But whoever or whatever was to blame, as Chris O'Donnell had already experienced, Mercury had changed from his Kensington market stall days – and not necessarily for the better.

Queen performed on two consecutive nights at Earls Court three days later. It was Queen Elizabeth II's Silver Jubilee year. A huge fan of the monarchy, Mercury adored all its pomp and circumstance, and this must partly explain the lavish expense this time on their stage effects at Earls Court. Besides the familiar smoke bombs, fireworks and elaborate lighting, a specially designed rig, in the shape of a crown, had been commissioned at a cost of £50,000. Ascending dramatically amid the smoke of dry ice, Mercury was in his glory, straddling the centre stage beneath it.

Such an ostentatious display at the height of punk was guaranteed to goad the critics, and in June *NME* attacked Mercury in a lengthy interview by Tony Stewart, entitled IS THIS MAN A PRAT? Stewart criticised Mercury's love of lavishly toasting his audience with champagne, as well as generally setting out to lampoon him. But the foppish Mercury turned out to be a good match for Stewart, a fact that was clear in the text of the article.

That year the Sex Pistols' 'God Save the Queen' became a UK number one, outselling Rod Stewart two to one. Banned from the airwaves, at least one major retailer refused to stock the single, and many distributors would not handle it. Their manager Malcolm McLaren calls the number: 'The most English, angst-ridden, toughest, mother-fucking rock song that's ever been written,' adding, 'that was to me, punk rock at its best.'

Queen and the Pistols were to meet one day, in a recording studio. 'In 1977, after the Sex Pistols signed with A&M Records,' Malcolm McLaren recalled, 'we all trucked off to Wessex Studios in north London. Queen were recording in studio one, and Chris Thomas, the Sex Pistols' producer, was in studio two. On entering studio one on his way next door, Sid

Vicious got down on his hands and knees and crawled through Freddie Mercury's legs. That was the day the Sex Pistols finished their second and most notorious single, "God Save the Queen!"'

The studio work under way was for Queen's new album, although Mercury made time for another attempt at production; this time for actor Peter Straker, a close friend. Straker, who had been cast in the original stage production of *Hair* and appeared regularly on TV, had decided to make a record. Mercury's newly formed Goose Productions had invested £20,000 in Straker's album, *This One's On Me*. Mercury produced Straker with Roy Thomas Baker, but only as a one-off. When Straker went on to record more material with Goose, Mercury's role was purely financial. In addition to Goose Productions, in time he formed Mercury Songs, a publishing company set up to handle his future solo work.

Queen recordings soon demanded his full attention, and on 7 October their tenth single was released. It was 'We Are the Champions', a sturdy arm-locking anthem, written by Mercury. The simple but rousing chorus sounded as if it had been around for years and was a guaranteed crowd-pleaser. Its promotional video was, unusually, to be filmed in front of a live audience. Bruce Gowers, the promo director of 'Bohemian Rhapsody' who had also shot their last three videos, was not available. So they enlisted the services of Derek Burbridge to control the crowd of 'extras' hired through the Queen fan club for the shoot at the New London Theatre Centre.

Released with Brian May's 'We Will Rock You' as the B-side, 'We Are the Champions' was immediately panned by the critics. But the fans took no notice, and it went to number two. Elektra also liked the new single enough to release it as a double A-side. They correctly anticipated massive airplay and were rewarded by its huge success in the States. 'We Are the Champions' found favour throughout Europe, too, holding on

to the number one slot in France for an impressive twelve consecutive weeks. Today the song still features regularly at major
world sporting events.

When *News of the World*, the album from which the hit
single had been selected, was released at the end of the month,
it topped the charts in nine countries. Two years on Mercury
was still reaping awards for 'Bohemian Rhapsody', but he came
to value most highly the one he was to receive on 18 October,
at a ceremony in Wembley Conference Centre, when 'Bo
Rhap' tied jointly with Procol Harum's 'A Whiter Shade of
Pale' to receive the Britannia Award for the Best British Pop
Single of the Last Twenty-Five Years. Queen received their
awards from TV presenter Michael Aspel.

The financial rewards of their continuing success helped
Queen out of their commitment to Trident. Finally they could
buy themselves out of the clause in the severance agreements
that had given Trident a 1 per cent share of six future albums.
But any pleasure derived from this development was dulled by
the band's growing awareness of management difficulties.

As Pete Brown explains: 'The problem was that Queen
didn't feel that John Reid was able to give them enough of his
time, and that didn't suit them. When Queen were brought on
board you have to understand that it was really the Elton John
office. Reid had been working at Tamla Motown and hadn't
been a manager before Elton picked him to handle his business
affairs. He duly set John up with an office, and all the staff had
worked for Elton for a long time already, so their loyalties lay
there. If Elton had a tour, that took priority, and with the different personalities in Queen, you can imagine how that went
down.'

It was Queen's lawyer, Jim Beach, who negotiated their way
out of the partnership, and with much less difficulty than free-
ing the band from their ties to Trident. 'Queen were doing an
outdoor video shoot for "We Will Rock You" in Roger's

garden,' says Pete Brown. 'It was unbelievably cold, with snow lying about a foot deep, which made it not a lot of fun for everyone hanging about, as you do on film shoots. People were growing very touchy as the day wore on, and the light grew poorer; then suddenly John Reid arrived and the band all piled into the back of Freddie's limo. That's when they signed the severance papers.'

As a penalty for opting out of their contract in advance of the agreed expiry date, Queen had to pay a substantial sum of money to John Reid Enterprises, as well as signing over a sizeable percentage of royalties on existing albums.

Years later, when referring to Mercury's grasp of finances, Elton John commented that his friend wouldn't know the price of a pint of milk but could tell you, to a penny, the cost of a bottle of nail varnish. And Mercury himself often airily claimed never to concern himself with the extent of his wealth, maintaining that as long as he had enough money to go shopping he was happy. But in reality Mercury wasn't anything like so naive. He was fully conscious of the fact that once again they had had to shell out big. He was equally aware that while the downside of this latest severance with John Reid did not impoverish Queen, it did leave them with the continuing headache of making the correct decisions concerning future management.

After much discussion, the band unanimously agreed that they would try to manage themselves. They would be assisted by Pete Brown and Paul Prenter – both of whom remained with Queen, although they had been employed originally through John Reid – as well as Jim Beach and Gerry Stickells. And this new arrangement came into effect just prior to Queen's tour of America, their second that year.

Joining the band this trip was Bob Harris. He was working on a Queen documentary and intended to gather more footage for it, as well as holding interview sessions with Mercury and the others. 'The idea was to knock all this together with the tour film and do a retrospective at that point,' says Harris. 'But, in fact, what ended up happening was that on my return to London I went to an editing room in Wardour Street, with only an editing engineer in my innocence, and, of course, progress was extremely slow. I just didn't have the time with all my other commitments, and eventually Queen took back the film. Bits and pieces of it have emerged in various videos over the years.'

More successful was the tour itself, which began in Portland, at the Cumberland County Civic Center, on 11 November. That night, for the first time on tour, Mercury sang his tender ballad 'Love of My Life'. The audience joined in, and thrilled that they sang so well, Mercury stopped and let the fans carry on alone. From then on, this became a feature of every gig. As Mercury said, no matter where they performed the number, the fans automatically knew their role without him having to say a word.

Witnessing this first-hand, Bob Harris agrees that 'Freddie was one of the most generous performers in the business. It was no ego trip when he got the crowd to sing back to him. He actually wanted them to communicate with him that intensely.' This is something that is made especially clear from video footage. Here Mercury can be seen, looking like a doting tutor, as he watches and listens intently to the crowd. His eye contact with the vast audience is acute enough, one imagines, to pick out a single person in the back row not joining in.

By the time they reached New York on 1 December, it was clear that this was the tour that marked Queen's conquest of North America. Back in February they had played the prestigious Madison Square Garden, at which time Mercury had vowed to better Yes's record there of three consecutive sold-out nights. They would do five in a row, he said. Eleven months on, although they fell short of that pledge, Queen were still booked to headline for two consecutive nights. Both shows turned out to be very special.

Soon afterwards, Queen paid a return visit to the Stadium in Chicago. It was a bitterly cold night, but in contrast to Chris O'Donnell's recollections of Mercury keeping fans freezing in the snow, Bob Harris has happier memories. 'It was an amazing experience,' he recalls. 'The stadium was the one used by the Chicago Bears, and because it was so bitter we were all presented with a beautiful team jacket. I wore mine until it literally disintegrated. We went from there – and temperatures of minus fifteen degrees – to Las Vegas just three gigs later and a wall of heat. We'd arrived a few days before Queen were due to play, and so had a bit of a holiday. Roger, his minder and I one day worked our way down two strips, frequenting every hotel, casino, bar and club in our path.'

In contrast, Mercury preferred to enjoy himself out of the limelight, as this second lengthy US tour provided him with the opportunity to scour the gay scene. In public he maintained the distinction drawn between his 'secret' homosexuality and self-confessed bisexuality. He was now approaching superstar status and to have admitted openly to being gay could have jeopardised his popularity. Despite his camp behaviour, and the fact that he saw his bisexual image as creating an appropriate mystique, he had a strong female following, many of whom continued to see him as a red-blooded macho man. Either not hearing or choosing to ignore any talk to the contrary they happily fantasised about Queen's energetic lead singer and his raunchy routine with the sawn-off mike stand.

Having embarked on this track, Mercury never went back, but there are those who wonder, even at this early stage, about how content he was with his decision. Says Chris O'Donnell, 'Freddie demanded so much of people and often too much, so that at times they fell short of his expectations. He loved the adulation he received on stage, but in his personal life behind the scenes I felt he wasn't really enjoying himself, not deep down.' If this is true, it wasn't something Mercury cared to admit, and indeed with disregard for his own health – and that of his countless one-night stands – he would continue to behave recklessly for a long time.

EIGHT

Alley Creeper

Within a matter of months it became clear to Queen that managing themselves was not working out, and they turned to their new accountant, Peter Chant, for advice on setting up a proper management structure. It was decided that Chant would be responsible for the band's business, accounting and tax. Jim Beach was persuaded to resign his partnership in the west London law firm of Harbottle and Lewis in order to become Queen's manager, heading up the newly formed Queen Productions Ltd. At the same time, they created Queen Music Ltd and Queen Films Ltd.

No self-respecting band could hope to chart now without a pop promo. But the publicity videos were also proving more complex and expensive to make. While they were financing their own videos, Queen's idea behind setting up the two film and music companies was to retain the all-important control of the video rights and license them to EMI for promotional use.

By now Queen were such high earners that British income tax regulations would cripple them if they were to spend more than sixty-five days out of the year in the UK. On their accountant's advice, the solution was to record and perform overseas. The income could then legitimately be channelled through a different company from Queen Productions and would be tax-free. So after the release of the single 'Spread

Your Wings' on 10 February, they embarked on a spring tour of Europe. While in Berlin to play the Deutschlandhalle, Roger Taylor crossed Checkpoint Charlie into East Berlin. While there, he saw a piece of graffiti that made such an impact on him that it was to inspire his cover concept for their forthcoming album later that year.

The tour wound to a close with a few British dates. Mercury's style was visibly changing. Always flamboyant, he had appeared before his public in silver lurex bodysuits, black leotards, often with a diamanté-studded crotch, and other equally subtle outfits. Now he favoured shiny black PVC. Prowling the stage, and extremely light on his feet, he once confessed, 'I rather fancy myself as a black panther.' He also liked dressing from head to toe in leather. Both styles strengthened his manly stage image, but many fans wondered if they liked the new biker image. In the late seventies, this was also a popular style among gay men on the nightclub circuit – especially in America where Mercury had lately spent some time. Perhaps he viewed his new look as a way in which he could fuse his two worlds.

With Queen's heavy touring commitments, specific periods had to be timetabled in to allow them to get down to songwriting. Mercury spent most of the summer with the other band members at the Super Bear Studios in Nice for this purpose. His contribution to *News of the World* had been his least major to date, but this time he produced almost half of the thirteen tracks – the most controversial of which was 'Bicycle Race'. The annual Tour de France passed through the French Riviera when Queen were there, and the inspiration for the number had come from Mercury's appreciation of scores of hard-bodied young cyclists. He watched them race, crouched low over their handlebars and poured into Lycra. The song was to back Brian May's 'Fat Bottomed Girls'. Together these tracks would provoke a small storm of outrage.

With more extravagant budgets for their video promos, the temptation was to be even more risqué. Promoting 'Bicycle Race' and 'Fat Bottomed Girls' gave them the ideal opportunity to indulge themselves. Deciding to stage a girls' bicycle race, Queen hired Wimbledon Stadium, sixty-five models and Steve Wood as director. There was one important detail: the girls were all naked. It was all seen as a cheeky prank by those involved – except for Halfords, the company that supplied the bikes. They were prepared to accept back the cycles afterwards, but refused to do the same with the saddles. Queen had to pay for sixty-five new leather seats.

When the record was released on 13 October 1978, the sight of a naked rear on its sleeve caused an outcry. Accusations of sexism were thrown at the band, and *NME* ran an unflattering photo of Mercury, with the caption FAT BOTTOMED QUEEN. According to Brian May, they received no complaints from fans, but certain chain stores refused to carry what they considered to be a semi-pornographic poster. Later copies of the single were sold wrapped, the cover model now modestly clad in a superimposed pair of briefs.

Impatient at the pious uproar, Queen quit Britain soon after for another US/Canadian tour. By now they were almost as famous for the salacious entertainment laid on at their after-gig parties as for their music. At one of Mercury's private gatherings, an army of dwarfs ran around with bowls shoulder-high containing thousands of pounds worth of the finest cocaine for his guests. Certainly the goings-on at Queen's Halloween bash in New Orleans made the newspapers coast to coast in America – and beyond – and went down in Queen folklore as one of their most infamous. Parties often lasted days, but this time they had a gig in Miami on 3 November, and so made do with a twelve-hour orgy of excess. This featured such exotica as a nude model served up hidden in a huge salver of raw liver, semi-naked girls dancing in bamboo cages suspended from the ceiling, as well as female mud wrestlers and topless waitresses, all for the delectation of the most bizarre cocktail of people imaginable.

Publicist Tony Brainsby had clashed with Mercury in 1975 for his presence on a Wings tour, instead of going on the road with Queen. After a three-year absence, he was back to handle the band's PR, and he remembers this particular party well: 'It was a pretty wild night. I took a party of press over. We flew from London to New Orleans, partied for twelve hours solid and staggered back to the airport, still not having been to bed. They'd hired a huge hotel ballroom, which had been made to look like a swamp. There were trees, masses of hanging creepy vines, dry-ice smoke pumping everywhere and snakes, not to mention strippers. All in all, a first-class party!

'I don't recall seeing Freddie take coke that night. Mind you, he was discreet that way, and, anyway, in those days, rightly or wrongly, doing cocaine wasn't really seen as taking drugs. It was more a trendy thing to do.'

What Brainsby did see Mercury do was to sign his autograph for a stripper in an unusual place: 'I've got a photograph of Freddie signing his name on a stripper's botty as she slightly bends over a table.'

Continuing to indulge his fad for PVC, in shiny black trousers, a short-sleeved checked shirt and braces, Mercury may not have wanted to be seen taking drugs that night, when he circulated as the life and soul of the party. But, afterwards, it could have been a different story, as Brainsby recalls. 'Freddie would regularly go straight off to a club to hang out, and God knows what he got up to then,' he says.

This party had doubled as pre-launch publicity for *Jazz*, their forthcoming album, which was released in Britain on 10 November. Meanwhile, the tour went on. Regardless of the outrage at home, Queen had included a free graphic poster of the nude bike race with the album. Like the British shops,

With Mary Austin in 1987 at his 41st birthday at Pikes Hotel, Ibiza. Although Mercury had ended his physical relationship with Austin a decade earlier, she remained, to the end, the love of his life and inherited the bulk of his estate on his death. *(Photo courtesy of Tony Pike)*

Kindred spirits. Mercury and German film actress Barbara Valentin relax in the studio during a break in recording. 'We shared a once-in-a-lifetime love. It was so special, and I still loved him,' Valentin said. *(Photo courtesy of Barbara Valentin)*

Barbara Valentin's unique friendship with Mercury survived throughout the eighties. In the late phase of his illness, the star tried to cut himself off from some of his friends, but Valentin recalls, 'My doorbell rang one day, and it was Freddie. He said "I can't stay away from you. Take me in and take care of me."' *(Photo courtesy of Barbara Valentin)*

One of many attempts at an early Queen publicity shot, taken in Freddie Mercury's flat at 100 Holland Park Road, London. Mercury would regularly veto any photograph he felt didn't flatter him enough. *(Photo courtesy of Ken Testi)*

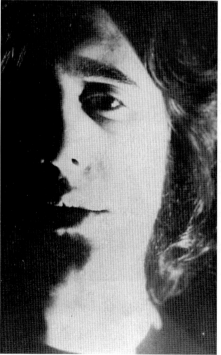

Queen's two party animals celebrate at Pikes. Mercury's friendship with Roger Taylor was strong and dated from the days when they survived on the tiny income from the stall that they ran together in London's infamous Kensington Market.

(Photo courtesy of Tony Pike)

Mercury's first manager when he fronted Ibex in 1969, Ken Testi also become Smile's first manager. When Mercury suggested renaming Smile as Queen, Testi remarked to him, 'You can't get away with that!' To which Mercury replied, 'But of course we can, my dear.'

(Photo courtesy of Ken Testi)

Freddie Mercury gets to the bottom of things here during the infamous 1978 New Orleans after-gig party. PR guru Tony Brainsby says: 'It was a really wild night – half naked dancers in bamboo cages, female mud wrestlers, snakes and strippers. All in all, in fact, a first-class party!' *(Photo courtesy of Tony Brainsby)*

(Left to right) Queen's manager Jim Beach, composer and close friend Mike Moran, Mercury, Spanish soprano Montserrat Caballe and promoter Pino Sagliocco are seen together in 1987 at the Spanish Embassy in London. A year later Mercury and Caballe were to headline at La Nit, the opening celebration for the run-up to the 1992 Olympic Games held in Barcelona. *(Photo courtesy of Pino Sagliocco)*

Surrounded by some of his closest friends at the Ibiza hideaway in 1989. Left to right: (back row) actor Peter Straker, promoter Pino Sagliocco, Mercury, his bodyguard Terry Giddings, an unknown associate, composer Mike Moran and Jim Hutton; (front row) hotelier Tony Pike and Mercury's confidante Barbara Valentin. *(Photo courtesy of Tony Pike)*

Close friend Kenny Everett was also a victim of AIDS. In 1975 it was Everett's unorthodox airtime blitz with 'Bohemian Rhapsody' that encouraged the single's release by EMI.

(Photo courtesy of Jo Gurnett)

The legendary Hollywood star Elizabeth Taylor, in her capacity as National Chairperson for the American AIDS Research Foundation (AmFAR), made a guest appearance at the 1992 Freddie Mercury Easter Tribute at Wembley. She described Mercury as 'an extraordinary rock star, who rushed across our cultural landscape like a comet shooting across the sky.' *(Bruce Weber: courtesy of Elizabeth Taylor)*

Mercury hides behind his tennis racket after a match with
Tony Pike at Pike's Hotel. *(Photo courtesy of Tony Pike)*

though, American stores considered it pornographic and banned its inclusion in Stateside copies. Probably stung by this, during the band's two-night stint at Madison Square Garden, several naked ladies on bikes were arranged to join them on the New York stage. During 'Fat Bottomed Girls' they circled Mercury, defiantly ringing their bells. The continuing controversy did them no harm. *Jazz* went to number two in the charts, and Queen received the Gold Ticket award in recognition of their performance before more than 100,000 fans at the Garden.

Flying home for Christmas, Mercury barely had time to touch base before he rejoined Queen in January for yet another European tour. The treadmill of recording and touring was beginning to get to him. Nevertheless he was cheered to learn when they reached Brussels for their gig at the Forest Nationale that, back home, the new single 'Don't Stop Me Now' had received two very good reviews.

Fatigue was setting in. Throughout Holland, Switzerland, Yugoslavia and Spain, with two return trips to Germany, they gigged nightly to enthusiastic fans, some of whom were fanatical enough to trail the band. When Queen reached Paris for the last three nights at the Pavilion de Paris, Mercury recognised faces that stared up at him from the front row. On the final night, he barked, 'Fuck sake! Are you lot here again?' But he was delighted by their devotion and proudly dubbed them 'the Royal Family'.

On occasions, as their personal manager, Pete Brown envied the fans. At least Mercury showed them his appreciation of their loyalty. Brown was experiencing problems with the band again. 'Wherever Queen went,' he explains, 'it was my job to make sure that the style and size of their accommodation was exactly equal. Their idea was that that way no one would have anything better than the other, but trying to put theory into practice was often near impossible.

'I tried my best, but that European tour, it didn't matter what I did, it wasn't right, and I'm sure it was a record that I managed to upset all four at the same time.

'My problem was that I could never develop a thick skin against it. It hurt me a lot sometimes, but I don't regret it. We had some good times.' Just as when Pete Brown forgave Mercury for assaulting him in a fit of temper, so once more he blames the hectic schedule: 'It was definitely the pressures. I guess you would have had to experience it to understand.'

The pressures could only have worsened during their subsequent third visit to Japan, this time for a much longer tour. It was a professionally fruitful visit, with numerous awards for top single, top album and top group. As summer approached, free time was scarce as recording commitments meant a confinement in Mountain Studios, Montreux. The complex was now up for sale. For tax reasons it suited Queen to own it, and Jim Beach approached the shareholders on their behalf with an offer to buy them out.

It was at Mountain that they were invited to write the music for a new feature film, *Flash Gordon*. Directed by Mike Hodges and starring the former American footballer Sam J. Jones, Max von Sydow and Topol, everything about the film version of Alex Raymond's 1930s comic-strip adventure was intended to be lavish. Certainly Danilo Donati had come up with impressively grand sets, and the film's producers felt that a pounding rock score by Queen would be a perfect complement. All four band members would contribute tracks; in Mercury's case, five of them, including 'Ming's Theme', 'Vultan's Theme' and 'Football Fight', which would partner Brian May's 'Flash' as a single at the end of the following year to coincide with the film's release.

Summer saw a rash of Queen releases, starting in June with *Live Killers* and the single 'Love of My Life', both recorded at various recent gigs. Then, because EMI received the 1979

Queen's Award to Industry, the record company decided to launch a 200-copy limited edition of 'Bohemian Rhapsody', pressed on blue vinyl. By now the band was busy writing new material, this time at a different location – Musicland Studios, Munich. It was here they would begin work on the film score, and here, too, where they would first meet record producer Reinholdt Mack.

Queen had never lacked a strong sense of their own importance; indeed Brian May has said that 'Part of you believes that the group is the most wonderful thing that the world's ever seen.' Almost proudly, May admitted that life could be difficult for outsiders around the band, declaring, 'We don't compromise with anyone else. If someone else comes along, he gets kicked out of the door very quickly or else can't stand the heat. It was pretty hard for anyone to sit with us as a producer or whatever, and the ones who managed it, managed it by having very strong personalities.' But, having already worked with many top groups, Reinholdt, known simply as Mack, had no need to be intimidated by Queen. He was to become the first outside producer since Roy Thomas Baker to work regularly with the band.

The only break in recording for four months was Queen's brief return to Shepperton Studios to rehearse for an open-air gig scheduled for August. At the Ludwigsparkstadion in Saarbrücken, Queen headlined with Voyager, the Commodores and Rory Gallagher, as support. Then it was back to Musicland Studios.

Munich was to play a big part in Mercury's future. While he was there he became close friends with Mack and his family. Because the star would go on to make the city his home for some years, he eventually bought himself an apartment there, but in the meantime he preferred the luxury of a suite at the Munich Hilton. It was here, while soaking in the bath, that he wrote an unusual song for Queen, but one that would give them their first American number one.

Mercury could compose a song in minutes, conjuring up melodies off the top of his head at a piano. Few can deny that Mercury was a one-off, unique in every way, including his style of songwriting. But, when he wanted, he could also be an incurable mimic, and 'Crazy Little Thing Called Love', the jaunty number he knocked together in record time, was a distinct pastiche of Elvis Presley. Perhaps this partly accounted for its strong appeal to the US public.

'It's not typical of my work,' Mercury said, 'but that's because nothing is typical of my work.' Recorded at Musicland, Mack, who had expected the whole band to turn up for the session, was surprised when, on the first day, Mercury arrived early and alone, anxious to get started. Apologising to Mack for the fact that he wasn't too adept on the guitar he was slipping over his head, Mercury clearly wanted to establish a particular sound before the rest of the band had the chance to turn it into a typical Queen number.

When released on 5 October, the record went gold. It also marked another first by featuring Mercury on rhythm guitar. The star strummed the three chords only fractionally better than the time he had plagued flatmates ten years earlier. When some sought to mock this musical debut, Mercury unceremoniously crushed them, retorting, 'I've made no effort to become a guitar hero, because I can't play the fucking guitar.'

What Mercury excelled at was surprising people, and he was set to do so again. For him it was the fulfilment of a personal dream. Since his days at Ealing College, he had been fascinated with ballet. He had attended performances in various parts of the world, but in particular he admired London's Royal Ballet Company and had become friends with one of their principal dancers, Wayne Eagling.

'I first met Freddie when I was producing a dance gala for mentally handicapped children,' says Wayne Eagling. 'I wanted to widen its appeal to more than just dance fans, and so I went to see my friend Joseph Lockwood, treasurer of the Royal Ballet, who was then also head of EMI. Originally I asked him if I could work with Kate Bush, but, unfortunately, Kate's manager didn't like the idea, so I asked Joseph to suggest someone else. He took five seconds to come up with Freddie Mercury, and it was he who initially brought Freddie along to the ballet school.'

It was an unforgettable first meeting, Wayne Eagling recalls: 'Freddie turned up already wearing tights and ballet shoes, and we all took one look at him and nearly fainted. I think some of the group thought, My God! What have we got here? because Freddie really made an entrance. We were to do two numbers, "Bohemian Rhapsody" and a new song called "Crazy Little Thing Called Love", which hadn't yet been released.

'I'll always remember, we were in the middle of rehearsing "Rhapsody", when in walked the choreographer Sir Frederick Ashton. He asked me what I was doing, then suddenly scowled at Freddie and demanded in a strangled voice, "And *who* is *he?*" A little embarrassed, I replied, "He's a famous rock star." Ashton looked Mercury up and down and snapped, "Well, he's got *terrible* feet!" Poor Freddie, and I thought he was being rather sweet, trying to point his toes so carefully, but fortunately he thought it was funny.'

Eagling wasn't Mercury's only acquaintance at the Royal Ballet. During these rehearsals he also worked with Derek Deane, another principal dancer, who fondly recalls the fun they had. 'We never stopped laughing,' he insists. 'Freddie was so Freddie. He became a great friend of Wayne's and mine, and I saw right away that he liked to think of himself as a good dancer, but he wasn't really. He more than made up for that though by being terribly enthusiastic.

'One of the first things that struck me was the interest he took in the whole thing, and he wasn't nervous either. It wasn't that serious, and he didn't have to do anything very strict. But still there was a big difference to what he was used to. On stage he did his own thing, whereas here he had to be where he was supposed to be at all times, or he'd throw the whole company out – and we kept trying to hammer that home with him.'

Mercury's eagerness was to prove legendary in the group. 'He would try absolutely anything,' says Deane. 'In fact a lot of the time we had to hold him back in case he did himself an injury.' After practice both at the school and on stage, there was the costume rehearsal. 'We were going through our paces when suddenly Freddie began to sing "Bohemian Rhapsody" without music,' Deane recalls. 'His wonderful voice just stopped us all in our tracks. We stared at him, awestruck.'

Mercury had bottled up his nerves for the big night on 7 October at London's Coliseum, but unnecessarily so, according to Derek Deane: 'The audience were major!' he says. 'In the main, ballet audiences tend to be quite stuffy, and never in a million years did they expect a rock star to arrive on stage – but they loved Freddie.'

'Basically we lifted him around all the time, tipping him upside down and throwing him about, but Freddie was a natural showman, and he thoroughly enjoyed it,' Eagling recalls.

Mercury remained friends with Deane and Eagling, often discussing the possibility of future projects. While spending time together, the contrast between the star's public persona and the private man was obvious, says Eagling: 'Freddie would slip in to see our performances and hardly be noticed. Then again, he loved his wild parties and being flamboyant. Even so, essentially he was a very shy man. He had to feel comfortable with you before he'd drop his guard.' When Mercury ended his association with the Royal Ballet Company, he took with him one of their wardrobe assistants, Peter Freestone, with whom he had struck up a rapport. Peter joined Joe Fanelli and Paul Prenter as another of his personal assistants. He was with the band the next month when they set out on what they called their 'Crazy Tour'. Instead of playing the famous, big venues, they took their music back to the smaller theatres.

As the decade drew to an end, the change in Mercury's style was pronounced. His hair had become gradually shorter, until now it just brushed his collar and only partially hid his heavy sideburns. On stage he was rarely out of leathers and had added a leather and chain cap to his biker ensemble. He may have recently performed ballet on a London stage, but when fronting Queen, his image was thrusting and aggressive. Rob Halford, lead singer with Judas Priest, called on Mercury to ride a motorbike round the Brands Hatch circuit to prove he merited his biker gear. Mercury neatly deflected his challenge by accepting the offer on condition that Halford first danced with the Royal Ballet. Halford was never heard from again on the subject.

In mid-December Queen played a couple of nights at the Centre in Brighton in the final two weeks of the tour. It was here that Mercury would meet the man who was to become his first live-in male lover. The star's weakness lay in the beef-cake variety, muscly men who looked like truck drivers, with big hands and, invariably, a thick black moustache. Still enjoying the gay scene to the full, after each gig Mercury would set off in search of local talent. It was on one of these excursions that he found the Curtain Club, where he was to meet twenty-eight-year-old Tony Bastin, a courier for the express-delivery company DHL.

Mercury took Bastin back to his hotel room, where they spent the night together. After three years of picking up a different man every night and discarding him the next day, like any other star-struck groupie, this time was different. They hit it off so well that before Queen headed back to London, the two men had exchanged telephone numbers and promised to keep in touch.

Queen ended the seventies with a Boxing Day charity gig at

the Hammersmith Odeon, organised by Paul McCartney, in aid of the Kampuchea Appeal Fund. It involved a series of concerts, including performances from Wings, the Who and the Pretenders. False rumours had circulated that the Beatles were considering re-forming for the event, which had at least increased the media's interest.

Mercury had once predicted Queen's life span as five years. He could not have anticipated that by the end of the decade they would have sold over 45 million albums worldwide. Already the fame, wealth and recognition he had so desperately craved were his in abundance, and professionally new challenges lay ahead.

In his personal life, he had the best of both worlds – something he managed to maintain almost to the end of his life. Mary Austin, although no longer his sexual partner, still loved him and worked closely with him in her role with Goose Productions. At the same time he indulged in the sexual freedom that he had exchanged their relationship for. With his escalating drug abuse, his existence had become a cliché of sex, drugs and rock 'n' roll. It was a lifestyle fraught with dangers, some of which he must have been aware. But not of AIDS. It would not be long, however, before the word would begin to be mentioned in whispers throughout the gay communities of the world.

NINE

Shifting Sands

Mercury's intention to keep in touch with Tony Bastin had to be put on hold for the first quarter of 1980. Work at Musicland Studios, on both Queen's new album and the *Flash Gordon* soundtrack, kept him in Munich; a situation that suited him. The city's reputation for a notoriously uninhibited nightlife was well deserved, and Mercury formed some of his closest friendships there. But weeks of excess, of combining heavy recording sessions with hectic nightclubbing, had begun to take their toll. It was fortunate that, in March, Mercury had to make a quick return trip to London.

The new single 'Save Me' had been greeted by the rock critics' usual disdain, but it scarcely mattered. Reviews had long ago served as the least reliable gauge of the band's global popularity. 'Crazy Little Thing Called Love', in addition to having topped the US charts, had repeated this success in five other countries. But Mercury's flying visit to Britain was not business, nor was it purely pleasure. He was primarily honouring a promise to Kenny Everett to make a rare television appearance on one of his zany weekly shows. As Everett announced contenders for the 'British Eurovision Violence Contest', a leather-clad Mercury joined him on set, holding a can of carbonated drink. He promptly yanked off the can's ring pull, so close to Everett that the fizzy contents spurted all over his face.

'Good start,' quipped Everett and carried on talking to the camera. Clearly unscripted, Mercury sprang on the comedian, wrapping his arms and legs around Everett's body and unbalancing them both. As they crashed to the studio floor, they rolled around in a mock brawl.

Mercury's friendship with Everett would survive into the mid-eighties, but tales would later surface of their acrimonious split after a bitter row over drugs. This, however, appears to owe more to fiction than fact. In 1995 Kenny Everett died of AIDS, but his agent, Jo Gurnett, says, 'Kenny admired Freddie like mad and adored everything he did. They were very good friends. Their falling out is a bit of a grey area, but I know that it was a minor disagreement between them, after which they just seemed to drift apart.'

'Freddie's career took him away a lot, and certainly Ev's television work occupied most of his time, too. Kenny didn't see Freddie latterly. He would have liked to, but it was just one of those things. Then Freddie was too sick, and Kenny himself was too sick . . . I remember Kenny, in the late stages of his illness, when he knew he was dying, saying about Freddie and their lost closeness, "Oh, well, we'll all be up there together, and maybe then we will make it up."'

For some time Mercury's London base had been a comfortable flat at 12 Stafford Terrace in Kensington, but he had succumbed to the lure of owning a status symbol luxury mansion. He had no desire actually to move house – content simply to possess something sumptuous of his own. Mary Austin had been watching the property market for him, and as it appears that Mercury was unwilling to move out of Kensington, this narrowed his options. Still Austin found a house that hooked him immediately.

Garden Lodge, 1 Logan Place, was a splendid twenty-eight-room Georgian mansion, set in a quarter-acre of manicured garden and surrounded by a high brick wall. Mercury went to view it and stepped first into the large entrance hall, dominated by the sweep of an elegant staircase. This alone was enough to win his heart. Everything had been built to the grand scale that the star adored. Massive double doors flanked the hallway and opened into well-lit spacious rooms. One room, in particular, was spectacular, with long artist-studio windows at one end and a minstrels' gallery at the other. The extensive garden ensured an appealing degree of privacy, and he swiftly decided to buy, paying £500,000 for it in cash. Garden Lodge had formerly belonged to Hoares, a banking family. As the new owner, Mercury impudently christened it 'the whore house'. He had great plans for extensive renovations, which he immediately set in motion. He then returned to pick up the reins of his life in Munich.

On 30 May 'Play the Game' became Queen's latest single. It fared respectably in the UK charts, but when its video was released, many fans were clearly unhappy. Their familiar Mercury was slipping away from them – replaced by a singer with cropped hair, no nail varnish and, what seemed to many the last straw, sporting a bushy moustache. In protest they flooded the band's Notting Hill office with gifts of disposable razors and bottles of black varnish. But Mercury proved impervious to the message.

When *The Game* followed a month later, their discontent grew. Queen had always boasted that they did not use synthesisers to create their music, yet on this album they had done so. Having made such an issue of avoiding this device, many of their devotees felt let down. They were not prepared to be persuaded by what they saw as the band's excuse that they had wanted to experiment with new technology. Not insensitive to their fans' wishes, still Mercury agreed with the others that it would be unwise to be restricted by the past.

A part of his own past was at this time threatening to return. Mary Austin had played a key role in realising Mercury's desire to own a property of note and was closely involved in all the renovations at Garden Lodge. Perhaps affected by this surface display of domesticity, Austin appears to have wished to rekindle their old romance. She is said to have asked Mercury to give her a child. But, when he'd ended their physical relationship, Mercury reputedly told her, 'I still love you, but I can't make love to you.'

For Mercury, four years on, that clearly hadn't changed, and his response to Mary Austin's very intimate request was gently to decline. 'I'd rather have another cat,' he said, which was not a facetious snub; his passion for cats was real and in time he owned about eight of them.

That summer, Mercury left with Queen to commence a mammoth tour. Starting on 30 June at the PNE Coliseum in Vancouver, it would end on 1 October with four consecutive nights at Madison Square Garden. It was during an internal flight between Boston and New York that Mercury met the handsome airline steward John Murphy. A former soldier, Murphy possessed the he-man physique guaranteed to catch Mercury's eye. Although they were to strike up a rapport, they slept together only once, in Mercury's Manhattan hotel suite. Their friendship, however, lasted several years. As with Joe Fanelli, who became one of the star's closest confidants, being discarded by Mercury as a lover didn't necessarily mean the end of the association. Mercury had an uncanny knack of turning yesterday's lovers into loyal companions.

The tour was arduous, while airtight security left the band cocooned to the point of suffocation – especially now that they travelled everywhere in private planes. Pete Brown recalls: 'Every day it was a case of arriving on a private airstrip, being ferried from the tarmac by limo to some plush hotel, hotel to gig and back the same route. It created a rarefied atmosphere that was driving them all mad.

'People imagine that it's a glamorous life, but it's a damned hard slog. Someone would ask me, "How was Boston?" and I'd reply, "Boston had orange curtains and a blue bedspread." They'd look at me funny, but that was what it was really like.'

To alleviate the strain, they took a couple of breaks, just long enough to get off the treadmill – and go home if desired – before returning to the relentless gigging. After one break, in August, John Deacon's 'Another One Bites the Dust', was released. Again it was a departure for Queen, but its distinctive bass line overcame fans' resistance and made it the darling of the discos. It was universally a smash hit, selling 4.5 million copies in America alone. There it presided at number one for five weeks, one of three Queen singles to go platinum in the USA.

Since the song depended heavily on a combination of this powerful bass line and a piece of tight drumming, it was not easy to perform live. But 'Another One Bites the Dust' was so popular that it couldn't be left out of Queen's repertoire – and, besides, the number gave Mercury an invaluable opportunity. His delivery of 'Another One Bites the Dust' revitalised his status as a sex symbol. His performance had an ambiguous appeal to all genders.

At the Forum in Montreal, a well-toned Mercury stalked on stage to a wild reception, wearing only a pair of white shorts, a white baseball cap and a red neckerchief. The shorts were so tight that they later elicited some risqué queries from the press. The star took pleasure in declaring, 'I don't have a Coke bottle down there. It's all mine.' Barefoot and thrusting out his hairy chest, he ad-libbed during the tricky instrumental section, moving closer to the edge of the stage, repeatedly taunting the audience with the urge, 'Bite it, bite it hard, baby!' while he rubbed his taut lower stomach in simulated ecstasy.

In October 1980, at the end of their most gruelling tour to date, Queen returned to Britain. A European trip was sched-uled for six weeks' time, and there were finishing touches to be made to the film score before then. At home, Mercury spent his nights with Tony Bastin and his days, during early November, at London's Anvil Studios. The cover concept for the album was his work, and he spent time experimenting with designs. When Queen went to Zurich to rehearse for their tour, Mercury surrounded himself with his usual entourage, whose hard core by now included Joe Fanelli, Paul Prenter and Peter Freestone. Only this time his lover went too.

'Flash's Theme' came out shortly afterwards as the single from the soundtrack album, and by making the top ten it far out-stripped Elektra's choice in the US; 'Need Your Loving Tonight' languished at a disappointing forty-four in the Billboard chart.

On 8 December *Flash Gordon* was released to rave reviews. Any pleasure from this, however, evaporated when Mercury heard that John Lennon had been shot – apparently by a deranged fan – on his return from Record Plant Studios around 11.00 p.m.. It wasn't just a brutal lesson on the dangers of how extreme adulation can mutate into fatal obsession. Recalling Hendrix's demise a decade earlier, with Lennon's death Queen felt they'd lost a hero. The following night at London's Wembley Arena, in tribute they played Lennon's 'Imagine'. They were so distressed that Brian May forgot the chords and cut to the chorus. This threw the overwrought Mercury off his stride. If the audience noticed, they didn't care; many were themselves already in tears. Mercury's own mark of respect to Lennon was 'Life is Real (Song for Lennon)', which would later surface as a B-side to 'Body Language'.

By the year's end Queen became the first band to enter the *Guinness Book of Records* – listed among Britain's highest paid executives. This achievement in no way diminished their desire for new territories, places where the spectacle of their live extravaganzas would be appreciated. In Rio de Janeiro their manager discussed arrangements with local promoters for a tour that would start in less than two months. The year 1981 was to mark the beginning of their love affair with South America.

Before that, in early February, the band returned to Tokyo. After the Japanese film première of *Flash Gordon*, Queen performed five sell-out gigs at the Budokan. The country that had started Queenmania had lost none of its enthusiasm, as shown by the annual polls in *Music Life* magazine. Mercury was voted top of his category, as was John Deacon, while Brian May and Roger Taylor took second place in their sections. Queen itself won the top award for best band, which added to Mercury's delight at being back in his beloved Japan.

Mercury had been fascinated by Japanese culture for years. By now rich enough to indulge himself, he had become a serious collector of Japan's art and artefacts. Heaven for Mercury was a shopping blitz there, when he spent money like water – and sometimes with no thought about how he was going to transport his purchases home. The downside of being away was that he missed his precious cats and had lately taken to making long-distance telephone calls to talk to them at all hours of the night.

Ten days separated this tour of Japan from their first visits to Argentina and Brazil. Mercury took advantage of the break to go to America to conduct some overdue business. His love of New York and his frequent trips there meant that he now wanted somewhere permanent to live in the city. He purchased a sumptuous apartment on the forty-third floor of a skyscraper at 425 East 58th Street, which he'd eventually furnish with priceless art treasures.

Queen were scheduled to play just seven gigs in South America, three at the vast Vélez Sársfield football ground in Buenos Aires and two at Brazil's Morumbi Stadium in Sao Paulo. Mercury later confessed to nervousness at the challenge, admitting, 'We had no right to expect the works from an alien country.'

But in the course of three weeks they had played to record-breaking audiences, and that tour marked their status as among the prime instigators of stadium rock. Queen didn't invent this – the Beatles had packed New York's Shea Stadium in 1965 – but the sixties had only the tinny public-address Tannoy, while Queen were experimenting with the new and sophisticated sound systems. The sheer scale of these events required this new technology.

This trip was certainly unusual. Before Queen arrived, the Argentinian intelligence service had taken a close interest in the tour. The country's unstable political climate made the concerts a likely target for a terrorist attack. Argentina's president, General Viola, also contributed to the heightened sense of occasion with a government delegation to greet the band. The mass hysteria at the airport was televised live on the national news.

There were special celebrations in Buenos Aires for Queen. These included a party at the home of the president of Vélez Sársfield – at which the band met the country's soccer demigod Diego Maradonna – and dinner at General Viola's official residence. Being treated as a visiting dignitary probably pleased Mercury no end, but perhaps his deepest joy came from their first gig on 28 February. In the middle of 'Love of My Life', he stopped singing at the usual point, when, as ever, the largely Spanish-speaking audience took over and sang back to him in word-perfect English.

The road crew experienced a few scares as they organised the transport of tons of valuable equipment through dense jungle. Then at the Brazilian border they encountered an overly bureaucratic customs official. Jim Beach and tour manager Gerry Stickells were worried that the band's equipment could be confiscated by corrupt officials and made elaborate plans for it to be spirited away immediately after the final gig. But, for all that, the last night at Morumbi turned out to be remarkable, and not only because the band played before the largest-ever paying audience in the world. The brief tour itself also grossed approximately $3.5 million. The prospect of returning later in the year was appealing.

Back in the UK for a short period before work on their new album was due to commence in Montreux, Mercury picked up where he had left off with Tony Bastin. While abroad the star had been fooling around with men and drugs, and Bastin wasn't as naive as to believe that Mercury had been faithful to him – but still their relationship continued to thrive. When he chose to be, Mercury could be very romantic and admitted, on occasions, to feeling intensely vulnerable when he imagined himself to be in love. He would lavish diamonds, luxury cars and substantial sums of cash on his man of the moment and felt that his best creative work flowed then, too. Yet he was also prone to dramatic outpourings on the raw deal he believed he suffered in affairs of the heart.

'Love is Russian roulette for me,' he once mourned, adding, 'No one loves the real me inside. They're all in love with my fame, my stardom.'

On the whole he was probably right. But since he could commit serial infidelity from within a relationship, he contributed greatly to the emotional hollowness of which he often complained. For all that, his passion for Bastin was real and would endure for several months more.

By summertime, work was almost done at Mountain Studios. The final album was a disappointment to many fans, but these sessions were to produce Queen's first number one single since 'Bohemian Rhapsody'. At the Swiss resort, among the select few with whom they frequently socialised was David Bowie.

Resident sound engineer Dave Richards invited Bowie over to the recording studio, where an impromptu jam session started. No one thought much of it until they realised they were co-writing a song. 'Under Pressure' would be finalised a couple of months later in New York and released on 26 October.

Bowie was to reveal that parts of the single made him cringe, but neither his fans, nor Queen's, shrank from buying it, and it catapulted to the top of the charts.

It was in New York that Mercury celebrated his thirty-fifth birthday; for the next few years his parties would prove legendary. Although he had purchased a luxury apartment in the city, he took over a floor of the Berkshire Hotel in which to host the event and flew over all his closest friends by Concorde. Typically lavish, it went on non-stop for a spectacular five days.

Queen regrouped mid-month in New Orleans to rehearse for their return trip to South America. With its first date in Venezuela at the Poliedro de Caracas, the tour was called 'Gluttons for Punishment'. This turned out to be rather apt. Touring the world meant frequent and unusual media experiences, but the slot on the live pop TV show Jim Beach had booked for the band was among the strangest. The show featured a string of lookalike stars, and when Queen were announced, there was confusion about whether or not they were the real thing.

Mercury had refused to appear on the show alongside his bandmates and he must have been relieved that he had refused to go, when the show degenerated into an even worse fiasco. An excitable man rushed on camera and grabbed the mike, announcing that the statesman Romulo Ethancourt had died. A two-minute silence was ordered. Moments later a second man rushed on and announced that he hadn't died at all. As all this happened in rapid Spanish, none of Queen knew what was going on, and they could only squirm with embarrassment.

More serious than being shown up on live TV was the fact that Ethancourt did die later that night, a development that plunged the country into mourning. Airports closed, stranding Queen, with their gigs cancelled, in the middle of a politically inflammatory situation. The country was ripe for revolution, and it was easy to believe the tales of how people – especially foreigners – just vanished off the streets. There was great relief when the airport reopened, allowing the band to fly back to safety.

After this the three forthcoming Mexican dates, due to start on 9 October, were not very appealing. Their nerves were still jangling when during the first of the gigs, at the Estadion Universitano in Monterey, the audience began pelting them relentlessly with rubbish. Boots, bottles and batteries rained down on Queen. The band remained on stage for one of their most energetic performances, as Mercury, Deacon and May darted from side to side to avoid flying missiles. Roger Taylor, although further back, was a static target behind his drums and particularly at risk.

Fleeing off stage at the end of the show, they felt dejected by the worst reception of their careers. They were astounded, then, when gleeful officials came over to congratulate them. Apparently the crowd's behaviour was the traditional show of appreciation. Of the two remaining Puebla dates, they played only the first, as tax complications meant they would not get paid. It was the excuse they needed, and the band boarded a flight for New York, vowing never to set foot in Mexico again.

Although Queen first formed in 1970 with Mercury, Taylor, May and Mike Grose, the band chose to consider themselves complete only when John Deacon joined the following year. Consequently, they designated 1981 as their official tenth anniversary, and in the last months of the year launched a series of special releases to mark the occasion. Each featured a specially commissioned portrait of the band by the Earl of Snowdon.

Greatest Flix was a novel compilation of all the videos for Queen's singles since 'Bohemian Rhapsody', followed by *Greatest Pix*, a book of photographs compiled by Jacques Lowe, and the *Greatest Hits* album. Ten years on, only three other albums had spent longer in the charts: Fleetwood Mac's *Rumours,*

Meat Loaf's *Bat Out of Hell* and the soundtrack of *The Sound of Music*. Queen rounded off their celebrations with two gigs at the Forum in Montreal. These concerts were filmed for possible release as a feature film of the band the following summer.

By early December Mercury had returned to Munich, ostensibly to continue work on Queen's new album. But the emphasis for him really lay more on spending time at clubs such as the Sugar Shack, a favourite haunt of the band's. Mercury was ready to plunge back into the so-called 'Bermuda Triangle' of the city's crowded gay scene. With its wealth of venues, he found the atmosphere there more relaxed and open than in London. And the places he enjoyed the most were the bars and clubs that drew an interesting mix of straight and gay people.

Mercury had found an apartment in Munich and installed his retinue of attendants there to ensure his life ran smoothly. Paul Prenter always accompanied him through the chaos of the nightclubs and witnessed first-hand the extent of Mercury's hedonistic indulgence. Relentless partying required a lot of stamina, and Mercury was using cocaine heavily just to make it through the night.

His evenings out were planned very precisely. Dressed to kill, he would go by chauffeur-driven limo to a club with his body-guard and personal assistants. Once outside the venue, someone would go in to survey the scene and report back to Mercury, before he himself would enter the premises. Once inside, it was often bedlam. The place would be heaving and boisterous anyway, but Mercury was like a gigantic magnet, and his pres-ence would instantly crank up the tension.

His worldwide fame had its drawbacks. As one of the most famous faces on the gay circuit, he was undoubtedly exploited for who he was. Yet Mercury was well aware of this and could turn it to his advantage when he wanted. If nothing else, it guaranteed a greater number of men willing to go home with him.

Someone who can corroborate this is the only woman, apart from Mary Austin, to occupy a special place in Mercury's heart. German actress Barbara Valentin was to meet Mercury one night in a Munich disco called New York. Herself a cult figure, closely associated with her work for film director Rainer Werner Fassbinder, she was popular in gay circles.

'I was standing in a crowd, and Freddie was close by, surrounded by friends and with his bodyguards hovering around,' recalled Valentin. 'I knew who he was, but we had never met, except maybe to nod and say hello in passing. Well, this particular night everyone was jostling about as usual, and Paul Prenter walked accidentally into my burning cigarette, and he turned on me and started shouting and swearing at me. I told him to watch where he was going and turned away. A little later he came back to apologise and introduce himself, so I said who I was.

'Next day Paul and I met for dinner, alone, and as we talked we realised that we saw each other's crowd something like at least three times a week in the same places. A few days later back at the same disco, Freddie and I then met. Nobody introduced us as such. We just sort of came together.'

According to Barbara, from that first moment they clicked. 'I adored him,' she said. 'We fitted together absolutely instantly, and we never separated for three whole days. He stayed at my house, I went to the studio with him, and we went out to the clubs together. We talked all the time, and Freddie told me, "My God! Finally I can talk to someone who understands the real me and what I want to do with my life." That was something he was needing badly.'

It is clear that Mercury found something very different with Valentin to the long-standing bond he continued to have with Mary Austin. Certainly it seems that the fun-loving actress's complete and natural understanding of his homosexuality filled some kind of gaping void in him. At any rate he rapidly developed a unique and tender relationship with Valentin, which spanned several years, and which she found difficult to define.

'We had an amazing time together whenever he was in Munich,' she said, 'and just like that first time, sometimes we'd spend days on end never parting. I loved him, I still love him, and he loved me. It was a once in a lifetime thing between us, so special. I wouldn't want it to happen again. I'm only grateful that it came to me once.'

Valentin and Mercury both adored nightclubs, and on many occasions visited the Bermuda Triangle together. Valentin saw just how many men, looking for rich pickings, homed in on the superstar the second he walked through the door. But Mercury was nobody's fool. He was a man who did nothing he didn't want to do. Playing the game, however, he enjoyed stringing along a few men at a time; then later, much to their delight, he would invite them back home.

At his flat, though, the tables turned as Mercury indulged in one of his favourite games. His groupies were to strip naked and parade before him in nothing but a selection of women's hats. His taste continued to lie in large-built men, and he would select his bedmate and summarily dismiss the others. His sex drive, possibly drug-propelled, still bordered on the unquenchable. Inevitably, as 1982 approached, his liaison with live-in lover Tony Bastin, who had flown to be with him in Munich, was rapidly heading for the rocks.

TEN

Cutting Up Rough

By January 1982 Queen realised that more discipline was necessary to pull together their new album. For a time they worked daily at Musicland Studios. Business of another kind, too, had to be transacted when Queen's EMI contract for the UK and Europe came up for renewal in the spring. Their association had proved immensely fruitful, and on 1 April it was cemented further to include the band's next six albums.

The following day war broke out between Britain and Argentina over sovereignty of the Falkland Islands. A sideshow to the issue was the Argentine authorities' ban on Queen performing in their country for the duration of the conflict. 'Under Pressure' was currently topping their charts and, unamused, they instantly banned it from the airwaves. When asked to comment on the war Mercury replied, 'It's our young men killing their young men. There's no glory in being blown to bits.'

A week later Queen embarked on the first of their touring commitments that would span the next eight months. By the time they arrived in France, their latest single 'Body Language' had been released, reaching only number twenty-five in the UK charts. This coolness by the fans was also reflected at performances. Perhaps too much time had recently been spent in Munich's clubland, for the band seemed unduly influenced by the unchallenging funky disco sound.

Experimenting with rhythmic rock was the official line, but loyal fans refused to be pacified. They could only be further upset when the album *Hot Space* finally emerged on 21 May.

Gone was the hard-rock edge, gone, too, was the familiarity of Brian May's dominant guitar work; replaced by the much disliked synthesiser. May himself wasn't keen on the album, and, in an unusual step, he publicly admitted as much. Possibly to boost this dip in their popularity, on 10 June, for the first time in five years, Queen appeared on *Top of the Pops*, performing their new release 'Las Palabras de Amor (The Words of Love)'.

By this time their UK/Euro tour had come to an end. There was now a decent break before they were due to go on the road again, and Mercury rushed back to Munich. His strained relationship with Tony Bastin was now at an end. They remained friends and even occasional lovers in the years ahead but never again lived together. It wasn't long, however, before there was another man in Mercury's life, Winnie Kirkenberger, a handsome German restaurateur. They had met in a bar, and Kirkenberger's looks very much fitted the stereotype of Mercury's ideal lover.

It is said that initially Kirkenberger did not realise who Mercury was until someone tipped him off. He was, in any case, hugely unimpressed. The story goes that when the time came to leave the bar together that first night, Mercury had announced that he had a car and chauffeur waiting. Winnie is said to have replied that he didn't give a shit, that he was walking home, and if Mercury wanted to be with him, he'd have to walk too. This butch display supposedly thrilled Mercury, allowing him to feel he was liked for himself and not his fame. But, it is a scenario that is hard to accept.

By 1982 Freddie Mercury was a superstar, one of rock's most distinctive figures. The gay scenes of London, New York and Munich had dominated his private life for the last five years.

Among those of his stratum of homosexual subculture, he was probably the most sought-after conquest. Just a rumour of his imminent arrival could be enough to create a buzz of anticipation, and at times his entrance into a club would stop the show. It defies belief that anyone from this social world could not have known Mercury.

The suggestion, too, that Mercury might have believed the old ploy of not being recognised – and so wanted purely for himself – doesn't fit his character. One of the many aspects of Mercury's make-up was that he was a thinker and a manipulator. He admitted that he enjoyed being in love, but that didn't mean he was a soft touch. The star was never too weak, as has been suggested, to make choices when it came to his personal life. For all his devotion to Mary Austin, and the claims that he yearned for a family of his own, he was able to sever that part of their bond that could have brought marriage and stability. He exchanged their secure heterosexual love for his desire to lead a full homosexual existence.

Even his choice of men, the rough tough type, seems significant. In public he was so flamboyant and loud, it is too facile to claim that he sought to be dominated in his private life. But it was his own way of domineering, the fact that he was always the more powerful in his relationships because his fame and wealth gave him the edge over the type of men he preferred, those with much less money and power than him. He also chose men who were not especially well educated, which was perhaps another way of ensuring he kept control, something very important to Mercury.

Reinholdt Mack came to believe, for all the star's sexual activity, that he was ultimately dissatisfied with his gay lifestyle. According to Mack, Mercury seriously considered giving up on his homosexuality and going straight. If that were so, it is also indicative of the strength of his willpower. In any event, and however it began, Mercury's relationship with Winnie

Kirkenberger, although far from monogamous, would span the next three years.

The next tour was mid-July, another of those gruelling Canadian/US trips that involved playing almost every night, in nearly every state and with frequent wild parties. Now thirty-six, Mercury admitted that he was beginning to dislike this kind of hectic schedule. In contrast to his days of painted fingernails and elaborate posturing in saucy leotards, his stage act had become more energetic. For the entire show he would repeatedly rush the length and breadth of the stage, up and down open flights of stairs. It was an extremely draining performance.

His tour preparation now focused almost as much on being physically fit as musically tight. The financial incentive, too, had gone. Said Mercury once, 'It's not a question of money any more. I spend money like it's nothing. You know I could be penniless tomorrow, but I'd get it back somehow.' But, still, the love of music remained. He conceded that there would come a time when he couldn't dash about the stage and added, 'But music will always be my thing.'

There was, however, a special pleasure for Mercury this tour. In January, while recording *Hot Space*, he had taken time off to sing backing vocals, along with Roger Taylor, on 'Emotions in Motion' by American rocker Billy Squier. Squier was to form a friendship with Mercury, and on learning of Queen's US tour he agreed to join them as their celebrity guest.

Starting at the Forum in Montreal, the tour ended at the Los Angeles Forum on 15 September 1982. It was to be, little did they realise, Queen's last ever American tour. Six dates in Japan followed a month later, ending with a massive outdoor gig at Tokyo's Seibu Lions Stadium. Then they returned to Britain in time to enter into protracted, though ultimately fruitless, negotiations with Elektra over the renewal of their contract. In December, as an interim measure, they signed all albums to EMI.

Splitting from the US record label coincided with Queen's decision to take a year off. This might have shocked their fans, but privately it had been brewing for a while. Living and working so closely for twelve years had taken its toll, with serious arguments within the band a regular feature. They were simply exhausted and getting on each other's nerves. A rest was required if they hoped to survive as a band. The music press did their best to turn their announcement that they would not be touring for the next twelve months into a three-act drama. But Mercury dampened their imaginations by declaring, 'It's got to the point where we're actually too old to break up. Can you imagine forming a new band at forty? Be a bit silly, wouldn't it?'

A year off cleared the way to undertake solo projects, and Mercury was quick to book time at Musicland Studios with Mack. He had nurtured aspirations of creating music without Queen for some time and was looking forward to the challenge. No sooner had he begun on his solo work than he got sidetracked. Producer Giorgio Moroder invited Mercury to collaborate with him. Moroder had won an Oscar for his music for Alan Parker's *Midnight Express* and was working on an updated version of the classic silent fantasy *Metropolis*. When Moroder's *Metropolis* was released the following year, Mercury's contribution to its soundtrack joined those of Adam Ant, Bonnie Tyler and Billy Squier among others.

Although Mercury's original plans had stalled, he was not in a hurry to rush out his debut solo album during Queen's year off. Indeed it would be two years before it surfaced. He meanwhile enjoyed spending some overdue free time with Winnie Kirkenberger, generally living it up in Munich. At times he overdid it, once ending up with his leg in plaster for six weeks. Rumours that he'd been involved in a club brawl were scotched, but when his jealousy was aroused, for all his foppish front, Mercury could be aggressive.

His drug intake must take some of the responsibility for his violent tendencies too. It was hard for friends to predict his moods. He was quite capable of flying into sudden uncontrollable rages, when he would demolish furniture and roar abusively at the top of his voice. Afterwards he'd remember nothing. Reports that once, in the grip of a sexual drug-crazed frenzy, the star tried to strangle Barbara Valentin are not true: 'That just never happened,' says Valentin. 'I don't know where that story came from.'

Mercury considered he knew the world's hottest spots, but he was always open to suggestion – particularly if it sounded risky. In New York, he visited the Gilded Grape, where he'd been warned he would need a bulletproof car and fast driver at the ready. Such ingredients were guaranteed to take him panting downtown, on the scent. After several weeks of manic clubbing and sex, he suddenly gave up his nocturnal city prowling for the sunnier climes of California.

He had arranged to meet Michael Jackson, who was working on his follow-up to *Thriller*, with a view to recording with him. But before that was possible, Mercury had something else to do. As he would later admit in a rare interview he gave to Radio One DJ Simon Bates, after weeks of excess he needed to get himself fit before undertaking any work with the health-conscious Jackson. 'There was an attitude built in there,' says Bates. 'Freddie felt that if he was physically in shape, he would be mentally disciplined.'

Mercury joined Michael Jackson at his private studio in Encino, where they completed 'Victory' and 'State of Shock'. Mercury was still using cocaine, and initially, while recording with Jackson, aware of his views on the matter, he would discreetly vanish to the toilet. But the necessity to disappear so often irritated Mercury. Although he was not in the habit of wilfully upsetting outsiders with his behaviour – be it drug-taking or homosexuality – this time he grew sloppy. Seemingly

Jackson witnessed Mercury snorting cocaine, and this was enough to freeze their friendship. As a result, the tapes of their two duets are unreleased. 'State of Shock' did surface a year later on one of Michael Jackson's albums, but Mick Jagger had replaced Mercury as guest vocalist.

That rare question-and-answer session between Freddie Mercury and Simon Bates took place in London, after work ended with the American superstar. Aware that Mercury was notorious for not giving interviews, Bates asked him anyway. He didn't look for the reason why when the star unexpectedly agreed to meet him. The interview took place at Queen's offices. When Bates arrived Mercury greeted him graciously, making him comfortable and plying him with Earl Grey tea in exquisite china cups. They talked about art, among other things. A formal ninety-minute interview followed.

'He was almost Victorian in his manner,' says Bates, 'very quiet, extremely polite with the tea and biscuits and chatting – and I don't say that as a criticism. He was very much the middle-class man entertaining a guest, and it was all quite charming. He also went out of his way to show an interest in what I liked. He was fascinated with art and clearly very knowledgeable.'

That Mercury was nervous quickly communicated itself to his interviewer, as Bates recalls: 'Yes, he was a little insecure. I had a Radio One producer with me, and when it came to the moment to start the actual interview Freddie didn't want to talk in front of him. We had to be alone.

'I asked him if there were any areas he'd rather not stray on to, and he asked me instead to run through what I wanted to cover, and when I'd finished he said he didn't want to talk about his parents. There were no preconditions as such, but he would indicate that he'd rather not discuss such-and-such. The gay issue never came up, and why should it? It had no bearing on his work as a musician.'

During the interview Mercury relaxed. Far from putting on his standard performance, he revealed quite a lot about himself. 'He was happy to talk about himself,' confirms Simon Bates. 'He freely confessed to being a party animal, and that he liked to enjoy life to the full. He also liked to travel with Queen's touring commitments, to get away from Britain as often as possible, he said. He believed there were three of him. One was professional and hard-working, the second was the party animal and the third liked to be alone.'

Although Queen had temporarily disbanded, they remained in touch. For the past six months each member of the band had been involved in their own personal projects. In July they got together at the instigation of Jim Beach. In addition to being Queen's manager, Beach had links with the film world and approached the band with a proposition. A film of John Irving's novel *The Hotel New Hampshire* was in progress, starring Rob Lowe and Jodie Foster. Would Queen like to record its soundtrack?

Mercury was interested at once, and, with John Deacon, he flew to Canada to meet director Tony Richardson. Having read the darkly bizarre tale during the flight out, the meeting in Montreal went well, and they agreed to start work on material for the film score. Fixing a date in August, Queen met at Record Plant Studios in Los Angeles. They had never recorded together in America, and the novelty of this combined with the break from each other had rejuvenated them.

As far as translating this new vigour on to the soundtrack went, however, the initial enthusiasm quickly fizzled out. Tailoring their music to the novel wasn't easy. They liked the work itself, and for a while they persevered. But it proved a mismatch. Disappointed, the band had no option but to pull out of the project.

Recently Queen had signed to the US label Capitol Records, so they concentrated on making their new album.

Recording was at the Musicland Studios, with a release date set for early 1984. The first single chosen from the album was a Roger Taylor number, 'Radio Ga Ga'. The video promo, extravagant even by Queen's standards, reached epic proportions. Director David Mallett used five hundred extras, all recruited at short notice from the band's fan club, and the shoot took place one late November day at Shepperton Studios. The fans were all identically dressed, and at each chorus their role was to clap their hands in sequence above their heads. It wasn't complicated, and they were soon performing like professionals – unlike Queen. Led by Mercury dressed in black trousers and jackboots with what looked like strips of a red bandage as a shirt, all four band members at one point messed up a take by clapping out of time. The finished product, however, was a tight-set routine that was later adopted by concert crowds the world over.

Mercury's thoughts were preoccupied by his solo album, which he had begun to work on in Munich at the start of the year. As producer Mike Moran, later one of the star's closest friends and co-songwriter, reveals, Mercury never deliberately set out to distinguish his solo work from his work with Queen. But Mercury's heart lay more in ballads, and while recording his own material he intended to explore this fully. He admitted he wrote commercial love songs, maintaining that what he felt strongest about in life was love and emotion. 'I'm not a John Lennon who sleeps in bags for I don't know how long,' Mercury insisted. 'You have to have a certain upbringing and go through a certain amount of history before people will believe in what you're writing about.' Be that as it may, Mercury never allowed any of his lyrics to reflect his personal experiences too accurately.

At this time he was still leading a hectic social life, and one night in particular stands out in Peter Stringfellow's memory: 'My Hippodrome club had been open for about a year when I held my first Monday night gay night. There was a specific sound in music then, which was very high energy and exciting and closely associated with the gay scene, and this was blasting out. I was on the balcony with my girlfriend on my way to have a meal when suddenly a weird atmosphere came over the place. There was a big buzz of excitement and everyone, about 2500 people, had stopped whatever they were doing and turned to look at something. I wondered what on earth it could be, then I found out. Freddie Mercury had arrived. He was dressed all in white, and it was literally as if the Queen of Sheba had walked in. The crowd went absolutely berserk.

'It was a powerful example of Freddie's personal power because, make no mistake, he had that power. A thunderous round of applause got up, which, of course, Freddie took entirely as his due. He wasn't at all embarrassed. In fact, quite the reverse. His attitude was, "Well, of course! *I've* just walked in. What can you expect?" A great mass of people surged forward, but his bodyguards immediately closed ranks, and you couldn't get near him any more. He moved off with his entourage and set up court at a far off table.'

According to Stringfellow, Mercury would never stay in his clubs if he himself wasn't present. He adds, 'But Freddie had changed since that first time we met in Leeds. By now he lived in his own world, doing his own thing, and few people got near him. I became, like so many others, a Freddie-watcher, and he was the biggest star. Really, no one could touch him.'

Unless, that was, he chose to reach out himself. Before Mercury returned to Munich he was to meet a man who was to become very important to him. He had gone to one of his favourite haunts, the Cocobana, a gay basement club in South Kensington. Quite late in the evening he approached a stockily built, dark-haired man who was propping up the bar. Mercury offered to buy the stranger a drink, to which the man replied, 'Fuck off.' Never one to press unwanted attentions,

Mercury walked away to rejoin his noisy entourage, without even discovering the man's name.

He was in fact Jim Hutton, an Irishman who worked in a barber's shop concession in London's Savoy Hotel and shared a house with his lover in south London. When Hutton's boyfriend joined him at the bar, he was quick to reveal the identity of just who he had so rudely rebuffed. Like Winnie Kirkenberger, with whom Mercury was still involved – and despite the sort of reaction Peter Stringfellow had witnessed – Hutton maintained that the name Freddie Mercury was not familiar to him. Mercury, at a quick glance, had looked quite skinny, and Hutton didn't fancy him anyway. For Mercury this couldn't have been the first time he had been rejected, and he probably forgot about it.

'Radio Ga Ga' was released on 23 January 1984 and went straight in to the charts at number four, rising two places, but ultimately denied the top slot by Frankie Goes To Hollywood's 'Relax'. It marked another milestone within the band, however, as now all four members of Queen had a top ten hit to their credit. Roger Taylor's success was to be marred briefly a week later, though, with an incident in Italy during Queen's first live performance in fifteen months.

At the beginning of February Queen headlined at an annual music festival in San Remo. It was there, backstage, that a row developed between May and Roger Taylor, which almost resulted in a fight between the two friends. When asked later about this, Mercury described it as a 'very heavy scene' that developed from some tomfoolery. 'It was Roger squirting Brian in the face with hairspray or something,' he said. 'They nearly came to blows. It was a very tiny dressing room, very hot, and the whole thing just snowballed.'

To Mercury it confirmed how much tension remained among the group. Quick to recognise the potential gravity of the situation, he leapt between the feuding men and poked fun at them mercilessly. Initially neither May nor Taylor was in the mood for Mercury's antics – which could have fanned the flames – but he was so relentless that they eventually dissolved into laughter, and sanity returned. Onlookers have since credited Mercury with more than rescuing the moment, convinced that, in fact, he saved the entire future of Queen. But if a story Mercury once told is to be believed, he didn't always get away with sending up his friends.

'One night Roger was in a foul mood, and he threw his entire bloody drumset across the stage. The thing only just missed me. I might have been killed!' Mercury exaggerated. That night in San Remo, 'Radio Ga Ga' went down a storm with the delirious crowd. Days later, on 7 February, Capitol Records released it in America as their first Queen single, where it lodged in the chart at number sixteen. In Britain 'Relax' refused to budge but in nineteen other countries the song hit number one, in some cases remaining there for weeks.

Having learnt the lessons of *Hot Space*, when their new album, *The Works*, was released later that month, it gave fans exactly what they wanted – lots of harmonies, a meticulous production and the usual clever musical arrangements. Above all, though, the material was much gutsier, mainly thanks to May's insistence. Their reward came when it stormed into the album charts at number two.

To follow on from 'Radio Ga Ga', the second single from *The Works* was 'I Want to Break Free', the video for which was again to be directed by David Mallett. So far Queen's videos had been imaginative, even outlandish, and certainly expensive, but on this occasion they decided to have some fun. Granada TV's *Coronation Street* is the longest-running soap on British television, and Roger Taylor suggested that they should each dress up in drag as one of the female characters from the show.

The video was split into three separate sequences. The first showed Queen in a crowd of moronic-looking futuristic miners. Filmed one chilly March day in a warehouse at Limehouse Studios in London's Docklands, it again featured hundreds of fan-club volunteers as extras. The next day the second and main section was shot in a Battersea studio, and for this the band dressed up in drag. Responsibility for this was automatically attributed to Mercury. But he shrugged this off, and when asked by one TV presenter how he had persuaded the rest of the band to dress in women's clothing, he quipped, 'They ran into their frocks quicker than anything!'

John Deacon became a buttoned-up, disapproving granny. Brian May emerged a vision in a long nylon nightie, with fluffy slippers on his feet. While Roger Taylor transformed himself into an alarmingly convincing, sexy schoolgirl, complete with gymslip and stockings. But still it was Mercury who was the most hilarious. Opting to send up the *Street's* barmaid, Bet Lynch, he wore a candy-pink skinny-rib sweater, over an enormous false chest, and a saucy PVC, split-sided miniskirt. Whenever he took great sweeping strides, there was a flash of white knickers. He had originally attended dress rehearsals in ambitious six-inch stilettos, but couldn't stand up in them and had to settle for lower heels. He once impudently announced that if he weren't a rock star he would have nothing to do, adding with a twinkle, 'I can't cook. I'm not very good at being a housewife!' In this video, he certainly knew how to use a vacuum cleaner.

But if the Battersea shoot was a lark, the third and final sequence, which featured Mercury without the rest of the band, meant the most to him. Especially because he worked for a second time with his friend Wayne Eagling. 'Freddie was inspired a lot by ballet,' says Eagling. 'He had wanted for a long time to appear as a great dancer, and this was his chance, so we made him Nijinsky. Trying to choreograph for someone who is not a ballet dancer is difficult, and it wasn't easy for Fred. Sometimes in frustration, I'd end up saying to him, "Well, just do what you would normally do then." But he was the ultimate professional and determined to get it right.'

Derek Deane picks up, 'Wayne had recreated the ballet *L'après-midi d'un faune* for Freddie, which had been made famous by Nijinsky. It begins with Freddie looking as if he's sitting on a rock, but it's really made up of a pile of bodies, which one by one come alive. Later there's a shot of Freddie rolling on his stomach on top of a line of rotating bodies along the floor. Now he *loved* that bit!'

Although filming the ballet scene took a whole day, it features less than a minute in the final cut. Mercury had shaved off his moustache for the part and altogether enjoyed the experience. When it was over, he wanted to repay Eagling for his efforts, but the dancer refused money: 'I did it as a favour for a friend,' he says, 'and didn't want to be paid, but Freddie kept asking me if there was anything *he* could do for *me*, and I replied, "Well, I can't sing, but I'd love to sing a song with you."

'So Freddie and I wrote and recorded a number together called 'No, I Can't Dance'. I was never so nervous in all my life. If you feel inadequate I think you're like that, and being beside Freddie in a recording studio I certainly felt inadequate. But the funny thing was, I could sing with him next to me. We had a great time.'

The critics had fun, too, when the video for 'I Want to Break Free' was released on 2 April 1984. It was obviously meant as a lark, but self-righteous accusations about outrageous transvestism and ludicrous claims that such blatant homosexual behaviour could corrupt Britain's youth were made. It didn't stop the single from reaching number three in the UK, as well as becoming a huge hit throughout Europe. Some South American countries even adopted it as a freedom anthem.

Although by this time Mercury considered Munich to be very much his home, he began commuting to London at weekends. He still showed no signs of slowing down socially and in some ways had even reverted to the reckless hunger he had often displayed during those extended American tours. Come April he was to meet Jim Hutton again by chance, according to Hutton. Mercury was eating out at a smart restaurant in Earls Court and spotted Hutton among the other diners. From that moment, it is said that Mercury tracked Hutton's every move relentlessly.

Coincidentally, Jim Hutton's two-year relationship with his live-in lover was ending. Hutton's home was Surrey, but he liked to drink in a gay pub in Vauxhall, south London. Mercury frequented Heaven, a nightclub under Charing Cross Station, but he had apparently started to instruct his chauffeur to detour first to Vauxhall. Hutton believed that Mercury had made it his business to discover where he socialised, and that he would send his personal assistant Joe Fanelli into the pub simply to satisfy himself that Hutton was there and alone. After this Mercury would continue on to Heaven. If this were true, Mercury himself was far from ready to admit it. In one of his coarser moods, he bragged about his life then, 'I'm just an old slag who gets up every morning, scratches his head and wonders who he wants to fuck.'

By summer 1984 Mercury was in training for the demands of a forthcoming European tour. The band flew into a storm of controversy by announcing that they intended to play at the Sun City Super Bowl in South Africa. This immediately antagonised the Musicians' Union, anti-apartheid groups and the press. Queen's publicists tried to offset this by insisting that the band was not political, and that the gigs would be before mixed audiences. But nothing made any difference, and Queen were not to emerge from this furore totally unscathed.

It was ironic that the title of their new single was 'It's a Hard Life'. The video was a study in screen decadence and included, among the extras, the voluptuous Barbara Valentin. But it took more than a four-inch cleavage to upstage Mercury in his scarlet costume elaborately decorated with a profusion of Cyclops eyes.

The Works tour started in Belgium on 24 August and welcomed among its session men newcomer Spike Edney, who had lately worked with the Boomtown Rats. Edney had been introduced to Queen by Roger Taylor's personal assistant, Crystal Taylor. 'They asked me to an audition in Munich,' Edney recalls, 'and I went assuming there would be a queue, only to find I was the only one. I knew all their stuff anyway, so that was me in. I was more or less with Queen from that tour right through to Knebworth two years later.'

On 10 September, between the last of the four dates at London's Wembley Arena and their German gig at Westallenhalle, Dortmund, Queen's new single 'Hammer to Fall' came out. That day also marked the release of Mercury's first solo single in his own name. Co-written with Giorgio Moroder, and one of the tracks from the *Metropolis* soundtrack, 'Love Kills' was a rock/disco number. Convention decrees that solo work often fares worse than a band's material. But Mercury's single defied this tradition by reaching number ten in the UK charts. This was three places higher than 'Hammer to Fall', a typical Queen rocker normally guaranteed to have vast fan appeal. 'Love Kills' also became a massive hit in London's gay clubs and elsewhere in Europe.

It was while singing 'Hammer to Fall' a fortnight later in Hanover that Mercury slipped awkwardly on a flight of stairs. He carried on with the show, but when doctors examined him later it was clear that he had damaged some knee ligaments. He was advised against performing – but with just a handful of dates remaining, the star ignored their warnings and finished the tour. Five days later Queen landed in Bophuthatswana.

They were committed to a dozen dates at the Super Bowl, and tickets had sold out in a day. However, on the first night Mercury was scarcely warmed up, when his voice, which lately had been troublesome, threatened to seize up. Aware that he was in difficulty, the rest of the band tried to rally him, but Mercury's voice only got worse. 'Fred walked off after three songs. He was in agony,' Edney recalls.

Having lived on the road for several years, Mercury could never be accused of having neglected his comforts. He toured in the height of luxury with his personal valet, a masseur and a chef. Apart from his use of cocaine as a stimulant, his travelling medicine chest boasted an array of vitamins and tonics, specially selected to help him maintain the high energy levels he required to keep going. But despite all this, and the pre-tour physical training, his weak spot was his voice – and the small, persistent and painful nodules on his vocal cords that beat him every time. Frustrated, Mercury once rasped, 'They disappear but return like corns. It's misusing the voice that does it.'

The specialist summoned to examine Mercury couldn't have agreed more, and Queen had no option but to cancel the following four nights. 'It caused a big scandal because there was no time to reschedule dates, but it just couldn't be helped,' says Edney. Angry ticket-holders were one thing, but there was worse to come, as many people felt that Queen had failed fully to think through the political implications of playing in South Africa.

Mandla Langa, cultural attaché and ANC spokesperson, says: 'People were infuriated. Queen came into South Africa at a time when we didn't need any external influence which could lend respectability to the Pretoria regime. Sun City was always regarded as an insult to any right-thinking South African and to perform there, in the midst of poverty and rage, cannot be rationalised as Queen doing their bit to break down barriers. The people who attended those concerts were overwhelmingly white, and institutions such as the South African Broadcasting Corporation revelled at their new-found connection with the Western world and gave Queen maximum airplay ... People here have long memories, and their music has never been embraced by black activists.'

For their pains Queen were placed on the United Nations blacklist of musicians who performed in South Africa – although their name was later removed – and in Britain the Musicians' Union came down hard on them for flouting their rules. Unmoved by an impassioned speech from Brian May when he faced the Union's General Committee in person, they fined Queen heavily. The band paid up, but only on condition that the money was donated to charity.

Having left for Munich straight after the tour, Mercury was as keen as the other band members to put all this behind him. For the first time Queen had decided to release a Christmas single, and work on it had begun at Sarm Studios in London. 'Thank God It's Christmas' was started during Mercury's absence in Munich. Later May, Taylor and Deacon flew to Germany with the tapes, where Mercury added vocals. It was released on 26 November but failed to reach the top twenty.

The battle for that year's Christmas number one was won almost as soon as it began for 1984 was the year Band Aid emerged with their charity single 'Do They Know It's Christmas?'. In early November Boomtown Rats singer Bob Geldof had been deeply moved by a special televised report by the award-winning BBC's foreign affairs correspondent Michael Buerk on the Ethiopian famine. Inspired by this he had hatched at short notice an ambitious plan to produce an all-star record, from which no one involved would take any profit.

Two weeks and many phone calls later, thirty-six established rock artists gathered, in the same Notting Hill studio Queen had lately used. They were there to lay down the song that had been hastily co-written by Geldof and ex-Ultravox singer Midge Ure. The stars included Cliff Richard, Phil Collins, Sting, Boy George, George Michael, Status Quo, Duran Duran and Paul Young. But Queen hadn't been invited; a fact that greatly upset Mercury, who later revealed, 'I would have *loved* to have been on the Band Aid record,' adding, 'I don't know if they would have had me on the record anyway. I'm a bit old.'

Age, though, had nothing to do with it. One reason, cited by the charity organisers, why Queen hadn't been asked was because the band had been on tour at the time and were unavailable. But this was not the case. What was true was that the clouds of controversy over the South African shows still hung over their heads – and perhaps this played its part. Or possibly, knowing that Mercury's voice was more distinctive than the others, it was considered inappropriate to have any one individual's stamp on what was intended to be a joint effort.

If it were the latter reason, this didn't cushion Mercury's disappointment at not being part of what turned out to be the biggest-selling single in Britain ever. Especially now that Queen had come under fresh fire from the critics for having released a batch of singles that were all tracks from one album. Shouts of fan exploitation were heard and contributed to an unhappy end to Queen's first year back together again.

ELEVEN

Wembley Wizard

The humble way in which Mercury expressed his disappointment at being left out of the Band Aid recording signals a change in his demeanour from the mid-eighties onwards. 'I was caught up in being a star, and, I thought, this is the way a star behaves,' said Mercury. 'Now I don't give a damn. I want to do things my way and have fun.' And, certainly, close friends and acquaintances, who knew him in his last six years, independently testify to a man in many respects more placid and mature. Queen's first public-relations consultant, Tony Brainsby, detected a marked change in Mercury, when they ran into each other around then.

'Freddie had gone to see Peter Straker appearing in a play,' Brainsby recalls. 'He was wearing a beautiful suit and looked very elegant that night. I wasn't meeting Freddie the rock star, but the sophisticated gentleman. What struck me most was how much he had mellowed. He wasn't fighting for stardom and recognition, clawing his way back from Queen's financial set-backs. He had become a charming, congenial man who enjoyed going to the theatre. He was a different person altogether and relaxed, perhaps not professionally but certainly personally.'

Professionally there was no time to relax, for on 12 January 1985 Queen were to headline at 'Rock in Rio', a rock festival held near Rio de Janeiro that was billed to outshine even Woodstock. Staged at a custom-built arena in the mountains at Barra da Tijuca and organised by Brazilian businessman Roberto Medina, the other guests on the star-studded bill included AC/DC, Ozzy Osbourne, Yes and Iron Maiden. Maiden's lead singer then, Bruce Dickinson, vividly remembers the event:

'The whole thing was an incredible circus. It was the first time I had been associated with anything that came near to Beatlemania. There were crowds besieging hotels, long-lens cameras poking into the poolsides and everything. Originally Iron Maiden didn't want to do "Rock in Rio". We were in the middle of a winter sell-out tour of America, and it would've meant cancelling a week's gigs to go to do one spot in one show. So we put really ludicrous terms to the organisers, like we wanted to be paid the equivalent of five sold-out shows, recompensed for lost merchandising sales, air freight costs, etc. They also wanted us to do two nights, and we said we'd only do one. But they just said OK, and it was a case of, well, I guess we're doing it then.'

Iron Maiden, formed nearly ten years before and named after a medieval torture instrument, had survived the stagnation in the heavy metal scene in the late seventies to emerge as perhaps the most definitive example of the New Wave of British Heavy Metal. With a hugely energetic delivery, the band's stage act by now was spectacular with elaborate lighting effects easily to rival Queen's. The single performance they had agreed to give was the one directly before Queen closed the first night.

'Everyone was helicoptered in to the site,' says Dickinson, 'but because of the opposition from town they weren't allowed to fly at night, so it was, like, five hours getting back in traffic. Anyway, once there we found a set-up like we'd never seen. There were roving gangs of security guards, all of whom looked in really bad moods.'

Like anything Latin, the show was behind time, but on top of that Maiden were fifteen minutes late in getting on stage. Dickinson explains: 'It was all pretty hairy. There was a furious row going on in the hallway, right outside our dressing room. Two gangs of security guards were going mental, waving pistols at each other, and their guard dogs were all snarling and tugging on their leads.

'We were hiding like cowards, scared to step outside. Then, like something out of *Monty Python*, our own security guy eventually poked his head cautiously round the door and said, "Hey, guys! Would you mind giving it a rest until we get on stage?" And they did! They all shut up, and we hurried past, but as soon as our backs were turned, they all started up again!'

Once on stage, Dickinson said, 'We were all nervous, and I didn't think the monitor engineer was very good. We couldn't hear ourselves properly, and I got upset, as you do at twenty-three in front of 500,000 for the first time.' But it was a good show for them ultimately.

After Iron Maiden, Mercury had to lead Queen on stage. He was presumably a little edgy himself, because the schedule was running late and his adrenaline was pumping at the prospect of performing before a record-breaking crowd. 'Rock in Rio' was not the first time that Bruce Dickinson had met Mercury; that had happened in Sydney.

'It was when I'd first joined Iron Maiden, first time on tour in Australia and Queen were there,' he says. 'Things were going incredibly well, and I can't remember how it came about, but we ended up being invited to Queen's after-gig party. We all ended up the worse for wear, of course, and Freddie was being very quietly outrageous, as was his way.'

Bruce Dickinson watched Queen's closing performance in Brazil during the early hours of the morning. It did not go according to plan. 'Two or three of their numbers didn't go down well with the crowd,' he recalls, 'then when they launched into "I Want to Break Free", they didn't really take to Freddie dressing up in women's clothes, but Freddie obviously didn't understand what was wrong.'

In Mexico an audience had hurled rubbish at Queen as their show of appreciation, but the cans and rubble now rained down on them alarmingly. Hiding his confusion behind a false heartiness, Mercury brushed aside the props and carried on singing. He worked hard to ensure that they earned encores, but the confidence with which he strode the Brazilian stage belied his inner distress.

Dickinson reveals, 'When Freddie came off stage, he broke down in tears. He just had no idea why the audience had reacted like they did. Someone was quick to explain to him that "I Want to Break Free" was regarded as a freedom song there, and they had resented him sending it up, but he was very upset.'

That Mercury hadn't guessed this came as a surprise to Dickinson. To his knowledge, the star had experienced something similar before. 'He got the same reaction once in America to "Another One Bites the Dust",' says Dickinson. "There is a white, homophobic – bonehead – bunch of people in the States, and there was a large minority who'd kinda worked out that Freddie wasn't one of us, if you know what I mean? When that minority grew, it put the lights out for Queen in America for a time.'

Of Mercury himself, Dickinson maintains: 'He was fantastic. Everyone says now how unique he was, but he really was. He managed to carry it off with camp aloofness and yet be taken completely seriously, which is quite an achievement. He was so good that he could be schmaltzy and take the piss out of himself, then, in a heartbeat, turn it around and stop the show with a number like "Who Wants to Live Forever". Now *that's* a front man.'

When for the second and last time Queen closed the show

in the early hours of 19 January, there wasn't a bust or wig in sight. Brazil's Globo Television had covered the festival, and Queen purchased the rights to their own performances with a view to a future video release.

Back in England Mercury lost himself again in the gay clubs, where the latest dress code was the 'high clone' look, comprising tight blue jeans and a white singlet. Suitably attired and having grown back the requisite bushy moustache, Mercury mostly frequented Heaven. It was here, towards the end of March, that he was to run into Jim Hutton for a third time.

According to Hutton, Mercury had been after him for months. Yet it was Hutton who switched socialising from Vauxhall to Charing Cross. In this venue, heaving with clubbers, Mercury is said to have spotted Hutton instantly and approached him once more with the offer of a drink. Queen had just headlined at the world's biggest rock festival – all of which had received substantial coverage in music magazines – and Mercury's debut solo single 'Love Kills' had been a massive hit in the gay clubs. Incredibly Hutton maintained that he still had no idea that Mercury was a famous rock star. However, instead of the curt response he had delivered a couple of years before, this time Jim Hutton countered by offering to buy Mercury a vodka. The star accepted Hutton's offer with the appalling gambit, 'How big's your dick?'

Resilient to such crassness, they danced most of the night together, then Hutton returned with Mercury's crowd to the Kensington flat. Fairly drunk, Mercury took time as always to cuddle his two cats, Tiffany and Oscar, before snorting more cocaine and eventually drifting off to bed with his date. In the morning they exchanged telephone numbers, but it would be summertime before they were to meet again.

On 9 April Mercury's second solo single 'I Was Born to Love You' was released on CBS, followed at the end of the month by his debut solo album *Mr. Bad Guy*. Recorded with

Mack at Musicland Studios over the previous two years, the album went gold, reaching number six in the UK charts. A melting pot of musical styles, ranging from light opera to reggae, the album would later be considered ahead of its time – but on first release it was savaged by the critics.

Mercury could ignore them, though, being preoccupied with another Queen tour of Australia and New Zealand. The trip had been dogged by anti-apartheid groups heckling them outside venues and hotels. But they had also been approached with an intriguing offer, as their session keyboard player, Spike Edney, reveals: 'I'd briefly rejoined the Boomtown Rats between Queen's Works tour and them going to Australia, and Bob Geldof rang me up in New Zealand. He was going on about an idea he and Midge Ure had to follow up the Band Aid single with a massive rock concert, and he wanted to know if Queen would appear on the bill.' According to Edney, Geldof was using him as an intermediary in case Queen declined. 'I told the band about the idea,' he says, 'and they were piqued by the prospect, in theory, but it seemed too unlikely a project ever to come off – and so they said no.'

Perhaps Queen were also still annoyed at having been left out of the Band Aid recording. When Edney relayed their refusal, he tempered it by saying that it might be worthwhile for Geldof to personally approach the band. In the early stages of putting together the international Live Aid show, it was not the case that all the superstars were clamouring to take part. Bob Geldof had become adept at massaging the truth as he played one artiste off another. His initial negotiating tactic with Queen was to stretch the truth, saying he already had accept-ances from David Bowie and Elton John – whom he had lured in by suggesting that Queen had said yes. But for the time being the band remained resistant to Geldof's overtures.

Queen left for a week-long visit to Japan for what would turn out to be their last tour of the Far East. By mid-May they had returned to Britain, their touring commitments for the year concluded. Mercury headed to Munich where he indulged in a different kind of play-off. His relationship with Winnie Kirkenberger had come under pressure through Mercury's association with another man, known only as Patrick. Neither appears to have been willing to give up on the star's attentions, and it was a less than attractive side of Mercury's personality that, recognising this, he shamelessly enjoyed playing one lover off the other. It indicated no genuine depth of feeling for either participant in this *ménage à trois*. Mercury thrived on his role as the puppet master, exhibiting once again his desire to wield control.

The Live Aid project had grown beyond all expectations. From a massive concert in aid of the Ethiopian Famine at Wembley Stadium in the summer, a parallel gig was to take place at JFK Stadium in Philadelphia. Queen began to reassess their position, although Geldof still had some persuading to do – or perhaps it was assuaging Mercury's bruised ego.

Bob Geldof revealed he had traced Jim Beach to a holiday hideaway. Queen's manager warned him that Mercury was very sensitive. Characteristically blunt and running out of patience, Geldof said, 'Tell him that it's going to be the biggest thing that's ever happened.' That had already become glaringly obvious, and too smart to resist any further Queen agreed to participate.

This ambitious live event was a mere month away when Mercury finally contacted Hutton and invited him to a dinner party at Stafford Terrace. On his arrival Hutton wasn't entirely among strangers as he had known Peter Freestone after they had worked together in the same London department store. He was also reacquainted with Joe Fanelli, whom Mercury, with his penchant for attributing people nicknames, had dubbed Liza. Used strictly in intimate company, Mercury was Melina, as in the Greek actress Melina Mercouri, famous for her portrayal of a prostitute in *Never on Sunday*. Paul Prenter was also present. There appears to have been a lot of tension that evening.

Melina himself was blissfully unaware of this, though, as he was hitting the coke hard that night. This wired him up, causing him to gabble incessantly. With Mercury's fantasy mate still the actor Burt Reynolds, he rapidly convinced himself that Jim Hutton was a near enough lookalike. Attracted to a certain vulnerability in Mercury, once again Hutton stayed the night. The following day the star went back to Munich, but from this point on Jim Hutton would become his regular lover, eventually moving in to live with him.

Unpredictable and fiercely demanding in his physical needs, Mercury's legendary libido would seem initially to have surprised Hutton. Once describing their sex as raunchy but not especially acrobatic, on the whole Mercury apparently preferred the less dominant role in their relationship. When unbridled lust turned to love, a special companionship developed between the two men, about which friends would later talk with much respect. Unlike Tony Bastin, who lasted two years with Mercury, Jim Hutton remained with him to the end of his life and came closest, among the star's gay lovers, to rivalling Mary Austin in his affections. At this point Austin lived in a luxury flat in Phillimore Gardens close to Garden Lodge. She was involved in his business and daily life, and she and Hutton were quite quickly introduced to each other. Mercury revelled in the passion of a new romance. He enjoyed playing roles, even if they were short-lived and subject to sudden change. For now he was content with his latest affair, and liked to follow steamy love-making by lounging with his lover watching television on the sofa. Hutton saw to his every comfort, and the star felt pampered and cherished. Until, that was, he had to step out of this cosy domesticity and return to his role as egotistical performer; which colourful persona he was about to assume for Live Aid.

Queen's slot was to start at 6 p.m. With satellite link-up, this meant they would be the first band to be seen on live TV in America. On 10 July they barricaded themselves in to the Shaw Theatre in Euston for three days of intensive rehearsal. Each band had been allocated twenty minutes, and to use this to best advantage Queen decided to restrict their show to their most famous hits. 'Later such a fuss was made about how ingenious Queen had been, but to us it was the obvious thing to do,' Edney recalls.

Mercury, though, was clearly proud of their strategy, as DJ Simon Bates recollects: 'I interviewed him again just prior to Live Aid, and he was particularly proud of the hard work they were putting into the Queen set. He said to me, "Wait until you see it. You'll be blown away!" And, of course, he was right.'

On Saturday, 13 July 1985, everyone at 12 Stafford Terrace was in high spirits. Mercury watched on TV as, at precisely 12.01 p.m., Status Quo took the Wembley Stadium stage before a packed audience and opened to the sounds of 'Rockin' All Over the World'. It was to be the first number of a mammoth sixteen-hour mega-gig, whose final line-up included Bob Dylan, Tina Turner, Bryan Adams, Paul McCartney and Dire Straits among other rock celebrities.

Mid-afternoon, dressed high-clone and wearing a silver amulet, Mercury left for Wembley in his limousine, accompanied by Jim Hutton. It was Hutton's first live Queen performance. Arriving with an hour to spare, the star swept into the private enclosure and settled into his trailer. Simultaneously broadcast live to over one billion people worldwide, Live Aid was the first time a concert on that scale had been attempted. Consequently, nerves were fraught behind the scenes. It was a show that required state-of-the-art equipment, that included a revolving stage, split into three segments, one for the band in performance, one for the next band to set up their equipment and one for the band just finished to dismantle gear. Considering the logistics, it was surprising that six hours into the event, they were running only half an hour late.

Following David Bowie's set, with Wembley hooked up to the JFK Stadium, Queen came on stage, introduced as 'the next combo' by comedians Mel Smith and Griff Rhys Jones. Within eighteen minutes, as Mercury predicted, they blew everyone away. All four played for all their worth, delivering a punchy, edited medley of their greatest hits, which got the Wembley crowd, Queen supporters or not, rocking on their feet. But, undeniably, Mercury, the star, shone the brightest.

He was nervous, but he disguised it well as he blasted into 'Hammer to Fall'. During Brian May's guitar solo, he dug the end of the microphone stand into his groin, pretending to play frantic lead guitar along its chrome rod. He took time out mischievously to torment a BBC cameraman filming from the wings; within minutes he had begun visibly to enjoy himself. By 'Crazy Little Thing Called Love' he was bathed in sweat, and the sheer magnetism of his performance was so alluring that he had the audience enraptured and eating out of his hand. As he prowled the length of the stage, to the stirring intro to 'We Will Rock You', he knew he had taken control. 'Do it!' he ordered the crowd to sing to him, growling, 'I like it! Sing it again!' Then plunging non-stop into 'We Are the Champions', he had the stadium swaying in a sea of arms, a moving display of unity. Love him or loathe him, Mercury was untouchable that day, and the watching world now knew it, too.

Fellow performer Paul Young agrees: 'I'd always liked Queen, but that was the night I said to myself: these boys really are fantastic. Their sound was amazing, and Freddie proved just what a showman he was.'

Leaving the crowd in a lather, Queen quit the stage. The

second Mercury reached his trailer, he gasped, 'Thank God, that's over,' and promptly downed a double vodka.

They'd done it, and they knew it, but never more so than when Elton John burst in shouting, 'You bastards! You stole the show!'

It was a sentiment echoed by almost everyone and upheld years later when the event was rescreened on Live Aid's tenth anniversary. Thin Lizzy's Scott Gorham recalls, 'Man, that was six hours of Euro wimp! Everyone was wondering, God, who asked them along? And then Queen came on, and there's Fred stickin' out his chest and daring the world not to like them. It was amazing, like the rebirth of Queen on the spot. When you'd seen those guys, who wanted to see the rest?' In fact Mercury did. The party animal ignored the lavish after-gig bash and went home instead with Jim Hutton – to settle quietly in front of the TV with his cats and watch the American half of the show.

Live Aid's effect was far-reaching. And the man in a sense responsible for it all was BBC newsreader Michael Buerk. 'When the whole Live Aid thing got going I was in South Africa,' he says, 'the one country which couldn't have cared less about the starving in Ethiopia. My original feeling, I must admit, was that it was a bandwagon thing which would die out in a week and wouldn't achieve anything in effective terms. I didn't see much connection with the pop world and dying people. Shows you how wrong I was.

'I didn't see the actual concert as South Africa didn't show it. But it certainly increased the level of consciousness about the situation, which in turn placed pressure on governments and inter-governmental departments around the world, and that was a good thing. Two million people were estimated to be due to die in that famine and in the end 800,000 did, so Live Aid was at least, in part, responsible for saving over a million lives.'

There had also been spin-off benefits. For some acts, taking part had rejuvenated their careers. Others say that Queen's appearance helped to redeem the band after the Sun City débâcle. What Live Aid certainly did was introduce Queen to a new generation of fans, and their popularity, worldwide, rose to an all-time high. Roger Taylor admitted to reporters on the eve of the event, 'Of course it is a wonderful cause and will make a pot of money for that wonderful cause. But make no mistake. We're doing it for our own glory as well.' It worked. Queen record sales increased five-fold, and Mercury's solo album *Mr Bad Guy* leapt back into the charts, tripling in popularity.

After Live Aid, Queen scattered again. Inspired by their triumph, their thoughts would turn to a major tour for 1986. They would be approached, too, about writing music for a Hollywood movie. At the start of July, Mercury had already released 'Made in Heaven', another solo single, and the next one was scheduled for some weeks away. But before all that he decided to take a holiday. He chose the Mediterranean island of Ibiza, an international resort notorious for its nightlife and lively discos such as Pacha, Amnesia and the Ku Club. This time, on Jim Beach's recommendation, he stayed for the first time in Pikes Hotel. The luxurious complex was owned by Tony Pike and would come to feature regularly in the star's life over the next five years.

Pike, with whom Mercury would become good friends, is a down-to-earth man with little patience for any form of pretension. Pikes Hotel enjoys a worldwide reputation as an exclusive and relaxing hideaway, and its regular clientele includes such stars as George Michael and the former Real Madrid goalkeeper, now heartthrob crooner, Julio Iglesias. But if anyone comes to the hotel with the intention of swaggering around, they either have to come down to earth or accept that nobody there is going to be impressed.

'We had one particular British TV actor staying here once who was so pompous,' recalls Pike. 'He was very strong on how great he was. On his arrival he immediately warned me that our main gates had better have strong locks on them because when word got around that he was there, the place would be under siege. It was a load of rot!' With this experience of ego-mania, when Mercury first set foot in the hotel complex, Pike had his reasons to suspect that he had more trouble on his hands.

'I first met Freddie just after Live Aid,' says Pike. 'I already knew Jim Beach through a mutual acquaintance, but I hadn't met any of Queen. So this particular day Freddie and his party of friends were due, and I got word that they'd arrived. I went down to the courtyard to greet Freddie personally, who gave me the campest of handshakes with an equally camp "Hello" to match, and that was it. He didn't say another word, and I thought, Oh, this one's going to be difficult.

'He had a whole entourage with him, which included Jim Hutton, Peter Straker and Peter Freestone. They were occupying the whole of the hotel's oldest part for easier security arrangements, and without another word Freddie brushed past me and disappeared. I stayed in the courtyard talking to some people, and minutes later he appeared out on a balcony above, when I clearly heard him say, in a way that I took to be criticism, that the ceilings were all very low. I looked up, just as Freddie looked down, and our eyes met. A split-second later he called out, "Only joking!" and laughed, which made me laugh, too, and broke the tension between us.'

For Mercury this was a place to forget being famous and unwind – in a way that was impossible in other sumptuous hotels, where staff are forever chasing tips through five-star treatment. In the past, precisely this kind of fawning had suited Mercury perfectly. Now he valued different things, and Pikes was the only place where he felt he was able to be himself.

'Freddie had such wonderful times,' says Pike, 'because he surrounded himself here only with friends, not paid employees but people who were with him because he liked them, and they him.' Pike got to know the star well over the years, and he maintains, 'The absolute truth is that he was a wonderful human being, very attentive to others' needs, would always apologise for anything untoward happening and was eternally grateful to the staff for doing really only what they're paid to do.'

Among those who invariably accompanied Mercury on holiday was Barbara Valentin, who, according to Pike, could be just as outrageous and funny as Mercury. 'We had some wonderful, crazy times together there,' Valentin recalls.

The length of his stay would depend on what else was going on in his life, but he enjoyed dinner parties, playing tennis – often partnered by Pike, who admits that Mercury was more of a poser than a player – and he could also be persuaded to entertain. 'He'd be lounging by the pool,' Pike recalls, and suddenly say, "Go and get the piano." Well, I mean, a piano is a heavy thing, but, no matter, six or seven men would stagger down to the poolside with it, and Fred would play and sing for everyone – and that ended up including absolutely everyone in the hotel, not just his own set.

'Sometimes he'd then get campy and start horsing around, throwing people into the water and generally having fun, which again would inevitably end up also involving other guests. But he never upset anyone who preferred to keep their distance from this kind of carry-on.'

About Mercury's homosexuality Pike goes on, 'In all the years Freddie came here, never in my experience did he push it onto anyone. Sure he loved to camp it up. He was gay, but he was very secure in that fact, and unless he was in the mood to caper, you'd never witness his homosexuality. In fact, most women that I saw found him very attractive indeed. He had a good physique and was a very masculine-looking man. He was also not one of those gay men in whose company you feel uneasy. I have experienced that, but never with Freddie.'

Although Jim Hutton always accompanied Mercury to Pikes, it was some time before Tony Pike knew the nature of their relationship. He explains, 'It was about their third trip, when one day I said to him, "Where do you fit in, then?" Jim is a very quiet and reserved person, very masculine, too, and by this time I knew he wasn't involved in music. There had been no demonstrative behaviour between them on any occasion, so I wasn't being crass, and maybe he gauged that in the few seconds he took to answer, because he looked me straight in the eye then asked, "Don't you know?" I shook my head, and he replied, "I'm Freddie's man." I felt a complete idiot and awful for prying when I hadn't meant to.'

Pike developed a deep regard for Hutton. 'He and Freddie never exhibited their love in public,' he says. 'No arms around each other or any other indication that they were lovers. Fred was so publicly the outrageous showman of rock, but in private I think Jim had a steadying influence on him. He was a very nice guy.'

On their return to London, Mercury set arrangements in hand gradually to move his belongings from his Stafford Terrace flat into Garden Lodge. He still wouldn't take up residence there himself just yet, but when he did, Jim Hutton would move with him.

The film for which Queen had been asked to write the music was *Highlander*, to be directed by Russell Mulcahy on a $20-million budget. Queen had agreed to this on condition that one of their numbers was used as the signature tune. Drinking vodka and chain-smoking throughout, Mercury worked with the rest of the band in Musicland, Mountain and Town House Studios on the new album. His solo single 'Living On My Own', released on 2 September, had barely made the top fifty, and his aspirations were clearly much higher for Queen's material.

All work was suspended, though, as he celebrated his thirty-ninth birthday with a spectacular party held at Hendersons in Munich. There was always a theme now to these parties, and this one was to be a black-and-white drag ball. During his stay in Germany he continued to dangle both Winnie Kirkenberger and Patrick on a string. He also flirted openly with other men, despite his clearly deepening involvement with Jim Hutton. Yet even with Hutton, perhaps at times feeling hemmed in, Mercury was capable of being imperiously dismissive. On occasions Hutton would leave Mercury on account of this, only to be repeatedly coaxed back.

Back working in the studio again, one track quickly emerged, written collectively by the band. It appealed strongly enough to everyone to become Queen's first and only single of 1985. 'One Vision' was released on 4 November and, riding on the wave of their renewed popularity, it reached number seven in the charts. It would also feature on a future soundtrack album for Sidney J. Furie's movie, *Iron Eagle*. A fortnight later yet another Mercury solo single came out, 'Love Me Like There's No Tomorrow'.

Critics attacked 'One Vision', viewing its lyrics as a Live Aid cash-in, but Mercury ignored the accusations. He concentrated instead on taking part in the fashion world's charity event, Fashion Aid, held at the Royal Albert Hall. He had become involved through his friendship with fashion designer Elizabeth Emanuel, who, along with David Emanuel, had designed Princess Diana's famous fairy-tale wedding dress in 1981.

'I was originally introduced to Freddie through Wayne Eagling at the Royal Ballet one night,' says Elizabeth Emanuel, 'and from then on there was a whole crowd of us who often got together. We went to the same places, the same parties and so on. When Fashion Aid came along, David and I had a whole section to handle, as well as a ballet section, which Wayne was choreographing. We were to do outfits for Michael and Shakira Caine, Anthony and Georgina Andrews, John Hurt, Robin Cousins and others. Jane Seymour was to model a wedding gown of ours, and I asked Freddie if he would partner her. He was up for it at once.'

Mercury already had a stylish military-type black jacket of which he was proud, that he had worn at his recent birthday party. He opted to wear this again, and the Emanuels simply had to design a sash to accompany it. 'He came along at the last moment, and it was all pretty chaotic. But he was a good sport to do it,' adds Emanuel.

On the night itself Mercury and Jane Seymour made a stunning couple, with the star's presence alone causing a stir. 'He was very much the star that night,' Emanuel recalls. 'You couldn't get near him for the crush. When I had first met him it was a bit like that – very much a magnet, swamped by people at every turn. But then I met him at the ballet when he'd go along to see Wayne dance, and he was a lot less formidable. When he got ill later, he often went quietly to the ballet, slipping in unnoticed at the back. He was a really nice guy and far removed from his flamboyant reputation.

'The funny thing is, in the beginning when he behaved outrageously, I got the distinct impression that it was in a strange way so as not to let people down who expected it of him.'

At the end of the evening Mercury and Seymour left for a hotel where a party was to be held, still dressed as bride and groom. Astonished hotel guests recognised the couple and hastily photographed them, believing they had stumbled on a celebrity marriage. Mercury found it highly amusing and did nothing to disabuse them.

As the year drew to a close, more sombre matters preoccupied him. In October the American matinee idol Rock Hudson had died of AIDS, which revelation had sparked off an intense public awareness of a disease hitherto publicly unrecognised. Although the medical profession knew little about the illness, enough was known to ring alarm bells throughout the world's gay communities. Three high-risk categories had now been identified: homosexuals, people who had unprotected sex with multiple partners and drug addicts. Mercury fell into the first two categories – and could have no way of knowing whether any of his innumerable one-night stands had been needle users. Clearly anxious, he secretly took an AIDS test, which proved negative. His huge relief, though, would be short-lived.

TWELVE

Death Knell

At the end of 1985 Mercury shocked Barbara Valentin and his friends in Germany by abruptly quitting Munich for good – leaving behind the life he had revelled in for years. He called himself a man of extremes and on occasions could effect sudden changes in his life with no apparent weakening. But he was not emotionless; indeed, his conversions nearly always had a serious reason. With hindsight his departure might have been linked to his fear of contracting HIV, but equally he appeared to those around him simply a changed man. In London he stopped trawling gay bars for just any pick-up, although he continued to cheat on Jim Hutton.

Infidelity in Mercury's personal life remained normal for him, and his only steadfast commitment was to Queen. Throughout January they worked on the soundtrack for *Highlander*. On the album's completion, their UK and US labels differed over which single to release first. Capitol Records opted for Mercury's 'Princes of the Universe', while EMI preferred Roger Taylor's 'A Kind of Magic', which was also the album title track. Both accompanying videos were impressive in their individual way.

For 'Princes of the Universe' *Highlander*'s star, French actor Christopher Lambert, agreed to recreate his screen character to enjoin battle against Mercury. And for 'A Kind of Magic',

Mercury portrayed a magician who temporarily transforms three vagrants into rock stars. Its sophisticated animation guaranteed its unique appeal, and when 'A Kind of Magic' came out on 17 March, it claimed the number three spot in Britain and shot straight to the top in thirty-five other countries. The album release, to be backed by a major tour already many months in the planning, was set for summer, and in the intervening time all four band members pursued their own interests.

In Mercury's case, having dabbled with ballet, he had now set his sights on the world of stage musicals – with a little help from his friend Dave Clark. Clark was staging *Time*, a lavish production with spectacular sets and ambitious special effects. Its theme was human survival, and the central character, a spiritual rock star, was played for the first year of its run by Cliff Richard, later replaced by David Cassidy. There was also to be an album featuring a variety of artistes, including Dionne Warwick, Stevie Wonder and Julian Lennon. Clark had asked Mercury to record a couple of tracks, as the show's star, now knighted Sir Cliff, recalls, 'Freddie got to record "In My Defence" for the album much to my chagrin, because the number was one of my favourites – and I'd really wanted to do it myself – but Dave Clark asked Freddie.'

It opened on 9 April 1986 at the Dominion Theatre, Tottenham Court Road. At this time Clark invited Mercury to dine with Lord and Lady Olivier; Lord Laurence had a cameo role in the musical in the form of a hologram. Mercury considered the great actor to be a theatrical legend and jumped at the chance. They met only once but, according to Lady Olivier, she and her husband knew that Mercury was a regular theatregoer, who had been to many of their productions at London's National Theatre.

On his best behaviour that night, Mercury felt nervous. But that soon evaporated when he complained to Olivier about the treatment Queen had received from the music press. Olivier's response had been a curt 'Fuck the critics!' Recalling that single meeting, Lady Olivier declares Mercury as 'a most pleasing and courteous dinner companion'. The show's reviews were also warm enough, and initially it drew capacity crowds. When Mercury's single 'Time' was released on 6 May, though, it failed to crack the top three.

Despite Mercury's complaint about bad reviews, when *A Kind of Magic*, the soundtrack album from *Highlander*, was released at the beginning of June, it charted at number one and eventually went double-platinum. Days later the band kicked off what would turn out to be their last tour. Called the Magic Tour, it began at the Rasunda Fotbollstadion in Stockholm, ending two months later with a massive outdoor gig at Knebworth Park in Stevenage, and proved eventful from start to finish.

Because of the criticism they had continued to suffer over Sun City, Queen had issued a press statement the previous December to the effect that they would never again visit South Africa. Six months on, they were greeted in Sweden by a chanting crowd of anti-apartheid protestors. Two days later the single, 'Friends Will Be Friends' was released; then when the tour reached France, Jim Hutton surprised his lover by joining him in Paris.

It was also in Paris that Marillion joined the tour. Says lead singer Fish, 'We'd gone to support Queen on the open-air gigs, which were to be the last live dates that they'd do.' Freddie was Freddie and kept himself to himself; a detachment that came as no surprise to Fish. He explains, 'To do what we do, we have to be very selfish. Therefore when you're talking of two solid cores of selfishness meeting, the odds are remote on you actually relating to somebody and getting to the point where you want to give something to each other intellectually.'

Marillion continued to support Queen when they arrived for a gig in Mannheim, Germany, where Fish remembers Mercury coming up with one of his more daft ideas for arriving on stage. 'It was during the sound check,' he says, 'and Fred thought he'd try going up in a cherry picker – which is one of those enormous crane-type things used for doing up the overhead lights. So he climbed in, and it got so far up, when he got scared. I'm not surprised, but that was it. He scrapped the whole idea.

'Freddie was, of course, the most outrageous front man. I watched him a lot during that tour, and I think he made me a little less self-conscious, simply because of his own performance. He was so cocky and totally self-assured, but then anybody who walks on a stage to perform in front of crowds of people *has* to have an enormous ego. It's an incredible feeling of power and satisfaction.

'There are so many different emotions involved. Some say it's like sex, others that it's like standing on top of a tall building and leaning over. You can't equate it with anything else, at least nothing that I've found so far.

'Freddie could switch himself on and off, as most people can. If you want to, you can turn on the stage stuff. There's a mechanism that you've got to learn how to trigger and how to control. Freddie was a master of it.' That night, Fish ended up on stage with Queen, dueting with Mercury on 'Tutti Frutti' as it was broadcast live on German radio.

On 11 and 12 July Queen returned to the scene of their Live Aid triumph a year before with two sell-out gigs at London's Wembley Stadium. The extra date had been added because of the demand for tickets, and both were classic nights. Over the years Mercury had dazzled fans with his stage wear; antics that he once laughed aside saying, 'It's just theatre. I love a nice frock!' During this tour his outfits, particularly the yellow-buckled jacket with tailored trousers, combined a rock-star look with a stylish maturity. But for those entertaining any notions that his talent for surprise had died, he was about to prove them spectacularly wrong.

Ending the final encore with 'We Are the Champions', their fans were in a frenzy. In tribute, Mercury punched one fist triumphantly in the air and spun on his heels off stage. He returned draped in a stunning red velvet silk-lined robe, trimmed with fake ermine and a six-foot train. Cradling his sawn-off microphone stand as a sceptre, he wore a jewel-encrusted coronation crown on his head. No other performer could have pulled off such a cheeky stunt – and with such style. He suited the regalia of an English monarch, and as the audience erupted with delight, he stood with his feet planted firmly apart, proud to receive their homage, as if he were, indeed, King Mercury. His ensemble was the work of designer Diane Moseley, and although both the cloak and crown were heavy, Mercury adored wearing them.

Energised by their shows, Queen's post-Wembley rave at the Roof Garden above Kensington High Street carved a place in the band's mythology. Over five hundred guests circulated in the beautiful rooftop restaurant, landscaped like a garden. Celebrity guests included Sir Cliff Richard, Sam Fox, Fish and Spandau Ballet, who were well acquainted with the band's reputation for laying on exotic entertainment. Anticipation was high, and no one was disappointed.

The uniform of every waiter was body paint, the work of German artist Bernd Bauer. Among the other delights laid on for the guests were a scantily clad woman on duty in the men's toilets and an equally underdressed gent in the ladies – ready to render *whatever* assistance was asked of them. That night Mercury made a point to be seen publicly with Mary Austin on his arm. Jim Hutton was nowhere in sight.

Although Mercury had recorded tracks for the album *Time*, he and Cliff Richard had not met until the night of the Roof Garden party: 'I have to say that previously I'd never been a fan of Freddie's in terms of his kind of vocals,' says Richard, 'but I certainly admired his ability, including his skill on the piano, and, of course, he was such an extrovert showman.

'Just the year before when Queen did Live Aid, although I myself couldn't take part as I was committed to a gospel charity gig in Birmingham, I managed to see snatches of the show, and the second I saw Freddie launch into his act it was obvious that he was going to completely steal the show. When they returned to Wembley during their Magic Tour I couldn't go to see them because I was on stage with *Time*, but they invited me to their aftershow party.

'These kinds of parties are always the same – crowds of people – most of whom spend hours lining up to meet the star for usually no more than minutes, so it's not really conducive to getting to know someone.'

Subsequently, Cliff Richard had the opportunity to meet Mercury at smaller gatherings, when, he says, 'Freddie invited myself and a group of people to a few of his private parties at his home.'

With a solitary gig in Manchester a few days later, Queen then returned to Europe. By this time fatigue was setting in for Mercury, and he tried hard to avoid straining his voice. Through Germany and Austria they performed, reaching Hungary for a gig at Nepstadion in Budapest. Queen played to a capacity crowd with a huge number of ticketless fans hanging around in vain outside the venue. Mercury had learnt a couple of verses of the traditional folk song 'Tavaski Szel', which further endeared the band to the Hungarian people. Much has since been made of this gig, with claims that Queen's performance made history as the first rock show behind the Iron Curtain. Certainly their appearance there would have been historic in terms of their own careers – but not in rock music. Nineteen years earlier the Rolling Stones had played at the Palace of Culture in Warsaw.

What did become a landmark gig in Queen's career was the Magic Tour's final date on 9 August at Knebworth Park, Hertfordshire, before a crowd of about 200,000. Held in 247 acres of magnificent parkland, against the backdrop of the romantic castellations of Knebworth House, it was to be Queen's last live performance. Says Spike Edney, 'The demand to see Queen had been strong enough to have staged a third night at Wembley, but that couldn't be arranged.' Gerry Stickells had then come up with the suggestion of an outdoor gig at Knebworth. The band agreed, providing he could guarantee a sell-out crowd.

Several rock groups have performed there, including the Rolling Stones, Frank Zappa and Led Zeppelin. Lady Chryssie Cobbold, whose family owns the Knebworth estate, remembers Queen as being different from the others: 'We have often entertained the groups before,' she says, 'during or after their concerts, but in the case of Queen they were not interested in coming up to the house.' With Mercury's passion for grandeur, it was a surprising decision as much as a missed opportunity.

The gig itself was spectacular. 'It was an amazing day,' recalls Spike Edney. 'We'd never played to such a large audience in the UK before, and it was incredible. No one knew at the time, of course, that it would be their last ever gig.' The party afterwards stands out in his memory, too. 'It was the usual Queen extravaganza, with everything from a fairground to female mud wrestlers.'

The band had been helicoptered in and out of the venue and Mercury, who had been especially tense with nerves before this performance, was the first to leave. Lady Cobbold confirms, 'There was a backstage party after the concert, but Freddie left straight after finishing the gig.'

The previous month at Wembley, Mercury had referred on stage to press speculation that Queen were on the verge of splitting up. He denounced the busy rumours with the cry, 'They're talking from here!' and pointed to his arse. But, in truth, as he had closed Knebworth with the words, 'Thank you, you beautiful people. Good night, sweet dreams. We love you,' the fact that the tour was over came as a huge relief to him.

Friction in the band had again been building. Mercury later confessed that there had been times when they had hated each other vehemently. Roger Taylor also revealed, 'Our rows are partially a conflict of musical ideas and partially ego problems.' Marillion's Fish, straight from the Magic Tour, has no difficulty understanding these all-too-common problems. 'Everyone in a band has to come to terms with ego,' he says, 'and understand that every member is important. And that as a band evolves to a point where there will be an incredible amount of friction as the pieces jostle for position, some bands don't come through that stage. Marillion didn't come through it. Queen did.'

Over the years Queen's clash of creative forces had turned confrontational. Yet Mercury believed that had there not been fighting – if, for him, it had all been made too easy – then the quality of his work would have suffered. 'I think because we all fight,' he said, 'you get the *crème de la crème*.' Even so, while recording in Munich, tempers in the band had flared too often for comfort. One or another band member regularly threatened to walk out, finding fault with everything – major or minor.

One major ongoing resentment had developed over 'Bohemian Rhapsody'. Once the single had sold over a million copies, why should Taylor receive the same writing royalty as Mercury? After all, Taylor had only written the little known B-side 'I'm in Love with My Car'. There had been contention of this kind for years, but Mercury felt that however heated their exchanges became, none of them got to the point of wishing to quit permanently. He remarked that 'The four of us have said that this chemistry has really worked for us. So why kill the goose that laid the golden egg?' He added, 'Through anything, we will just carry on until one of us drops dead or something.' Under the circumstances, it was nevertheless advisable to take a second break.

This time Mercury found time finally to take up residence in Garden Lodge, although he continued to maintain his Kensington flat. Joe Fanelli, Peter Freestone and the two cats were among those who moved in, too, along with Jim Hutton. At this time Mercury and Hutton entered into an unusual arrangement, whereby, despite the vast difference in their earnings, Jim Hutton, in effect, paid rent to his superstar lover. This would eventually cease, but in the beginning Mercury took half Hutton's barber's wage as board. According to Hutton, he was happy with this, believing that it preserved his independence.

With a lot of free time on his hands, Mercury could indulge whatever whim took his fancy, and it was around this time that he enjoyed his one experience of appearing in a stage musical. *Time* was still playing to full houses at the Dominion Theatre, and Mercury was delighted to take part in a one-off special, as Sir Cliff Richard recalls.

'We had finished the show,' he says, 'but stayed on to do it all over again for a midnight charity performance, and Freddie joined me on stage to sing a couple of numbers – "Born to Rock 'n' Roll" and the final song "Each and Every One of Us".' Doubtless Mercury suffered his usual pre-performance nerves when straying into unfamiliar territory, but both he and Cliff Richard ended up enjoying the experience. 'It maybe didn't last long, but at least I can say that I've performed on stage with Freddie Mercury,' says Richard.

Although by no means a diehard Queen fan, Sir Cliff Richard admits that now and then one of the band's numbers would impress him. He has, however, no doubt about where their strength lay. 'Freddie had an amazing grasp of vocal harmonies and to me *that* was absolutely the core of the Queen sound,' he says. 'He was never shy of multi-tracking either and would produce layer after layer of sound – a whole blanket of sound really, and that was peculiar to Freddie. It anchored Queen's style to the point that you instantly recognised their work anywhere, anytime.'

As to the probability that Mercury might have branched into stage musicals in the future, Richard believes, 'I think he very well could have been drawn there. Perhaps he wouldn't have encountered anywhere near the same success – but that usually happens. But a performer of his calibre would always bring a certain audience with him to start with and would've reached out to a new one after that. He'd certainly have been capable of doing it.'

What Mercury was more than capable of doing was spending money. All this unexpected leisure time meant he could increase the frequency of his short but intensive shopping trips to Tokyo to buy expensive works of art and antiques and extend his collection of Dresden china. But his main home base from now on would be his sumptuous mansion, now extensively renovated and refurbished. Three rooms on the third floor had been knocked together to make one huge master bedroom – dominated by an enormous bed – with a splendid balcony.

In the garden he had special pools built and filled with his favourite exotic koi carp fish, and over the years he would accumulate another six cats on which to dote. Whenever he returned home, eight bundles of fur would converge to welcome him. When one once went missing he was so distraught that he organised a search party and was ready to put up a £1000 reward for its safe return. His close circle of friends often dined at Garden Lodge, and Peter Straker in particular was a frequent visitor. He and Mercury often talked the night away, listening to their favourite music while Jim Hutton waited upstairs in bed.

Although Mercury had stopped stalking the gay scene, he still couldn't resist occasional clubbing. Sometimes he'd pick up a man and take him back for the night to his Stafford Terrace flat, while Hutton was at Garden Lodge. When Hutton found out about these assignations, his retaliation could lead to terrible rows. The star didn't like the thought of being paid back in kind. Applying blatant double standards, on at least one occasion he threw Hutton out in a rage, although when he'd calmed down he always pleaded with him to return. Despite his sycophantic and elastic entourage and the genuine love of his select inner sanctum of close friends, Mercury had a fear of loneliness – and often dealt with this by spreading his options.

He seems to have not been able to commit himself entirely to one person. It is clear from his own comments over the years that he was conscious of being in a very difficult position. To Mercury, dropping his guard and allowing someone access to his inner self had resulted too often in being, as he put it, 'trodden on'. He declared, 'Because I'm successful and have a lot of money, a lot of greedy people prey on me. But that's something I've learnt to deal with. I'm riddled with scars, and I just don't want any more.' He once gave this as an excuse for some of his most outrageous behaviour.

He wasn't alone, however, when, soon after moving in to Garden Lodge, he hosted his fortieth birthday party there. Guests were invited to arrive at the 'Mad Hat' party wearing a hat, and a variety of silly, sometimes rude, confections turned up. Although Mercury had commissioned several special designs for himself, he ended up choosing none of them.

Ten days later the ballad 'Who Wants to Live Forever' was released. Then, mid-October, Queen received an award from the British Video Awards for the best live-performance video for *Live in Rio*. Brian May and Roger Taylor went along to attend the ceremony – but without Freddie Mercury, who had his own reasons for not showing up then.

On 13 October 1986 the *News of the World* ran a story, which the daily tabloids picked up the next day, revealing that Mercury had undergone a secret AIDS test at the end of 1985. The star was furious but not able to discover how the press had got hold of their information. Mercury was already edgy when he received an unexpected visit from John Murphy, the airline steward with whom he had remained friends after a one-night stand. Murphy's current lover was dying of AIDS, and Murphy himself, looking cadaverous and frail, was also clearly ill with the disease. By the second week of November both men were dead.

Trying to calm his rising panic, Mercury no doubt reminded himself how brief his liaison with Murphy had been. But this was cold comfort when just weeks later he received the news that his lover of two years' standing, Tony Bastin, had also just died of AIDS. Too many gay acquaintances were dead and dying – or just scared and shaken. Mercury's initial reaction was hardly to move from home. People who did meet him noticed that he seemed very preoccupied. He must have been terrified, but it was not a state in which he intended to stay for long.

His solution to his anxieties was to distract himself with work. In January 1987 he began to record at the Town House Studios with songwriter/producer Mike Moran, who became one of his closest friends. 'Freddie and I met in the early eighties,' says Moran, 'but the first thing we did together was when he recorded a couple of numbers for Dave Clark's stage musical *Time*.' That experience led Mercury to ask Moran to produce him when he wanted to record a cover version of the Platters' hit 'The Great Pretender'.

'"The Great Pretender" was the first cover Freddie had done in his own name,' says Mike Moran. 'He had been attracted to the number, because apart from really liking it, it was very him. He was a terrible show-off anyway. After we put down the track, I said to him, "We really ought to think of a B-side," and Fred replied, "Oh, bloody hell! I'd forgotten about that," Well, it was very late one night, and we were the best part of a bottle of vodka down, when Freddie started playing flashy piano, and he suddenly turned and said to me, "Wouldn't it be fun to do something classical?" "Exercises in Free Love" was the product of this. There aren't any lyrics. It's more like Freddie flexing his scales.

'After that he asked me if I'd be interested in working with him on a bigger solo project. Typical of Freddie, he had no idea at that moment what it would be, but we booked a whole load of studio time just the same and started work. The first thing we wrote and recorded was the track "All God's People", which actually ended up on Queen's album.'

While all this was going on, events were at work that would eventually mesh with what Mercury and Mike Moran were doing. The Spanish leg of the Magic Tour had been handled by the top Madrid-based concert promoter Pino Sagliocco. It was Sagliocco who produced Ibiza '92, the celebrations that led up to and included Spain's role as host for the 1992 Olympic Games. Although others, including Mercury himself, later claimed the credit, Sagliocco was the man responsible for controversially bringing together Freddie Mercury and Spanish soprano Montserrat Caballé. Sagliocco's connection with Queen had initially come through Roger Taylor who owned a villa in Ibiza, and it was while organising his part of the 1986 tour that he first met Mercury.

'I tried to get Roger to convince Freddie to let me arrange an interview,' says Sagliocco, 'but it was a very difficult thing because he did not like to give interviews, and everyone told me he would not do it. Queen were in Spain in August, which is a really weak time to get promotion, and the programme I wanted Freddie to appear on was not to be shown until October – but it was called *Sixty Minutes of Spain* and to be seen on this show makes a big impact.

'One night we were in a disco, and I was hassling Roger again to have another go at Freddie, and I don't know if it was the vodka talking but suddenly Freddie said yes, he would do it.'

Mercury's interview was recorded at his hotel before Queen left Madrid and screened several weeks later. Sagliocco recalls, 'When I watched this programme I was thinking of my main opening for a TV special to be held at the Ku Club in 1987. During the show Freddie was asked which Spanish singer he admired most and he replied, "Montserrat Caballé." At that moment the idea came into my head, why not get Mercury and Caballé to perform together for the Olympic celebrations?'

Driven on by the challenge of pulling off this remarkable duet, Sagliocco swung into action. 'I sent a fax to Gerry Stickells in Los Angeles,' he says, 'who told me to contact Jim Beach – who would ask Freddie on my behalf. At the same time I contacted Montserrat through her manager.' It was far from easy to get the two stars to say yes and as time passed an edge of desperation crept in – until Sagliocco was forced to bend the truth.

He recalls, 'Neither Freddie nor Montserrat would do it at first, and then Freddie said yes, thinking I had an agreement with Montserrat.' It got to the point that Sagliocco was scared to admit to Mercury, by now fired up by the prospect, that Caballé hadn't yet agreed. He admits, 'By now Freddie's only concern was that Montserrat would like his work so how could I tell him the meeting was not yet fixed?'

It was late February 1987. 'The Great Pretender', produced by Mike Moran, had been released and had gone to number four in the UK charts, giving Mercury his biggest solo hit. He was already in buoyant mood when news from Sagliocco delighted him even more, as Moran recalls.

'We'd left the studio late one night and gone home,' he says, 'when in the early hours Freddie rang me, very excited. He told me he had had a call from Spain that Montserrat Caballé wanted to meet him, and we were going over to Barcelona on Saturday. A little sleepy I sat up and asked suspiciously, "What do you mean *we're* going to Barcelona?" He replied, "Well, I'm not fucking going by myself!"'

According to Moran, the prospect of meeting Montserrat Caballé terrified Mercury. 'He got himself worked into a right state,' he says, 'and was rushing about panicking. He kept saying, "First I'll have to work out what samples of my work to take along. What can I take?" I grabbed hold of him and said, "Freddie. You're famous! You don't need samples of your work," but he insisted that he did. Eventually he said, "I'll play her this thing," which was the B-side to "The Great Pretender".'

The assignation took place at the Ritz Hotel in Barcelona. 'We got there first,' Moran recalls, 'and Freddie was still fussing like a mother hen. He wanted the sound system set so that all he had to do was press a button. We waited, and then Montserrat swept in with an entire retinue behind her. The hotel staff were bowing and scraping, almost walking backwards before her, which made Freddie even more nervy – but she was really good fun and everyone, except Freddie, loosened up the more the champagne flowed.

'All of a sudden, at a break in the chatter, Freddie burst out to Montserrat, "Well, can I play you this then?" The thing is she got the wrong end of the stick, because he somehow introduced the track by saying, "This is me, pretending to be you," and he played "Exercises in Free Love". She listened carefully, glancing quizzically at Freddie, and a few of us thought, what's she making of this? Then when the track finished she asked, "You wrote this for me?" Freddie had now realised his mistake but made matters worse by saying, "If you want, you can have it." He turned and asked me, "That's OK, isn't it?"'

Confusion aside, the reality was that Montserrat Caballé liked the track very much. 'She's this grand diva, and here she was suddenly announcing, "I'm performing at Covent Garden next week. I will perform this number and you" – she pointed at me – "will accompany me." And sure enough, in less than a week, we did it at Covent Garden. Freddie was more nervous on that occasion than at anything I'd ever seen, and he wasn't even performing.'

Moran reveals that 'Before a gig you could never talk to Freddie. He would be so uptight and want to be alone. He'd bawl out anyone who intruded on him at this time. But at Covent Garden he was so nervous for me that he suddenly burst into my dressing room as I was getting ready and began flapping about, talking ten to the dozen. Eventually I snapped, "For fuck sake, Freddie, go away and leave me alone. You're doing the same to me that you hate people to do to you!" It was nice, all the same, that he was thinking of me.

'Montserrat had asked Freddie where he would like her to place "Exercises in Free Love" in her programme, and he hadn't liked to suggest. She kept at him, though, and eventually he said, "Why don't you do it for an encore?" And she replied, "Which one? I usually have eight." Freddie just gaped at her.'

Pino Sagliocco had also attended the meeting in the Barcelona Ritz, and he recalls that by the end of the night there was a chemistry between the two stars. After that Covent Garden performance, Caballé accompanied Freddie back for dinner at Garden Lodge. 'Later the three of us grouped around the piano,' says Moran, 'as Freddie tried to teach Montserrat to sing gospel, which was a bit painful, but they became very good friends, and her parting shot was, "Do me a favour? I really enjoyed this. Would you and Mike write me a piece about Barcelona?" Freddie replied, "Oh, of course," and promptly forgot all about it.'

Soon after his glib promise to Montsy, as Mercury nicknamed the opera star, around that Eastertime he received some traumatic news. In the hope of allaying his mounting anxieties he had again undergone medical tests, one of which involved the removal of a small piece of skin from his shoulder. When the results had come back, he learnt from his doctors that he had AIDS.

The implications were horrendous and hard to absorb. Mercury confided in very few people, and it seems likely that only Mary Austin and Jim Hutton knew at this early stage. Following consultations with the best available specialists, his treatment began straight away. Mercury told Hutton that he would understand if he wanted to leave him, but his lover opted to stay – and it was only at this point that they began to practise safe sex. Considering the growing awareness of the disease over the previous years – and the acute anxieties brought on by the deaths of two former lovers – it seems almost criminal that Mercury had not thought it essential before this point to use condoms. It was too late for the star now, but it was to be hoped that that was not the case for his lover.

It must have taken an act of incredible willpower to show an untroubled face to the rest of the world, to those people close to him personally and professionally. But that's precisely what he did. Although secretly undergoing a battery of further tests, Mercury understandably wasn't ready to deal with such a harsh reality. He fell back on an ability he had cultivated as a child to conquer fear and block out emotional pain: initially he denied that anything was wrong. To do this he tried never to refer directly to AIDS again. He just got on with his life, throwing himself into a whirl of activity. Perhaps in that sense it was fortunate that Montserrat Caballé, oblivious of any problem, had been bringing some pressure to bear on him.

'She had been calling Freddie from all corners of the world,' says Mike Moran, 'asking how he was getting on with the song he had promised her. Freddie eventually came to me and said, "Fuck sake! We'll have to write this bloody song!" So we sat down and in pretty short order co-wrote "Barcelona". To let her hear it, Freddie recorded both parts, and we sent her a rough tape of it. She got back to us instantly, saying she loved it.

'Opera stars are booked about five years in advance, but because time was so short she cancelled a huge engagement – I think it was at La Scala – and whizzed over to London to stick her voice on "Barcelona". It was all recorded in London, except for when I went to Spain to get her vocals on the B-side, "Exercises in Free Love".'

Before long Montserrat Caballé had visions of them recording an album together. According to Moran, 'Freddie and I both thought, Oh, my God! And I just knew it wasn't going to be an easy thing either to combine those two. We had originally, don't forget, been going to work on a Freddie Mercury solo album, but this took up so much time. And then there were two Queen albums in the offing, *Innuendo* being the last one – by which time Freddie was very poorly. And so we never got to do his intended solo album.'

Work began on the Mercury/Caballé album in April. Pino Sagliocco's Ibiza '92 festival was due to open with the TV special at the Ku Club the following month, at which Mercury and Montsy were to headline. But before that, in early May, Freddie was defeated again, this time when his former personal assistant Paul Prenter sold his story to the *Sun*.

Prenter claimed that Mercury had recently rung him, panicked that he might have contracted AIDS. Prenter made other lurid revelations about the star during his wild days, including how he would drink two bottles of vodka a night and had shared lines of cocaine with a handful of other named superstars. He also blew Jim Hutton's cover by naming him as Mercury's current lover. Friends later swore that Prenter had always been a shifty character, who had spent years ripping off the star for money and drugs.

Prenter was said to have been paid £32,000 by the tabloid to dish the dirt, and for that he had thrown in private photographs of a lasciviously grinning Mercury, entwined with a variety of previous male lovers. It was a three-day serialisation and aimed at inflicting maximum damage on his former employer. While Mercury, already struggling to hide from the truth of his illness, was devastated, his friends were furious; made more so by what they saw as not only Prenter's gross disloyalty but also his ingratitude.

The previous year Prenter had been made redundant after eight years in the star's employ. Afterwards, when he had almost immediately fallen on hard times, Mercury had let him stay rent free at his Kensington flat. It was there that he alleged he had received a frantic call from his ex-boss in the early hours of one morning, during which, he claimed, Mercury unburdened his fears.

Freddie Mercury had a reputation among friends for having a very forgiving nature. Presumably hoping to play on this, Paul Prenter tried ringing him at Garden Lodge in the midst of the exposé. But this time Mercury refused his calls and never spoke to the man again. Deeply hurt and very fragile, he left Britain and headed straight for the sanctuary of Pikes Hotel. The Ibiza '92 festival was due to kick off soon anyway, but he needed the peace and security that he could be sure of finding there – even with a *Sun* photographer hot on his trail.

Roughly two weeks later, as Pino Sagliocco had dreamt, Mercury and Montserrat Caballé headlined at the Ku Club. Spandau Ballet, Duran Duran and Marillion also took part in the TV special. The opera singer and the rock star closed the show together by performing 'Barcelona' against a stunning backdrop of fountains and fireworks.

But behind the pizzazz lay a sad reality. Fish clearly recalls how shocked he felt when he came across Mercury here. 'I thought I'd go see him,' he says, 'and say "How ya doin'?" you know, and he was, like, really drawn. There were about three or four close friends in the dressing room with him, and it was like someone had fuckin' died! I thought, Something really heavy is going down here, and I'm not part of it. So I got out of there fast.

'At the time the people around him were saying things like, he's got a kidney complaint or a liver problem – stuff like that.

But having glimpsed some of Freddie's excesses, it wasn't so hard to put two and two together.'

For those close to Mercury, there wasn't a lot of guesswork required. The signs of his illness had begun rapidly to show with the usual development of Kaposi's sarcoma, or KS, an otherwise rare cancer. It resulted in large dark red marks surfacing on the skin of his hands and face. Treatment for these early telltale marks is to neutralise them with special lasers. They fade, but slowly, and usually leave blemishes, which are best covered by make-up; in itself a giveaway sign. At the Ku Club Mercury had not been able fully to disguise these marks; something that Barbara Valentin remembers only too well.

'Freddie and I never spoke about his HIV and AIDS, but he knew that I knew,' Valentin says. 'It was in our eyes whenever we looked at each other and was a silent understanding between us. When I joined him in Ibiza for this TV special, I saw straight away that he had not been able to hide the marks on his face properly – and so, before he and Montserrat performed, I said nothing but took Freddie away with me to another room and used my heavy professional make-up on him to make him look better.'

But Barbara Valentin's help had come a little late. Says Pino Sagliocco, 'There was an incredible party afterwards, and everyone had a good time, but I think we already knew then that Freddie was sick. He was not telling anyone anything, but as soon as he arrived we saw that he had begun to get these strange blemishes on his face. We were told it was his liver, and, of course, he did drink too much – but all those spots?'

Tony Pike also harboured unspoken fears. 'By this time,' he says, 'rumours had begun circulating that Freddie had AIDS – but then you don't ask a friend if he is terminally ill, and no one ever spoke about it. It was just not discussed. Those around him would have categorically denied it anyway.'

Once home, Mercury had writing and recording commitments with Mike Moran ahead of him for his album with Montserrat Caballé, and there was a Queen album looming, too, after their year apart. Possibly hastened by the recent press revelations, Hutton had recently left his job at the Savoy Hotel and officially become the gardener at Garden Lodge. During August Barbara Valentin paid Mercury a welcome visit, but soon after that he began withdrawing more and more into himself. Around this time, as his treatment stepped up, Mercury was upset when his precious koi carp began dying off for no apparent reason. He made up for it by acquiring yet more kittens.

But for all his attempts to hide from the truth, Mercury must have agonised a million times about how he was going to cope when his illness worsened. Yet he refused to crumble. He certainly had no plans to avoid celebrating his coming birthday in style. To host this party he chose to return to Pikes. Tony Pike was happy to accommodate him, but things almost went awry, as Pike recalls.

'Freddie's forty-first was originally going to be arranged in conjunction with Elton John's manager John Reid. That was until he and Jim Beach had a massive argument. Beach had been four hours late for their rendezvous, through no fault of his own – he and his family had been caught in a terrible storm at sea – but Reid, unaware of the circumstances, was fuming at being delayed so long. As a result, he promptly cancelled the party. When Freddie found out he called me and said he wanted a do regardless – just something for a hundred people instead of the previous two hundred and fifty – which, from a business point of view, was rather disappointing.

'The story of the bash being called off had somehow appeared in an English newspaper, and when Freddie read it he was incensed. He told me that he wanted the biggest party the island had ever seen, and I said, "But, Freddie, there are only four days to go." He replied, "I know you can do it."'

Pike didn't let his friend down. In the end there were seven hundred guests, of whom more than half sat down to eat. For their enjoyment he arranged a host of exotic entertainers including flamenco and fantasy dancers. Extra staff were hired, and altogether over eight hundred people packed the place.

Two elements of the celebration feature strongest in Tony Pike's mind: 'Firstly, I had arranged for a special cake to be made in the shape of the Gaudi Cathedral, but when the plane it was in landed, the cake collapsed. It was a disaster, especially at such short notice, but we hurriedly made him a replacement cake, two metres long and decorated with the musical notes to "Barcelona". Six men dressed in white and gold uniforms carried it in, but nobody ended up having room for cake. And as the high jinks began, my secretary at the time, a rather portly English lady in her best silk suit, ended up being thrown into it.' Then there was the champagne. 'We opened three hundred and fifty bottles of Moet & Chandon in less than one hour,' recalls Tony. 'After I was dressed I'd gone to check on the champagne only to find that the ice was in the vats but no bottles, and we all had to frantically empty out and start again. We just got it chilled in the nick of time.'

Pike had hired a professional decorator from Barcelona, and the hotel was hung with black and gold balloons, which had taken three days to blow up by machine. They were helium filled, and in the middle of the party there was a near disaster. 'There was this guy trying to impress the girl sitting on his knee,' he explains, 'and he thought he'd put a lighter to the balloon above her head to make it pop, but instead, the whole thing went up in a gigantic sheet of flame.

'The problem was we had had extra electricity supplied, and the massive overhead cables on the roof caught the blast and began to melt. It could have been catastrophic. I'd been elsewhere talking to Mike Moran and didn't know anything about it. As I returned to the party, someone anxiously asked what I was going to do about the fire, and I replied that I'd see to it tomorrow. I ended up with a "My God, that's a cool guy!" reputation that night.'

Having nearly missed out on his annual celebration, Mercury ended up with one of his best ever parties. He especially enjoyed the spectacular fireworks display that rounded it all off. 'He must have seen so many displays,' says Pike, 'but it was like he was a little boy, seeing one for the first time.' That night Mercury was the perfect host. He had allowed in none of the usual photographers and appeared happy, going out of his way personally to greet as many guests as he could. No one would have guessed that his white cell count had dropped significantly, although earlier in the day at the hotel friends had noticed, with alarm, some new and strange marks on the star's legs.

For Tony Pike the pleasure of having provided his friend with a party to remember was almost denied when the time came to present the bill. It was huge – his biggest ever account – and had been meticulously itemised. 'I gave the bill to Jim Beach,' he says, 'who naturally went through it carefully. There were items on it like 232 broken glasses, and suddenly he pointed to one entry of four vodka and tonics, and he said, "Take it away. We did not have any vodkas."

'I said that if it was on the bill, then someone must have ordered the drinks, but Beach repeated that I should take the bill away and not give him something with items on it that they didn't order. He repeated, "No one ordered four vodkas."

'As far as I was concerned the bill was correct and was about to stand my ground, when a quiet voice cut in and asked, "Is there a problem here?" It was Freddie, and I explained the situation to him. He replied, "Yes, it's correct. I bought those for the bar staff." So that was it.'

Mercury's dignified way of settling the impasse didn't surprise Pike. In the two years that he had already been coming to Pikes, they had become close friends. 'Freddie, myself and a handful of others would often talk for hours on end,' he says. 'He was the greatest raconteur I ever met and he'd never sit down while he was telling stories. His gestures were just mesmerising, but, between the hands and the voice, you could see everything he was describing. On one occasion he and I got talking before dinner, and someone came in to remind him of the time. He politely said he knew, but not to disturb him again as he'd be out shortly. Five hours later we were still talking. He just kept going, and the time flew by.'

The single 'Barcelona' was released first in Spain on 21 September, where shops sold out within hours. Says Pino Sagliocco, 'It's still played at every official event in Barcelona. It's like a national anthem here.' Then just over a month later it was released in Britain, where it peaked at number eight in the charts. In 1992 the BBC were to adopt it as the official anthem for their coverage of the Olympic Games. But the music press were hopelessly perplexed when they first heard it. Reminiscent of their reaction to 'Bohemian Rhapsody', they had no idea what to make of it, as their polarised reviews reflected. Some critics described Mercury as a total embarrassment to the rock world, while others deemed the song a brave and ingenious digression; a view shared by many fellow performers, including Cliff Richard.

'I thought "Barcelona" was terrific, and again, Freddie dared to do it,' he says. 'It was a most unlikely project for a rock star to tackle and was always going to have the stun factor, but it was a lot bigger an achievement than that.' Cliff Richard also holds strong views on the subject of critics and their persistent attacks on performers. 'Our industry is so small-minded in that respect,' he states. 'It's the tall poppy syndrome. They can't wait to cut someone down who is doing too well. I just wish they would start from the standpoint of a performer's ability and popularity among the fans, instead of being automatically non-supportive when someone makes a move in a new direction.'

Once sensitive to media attacks, Mercury now had more

vital concerns. During filming of the video to accompany 'Barcelona', his white cell count had dropped again, this time alarmingly – and his doctors once more intensified his treatment. With the *Sun*'s exposé still fresh in people's minds, rumours were circulating in the press about the star's health. In November, in a rare interview with a women's magazine, he lied outright, saying, 'Yes, I did have an AIDS test, and I'm fine.'

He was far from fine and had a long way to battle yet. But he continued to prefer not to have his illness mentioned and had been depressed lately by the news that Nicolai Grishanovich, a lover he had shared in common with Kenny Everett, had also contracted AIDS.

Mercury had once maintained, 'I don't expect to make old bones. What's more, I really don't care.' It was the kind of careless rock 'n' roll quip that's easy to make when twenty-something and in robust health, but he must have felt differently now. Utilising his strong willpower, after a decade's abuse of cocaine, he cut out drugs altogether, adopted a healthier diet and cultivated a more mellow attitude towards many things. Life had suddenly become a great deal more precious.

THIRTEEN

Seeking Sanctuary

In January 1988, Mercury rejoined Queen at London's Town House Studios to start work on their first studio-recorded album for three years. His collaboration with Mike Moran also continued on the Montserrat Caballé album. Each would take roughly a year to make, as Mercury was appreciably slowing down now. He was having regular medical check-ups, and his physical appearance would soon start noticeably to change. His enthusiasm for both recording projects, however, remained undiminished; a fact that now attracts great admiration.

'Freddie was an immensely creative man,' says Mike Moran. 'He could do almost anything musically, and he worked amazingly hard in the studio. His attitude was always, "I *will* do this," and that didn't change when he became ill. Most amazingly, he was still there. He'd work himself into a frenzy in the studio and was a perfectionist to the last. He would not leave anything to anyone else, even when he was latterly very sick. If the tiniest thing bothered him, he'd keep at it until he felt it was right.

'He kind of made it clear, without explaining why, that he would come in when he could, and if he did, he was the same old Freddie. I mean, he'd get tired and would suddenly just call a halt saying, "Right, that's it. Got to go." But when he was there, he gave it his all. As far as the *Barcelona* album was concerned, the whole thing also took so long because logistically trying to get Montserrat's vocals on the tracks was often a nightmare. And that was on top of all the songwriting.'

To alleviate the creative workload, by spring Mercury and Moran had invited on board the considerable talents of lyricist Sir Tim Rice to help out on two of the eight album tracks required for *Barcelona*. With a string of the world's most famous stage musicals to his credit, Rice would later win an Oscar for Best Original Song for Disney's *The Lion King*. In 1988 he co-wrote 'The Fallen Priest' and 'The Golden Boy', from which point his friendship with Mercury developed.

'My first connection with Freddie came about when Elaine Paige wanted to record an album of Queen songs,' Rice recalls. 'It was originally my idea that she should. I'd always been a great fan of the band, and I thought it would be a different thing for Elaine to do. I think the album was actually one of her best.

'But the whole idea came as a complete surprise to Freddie. We had approached Jim Beach with our suggestion, and Freddie was rather flattered because he, in turn, much admired Elaine's work. He took great interest in the project, and we went to a couple of dinners at his home to discuss it. It didn't end up just Mercury compositions on the album, and indeed Freddie was often the one to say, "Well, have you thought about doing this one?" and so on.

'Freddie was busy working on the *Barcelona* album, and he asked if I would put lyrics to a couple of tracks that he and Mike Moran had in mind. He gave me tapes to work with and I wrote some lyrics which Freddie liked, so they went ahead and recorded them.' Tim already loved the single 'Barcelona'. 'I thought it was absolutely wonderful,' he states. 'I don't think Freddie had an operatic voice. Obviously his was more a rock voice, but then most opera stars couldn't get near a rock song. For instance, Montserrat Caballé couldn't sing a Pretenders' number. However, if Freddie had trained from childhood, he could very well have sung opera. He wasn't that far off it.'

As to Mercury's solo talents, Rice believes, 'I personally think he flourished best as a songwriter within the context of Queen. He may have been their main songwriter, but the other three in their various ways gave him inspiration. Latterly, of course, the tracks were all credited to Queen, so you never knew whose song it had originally been.'

In many ways Mike Moran agrees with Tim Rice on Mercury's work outside Queen. He says, 'It's always a weird thing, but it's generally the case that when someone steps out of a band to do solo work, it's not easily accepted by the fans. Freddie's own view was to do something and just be himself, and if it sounded very reminiscent of Queen, that couldn't be avoided. He never set out to say, "I'm going to be different from Queen." Even with "Barcelona", although there is a diva shrieking away, with the multi-vocals from Freddie it still smacked of the band a little bit.

'You get instinctively drawn into how Queen do things, regardless. When we did "All God's People", which ended up on *Innuendo*, Brian did guitar on it. They had a rule, no more than two Queenies on anything solo or it would constitute Queen. With a track like that, which featured Freddie's voice and Brian's guitar, it was so strongly identified with the band that it ended up hard to divorce the two anyway.'

Reluctant to leave home when not at the studio, Mercury threw more dinner parties at Garden Lodge. His guest list was on a smaller scale than before, but they were intimate and enjoyable affairs, conducted at a pace more suited to his state of health now. In addition to his core of close friends, his guests included Tim Rice and Elaine Paige, then his long-standing girlfriend, and actress Susannah York.

Susannah York recalls, 'Because my taste in music is classical and soul, I hadn't previously paid much attention to Freddie or Queen, but we had a mutual friend in Peter Straker. It was one night when a bunch of us after a performance went to a club, where Peter was to join Freddie, that I met him for the first time. He was great fun, very warm and had tremendous spirit.'

One Sunday at dinner Mercury made York a surprise offer. 'He had so much charm,' she explains. 'He offered me the use of his New York flat whenever I liked, and I was touched by the spontaneity of such a generous offer. Inwardly I suppose I didn't take it seriously, and I hadn't any occasion then to be in New York, but the next time we met, Freddie took me aside and said quietly, "You didn't take me up on my offer." He assured me, "I really meant it."

'Freddie could be very manipulative in his relationships, which can be very easy when you reach a position of power, but having said that, he was generous to his friends and he'd support something like going to see a play of Peter's or even mine. Primarily he came to see me to please Peter, I think, but then he came later for me in my own right. If I was ever going out with Freddie and Peter, I always looked forward to it immensely because I knew I'd enjoy myself in Freddie's company.'

Another guest at these dinner parties was Sir Cliff Richard: 'The first time I went there I was amazed that there was a house there at all,' he says. 'It is so tucked away, set well back off the road. Suddenly you're in an oasis, a real country garden. It was a beautiful house with fabulous gardens.

'Freddie was always surrounded, even at parties in his own home, but what I did notice at these affairs was that he seemed to have to live out the whole fantasy all the time. He had lots of people looking after him, ready to do his bidding at all times – he carried the "star thing" into his private world, too. I mean, you just knew that he'd never, in a million years, ever do the washing-up himself, for instance. He loved the mystique, I think.'

The care that Mercury took to ensure the excellence of his intimate dinner parties left an impression on Mike Moran. 'There was nothing cheap about Freddie,' he declares. 'It always had to be the finest champagne and food, and his attention to detail was amazing. He'd personally triple-check everything. I've been at his house, about to leave to come back later for dinner, and found Freddie fussing about the table, checking place settings, china and cutlery and getting himself into a state. I'd say to him, "Hey, Fred. It's only us," to which he'd reply, "Oh, that's not the attitude" – and carry on fussing.'

Through working together so closely Mercury and Moran developed a strong bond. 'He was an absolute sweetheart – fab, considerate and kind, and a very loyal friend,' says Moran. 'He was an intensely private man and kept about him only a very small circle of friends. My wife and I were fortunate to have been two of those. We went to all his anniversaries, like birthdays, and never missed his Boxing Day dinner parties.

'In lots of ways he was a happy man. He thoroughly enjoyed his beautiful home and the company of his friends, loved his big garden and, of course, his cats. When Tiffany, the long-haired Persian, died Freddie was absolutely heartbroken. He was a highly intelligent man too. He read avidly and had a vast knowledge of art and history.'

These sentiments are echoed by Tim Rice, who says, 'I found Freddie a very sophisticated and charming man. I mean some evenings at his house were sort of boisterous – he was a great entertainer in private, too – but he was always jolly and eternally generous. And he had a great knowledge of artistic things, of Japan in particular, but art in general, and was an absolutely fanatical follower of opera.'

Socialising at home was about the limit to Mercury's strength that summer. Although he did slip abroad for a holiday, he avoided his usual haunts and headed instead for the tranquillity of a rented lakeside house in Montreux. There he spent hours watching the television or taking slow walks along the shore with Jim Hutton. At home he stepped up his now regular visits to his parents, too. Because of their son's rejection of their way of life, relations between them had been strained for a long time. Parsees consider homosexuality unclean, and Mercury's reputation for wild, decadent behaviour had caused a rift. But his family remained very important to him, and he helped them whenever he could. Healing the breach, he obtained the finest medical treatment money could buy when, at one point, Bomi Bulsara took seriously ill.

His parents occasionally came to visit at Garden Lodge. This was a world of splendour away from the same modest semi in Feltham from which Mercury had gone to school. They refused his frequent offers to buy them a new home. During these visits a charade was staged for their benefit, whereby Jim Hutton was introduced as the gardener, and there was no hint of their true relationship. No word of his illness, at least at this stage, reached them either. Although with their son's weight loss and the marks on his skin, even if they didn't specifically know what was wrong, it must have become clear to them that he was not well.

Mid-October would finally see the release of *Barcelona* and also the single 'The Golden Boy'. Before that, on the 8th, Mercury took part in what would be his last live performance. La Nit was a huge open-air festival, held in Barcelona, on the Avinguda de Maria Cristina – the equivalent of the Mall in London – that would officially launch the four-year run-up to the 1992 Olympic Games. Mercury and Montserrat Caballé were to perform with the Barcelona Opera House orchestra and choir on an enormous stage set in front of the beautiful fountains in Castle Square. For organiser Pino Sagliocco and Tony Pike, there to enjoy the spectacle, it was a night to remember – and not just because, at the last moment, Mercury had to mime.

'Freddie was anxious about the whole thing,' says Pino Sagliocco, 'but he had worked on the project with Mike for a whole year, and he admired Montserrat so much that he never stopped saying that this was a dream come true for him. He was possessed about it. Everyone had thought I was a lunatic matching these two, and people made attacks on why Montserrat was doing this, but there was nothing wrong with cross-culture. It worked. Freddie was an extravagant personality. Montserrat is recognised as a diva, but Freddie was also a diva. Both were great artistes and totally inspired.

'I never saw anyone with such belief as Freddie. He was professional all the way and he always delivered 100 per cent. Not many have the drive to make something happen. But he was unique in that way, and it was a privilege and a pleasure to work with him. For me, having built this Ibiza '92 show, it was great to have Montserrat and Freddie open it – all that power of music. It was a piece of art.'

Although Sagliocco describes La Nit as magical, putting on the actual show, he admits, was hell: 'The universal feeling in my camp when it finished was, thank God! I financed it with mainly Japanese money. I assembled the artistes and had great difficulties in sorting problems out, like one performer at the last moment would refuse to go on stage with another and so on.'

Among the other participants in the colossal event were Jerry Lee Lewis, Dionne Warwick and José Carreras, as well as Rudolph Nureyev – who also had AIDS. With this being Mercury's first public appearance for a long time – and the rumours rife about him – some sections of the press were in their element, trying to link Mercury with Nureyev. 'The stories were bullshit!' confirms Sagliocco. 'Freddie and Rudolph were never involved. They never even said hello.'

Mercury and Montserrat Caballé were to close the show with two songs, but the nearer the time came to take the stage, the edgier he got. Tony Pike recalls that 'Freddie had been extremely nervous earlier when he was introduced to the King and Queen of Spain, anxious about how he looked etc. As time marched on, Peter Freestone was the only person he allowed near him for about the last half an hour. We kept out of his way, but I caught sight of him – and he was pacing up and down dressed in his suit, deep in thought and lipping various phrases from the songs.'

It is impossible to tell whether it was nerves or ill health, but just prior to joining Caballé on stage, Mercury complained of a sore throat and insisted that they should mime. With two such experienced stars, this might have worked. But, much to Mercury's great annoyance and embarrassment, a technical hitch made the tape play too slowly and so mismatch the lip-sync. His friends maintain that either no one really noticed, or they didn't care.

'It was a fabulous setting in the old place,' says Pike, 'and a magic moment in entertainment when, just as Freddie hit that last "Barcelona!", the sky exploded with fireworks.'

While Pino Sagliocco maintains, 'I honestly never found out why it was suddenly to be mimed. The song was very compli-cated and to perform at that level perhaps it made it easier, but no one cared because the occasion was so wonderful.'

During Mercury's brief stay there, Pino Sagliocco was among those who could not help but notice the change in his friend; the dark marks on his face, now hard to disguise despite the heavier make-up. 'Freddie always showed integrity,' he says, 'even when he was dying. But there was a feeling about him right then of being totally closed in in his own world. He wanted to write and record, and not tell the world his troubles. Perhaps he feared coming up against prejudice. And, anyway, no artiste wants to be seen that way.'

Jim Hutton had accompanied his lover to La Nit. Says Sagliocco, 'He and Freddie were very happy together. They were established and a really close couple. Jim was like a wife to Freddie, and Freddie loved him dearly.

'I would say that Freddie was too generous to some people.

When someone becomes a huge star, sometimes people around the star abuse him. And it's often they, and not the star himself, who is trouble. But Jim was never like that. He never used any power because of his position. He always discreetly kept in the background.'

After miming his performance that night, Mercury then compounded the speculation around him by cancelling his press conference. One of the few media people he did speak to was Simon Bates back in London. 'Freddie rang me,' Bates says, 'and we talked on the phone about "Barcelona". He was very ill then, but again it wasn't something I asked about. It was definitely not an area to intrude upon.'

From that point on, life for the remainder of the year seems to have become increasingly stressful. Perhaps the strain of having appeared in public – or of not having been able to perform – had brought his weakness home to him. That Mercury was a natural showman was true during his long quest for success, and remained so as he reigned supreme at the top of his profession. The fact that his doctors had diagnosed his condition as terminal didn't remove any of that overnight. He was just not physically capable of performing any more and had bleakly been forced to acknowledge this. But that is not to say that coping, emotionally, was easy.

Leaving aside for the moment the reality that he was having to face the prospect of a horrible and premature death, no one who had received so much adulation for so long – who'd derived such intense nourishment from it – could suddenly switch it off. He said himself that performing live was so much in his blood that he would be vulnerable without it. And he had to have felt its lack with an acuteness bordering on agony. His distress was causing stormy rows with Jim Hutton that shattered the illusion of tranquillity at Garden Lodge. Some of the arguments were quite vicious, and most ended in tears. The strain of keeping his illness to himself was clearly too much for him.

It hadn't helped, either, that he had severed all contact with some of his friends, only to miss them terribly. The closest friend he had been avoiding for months now was Barbara Valentin, the person he had said he felt best understood his chosen way of life. But that was one battle he was about to lose.

'When Freddie had suddenly quit living in Munich I knew he was worried that he had HIV,' said Valentin. 'I knew he went hurrying back to London to hide – but there was nowhere to hide. Soon after the special concert with Montserrat in Ibiza, I began to see less and less of Freddie. I rang Garden Lodge often, but he would not take my calls. That Christmas I tried again, but this time was told by someone there to stop calling, and, I thought, OK. Fuck this.

'But, then, about eight months later my door bell rang one day, and it was Freddie. He just stood there and said, "I can't stay away from you. I can't live without you in my life. Take me in and take care of me." And I did. He was in a lot of emotional pain, and he *had* to work out a way to live with his illness. But it was very hard.'

By January 1989 Queen's album was finished. Because of past rows over money, Mercury suggested that it would be fairer collectively to credit all tracks to the band. And that, equally, the royalty earnings should be a four-way split. Work was due to start on a new album, which would mean frequent trips for Mercury to Mountain Studios in Montreux. In the meantime his latest solo single, prophetically entitled 'How Can I Go On', had just been released. It had barely scraped into the top 100 but the star little cared.

The progression of his illness meant that the marks on his skin, where visible, as on his face, were becoming harder to hide with make-up alone. So, to help his disguise, he grew a beard. Although not ready to share his troubles with anyone apart from the two or three friends who were sworn to secrecy, Mercury was thinking ahead. He had decided gradually to start utilising his vast wealth. One of his first decisions was to make huge donations to various cat sanctuaries. He would later establish certain close friends in substantial new homes.

The first single from Queen's new album was released on 2 May, a belter entitled 'I Want It All'. Its video had been shot in Pinewood Studios without an audience and was the first public recognition of how Mercury was drastically changing. Dressing conventionally in a collar and tie and sporting designer stubble proved little distraction for the shock of realising how much thinner he was – his face was gaunt and almost haunted under the studio make-up. He sang as powerfully as ever, though, and despite the fact that he was clearly much less energetic, his delivery remained defiant. The single charted instantly at number three, giving the band their highest entry to date.

Ten days later *The Miracle* followed. It was a stylish album complemented by an inspired sleeve design, the work of artist Richard Gray. Using advanced computer graphics, Gray had created a striking effect of fusing the band's four faces. Working on their new album, in Montreux, Queen got together one night in a restaurant. Taylor, Deacon and May had been told no more of their lead singer's illness than any outsider, but clearly each harboured his own suspicions. It seems they anticipated with a sense of foreboding that their friend was about to give them some devastating news. Perhaps he had intended to confide in them, feeling the pressure recently of the burden of keeping his illness a secret. But, although Mercury admitted to his friends for the first time that he was not well, he shied away from revealing the truth.

Not able to tell the band, Mercury certainly wasn't about to confess days later, when for the first time in nearly ten years, Queen were interviewed together on radio. It was DJ Mike Read's coup, and for an hour he subjected all four to a question-and-answer session. When the question arose about why Queen no longer toured, Mercury took the blame by saying that he wanted to change the cycle of album-tour-album-tour. For many, it was an unsatisfactory reason, and as time passed the queries kept on coming.

Eventually Mercury partially confessed: 'I can't carry on rocking the way I have done in the past,' he told persistent reporters. 'It is all too much. It's no way for a grown man to behave. I have stopped my nights of wild partying. That's not because I'm ill, but down to age. I'm no spring chicken. Now I prefer to spend my time at home. It's part of growing up.'

Over the next six months, four further singles emerged from *The Miracle* – 'Breakthru', 'The Invisible Man', 'Scandal' and the title track itself. The first and last of these spawned unusual videos. For 'Breakthru' Queen were filmed playing aboard a speeding vintage steam train on the Nene Valley Railway near Peterborough. Although the shooting lasted three days, Queen were there for just one of these. With the now familiar designer stubble Mercury looked good, albeit a shadow of his former self.

For 'The Miracle', probably in an effort to involve the star on screen as little as possible, child actor band look-alikes had been hired, who mimed to the song. All were well cast, but Ross McCall, who beat off stiff competition at auditions to play Mercury, fittingly stole the show. So much so that when the band joined the kids on film, for the last minutes of the track, Mercury found himself imitating McCall. He later quipped to Ross, 'How are you fixed for doing a tour?'

While these releases kept Queen in the public eye, the band were busy on their new album in Switzerland and London. Mercury had grown steadily weaker and could manage less time each week in the studio. He had been forced to give up smoking because of respiratory problems, and singing exhausted him more than he allowed anyone to see. In December Queen released *Queen at the Beeb*, an album of early recordings made for the BBC.

But, it wasn't the past the watching press was interested in. Having had their antennae tuned in for some time, they were now seriously alert. Media speculation about what was wrong with Mercury multiplied by the week. The pressure on the band was considerable. While the star himself had become adept at avoiding journalists, the other three band members were hounded by the press at every opportunity. Forced to lie and say that Mercury was fine, each was burdened with the knowledge that their lead singer's plight – and their own – could only worsen.

FOURTEEN

Silent Sorrow

Work on Queen's new album, already ten months in the making, looked set to take even longer than *The Miracle*. In the end its production spanned the whole of 1990, too. But, with Mercury's state of health dictating the pace, there was nothing anyone could do. When it had come to the crunch the previous year, Mercury had shied away from admitting to the rest of the band that he was battling against AIDS. Although it remained unspoken, each believed that this would be the last album they would record together.

For close friends such as Mike Moran it was a hellish state of affairs that someone they cared for deeply was suffering so much. Yet because of his decision not to discuss his illness openly they were not able to reach out to him. It was a very painful time, as Mike Moran recalls.

'Freddie showed immense bravery, and none of us really knew just how ill he was,' he says. 'He didn't want to be a burden to people and certainly didn't want anyone to feel sorry for him. For about three years it was awfully difficult for us, but we coped by going into denial – the way you do when you don't want to face the fact that someone you love is dying. And there were often times when we'd say to each other, "He's looking a bit better today, don't you think? Maybe, right enough . . ." We'd semi-convince ourselves that he was going to be OK. It was all a case of not wanting him to go.'

Apart from recording when he was able, Mercury now lived reclusively, and, conscious of his looks, the last thing he was likely to welcome was any public engagement. But this year the British Phonographic Industry chose to honour Queen for their outstanding contribution to British music, and in mid-February that meant being presented with an award at their ninth annual ceremony, held at the Dominion Theatre. The evening was hosted by Jonathan King, and the band, in formal dinner dress, received their award from BPI chairman Terry Ellis.

Mercury couldn't win this time. Had Queen turned up without him – whatever the excuse – it would have provided the press with more fuel to fire the rampant speculation about his health. Inevitably, when he did appear on stage, keeping well to the back and watching as Brian May delivered the acceptance speech, his hollowed features and gaunt frame were so pronounced that it sparked off a rash of new rumours.

Queen made a quick getaway that night, shunning the official BPI dinner for the attractions of their own special party at the Groucho Club in Soho. They had celebrated 1981 as their tenth anniversary. For the purposes of this party, they decided to make 1990 their twentieth. Mingling with over four hundred guests were celebrities and Queen employees past and present. Many people were privately shocked – hardly able to recognise the star in their midst.

Mercury tired easily now, and looking drawn and feeling not very alert, he tried to slip quietly away from the party. A press photographer lurking in the shadows outside had been hoping for just such an opportunity and snapped him leaving. Looking haggard and preoccupied, Mercury's picture was splashed across the front page of a national daily newspaper next day. Fans and friends, already jittery, became downright anxious.

Mercury must have known that he was fighting a losing battle with the press, but again he tried to scotch the rumours. Publicly he reiterated that he felt fine and categorically he denied that he had AIDS. He was clearly in no condition to go on tour, but that didn't stop journalists questioning him about the cessation of live Queen performances. All he would say on the matter was that nothing was planned for the foreseeable future; that they had recording commitments in the studio. His private life in Britain was becoming non-existent, and he quit London almost immediately thereafter for the haven of Montreux.

Returning to his rented Swiss lakeside house, he honoured his work commitments as best he could, but mainly he resumed his strolls by the water's edge. For some time he had been plagued with skin sores and weeping wounds, and when walking gradually became too painful, he took to sitting by the lake and sketching waterfowl. Sometimes he would also write songs. The disease made him extremely susceptible to infection and fatigue, however, and although he derived solace from these excursions, he often felt too drained by them and had to cut them short. Soon afterwards he slipped back, undetected, to Garden Lodge. Around this time Mary Austin, who had created a personal life for herself apart from Mercury, gave birth to a son.

Mercury's own condition had lately taken another turn for the worse. He had been fitted with a small catheter on his chest, which fed him his medication intravenously. He was experiencing the usual disruption in sleep and the ever present risk of infection meant that he and Jim Hutton now slept in different rooms. He still celebrated his forty-fourth birthday lavishly but surrounded himself with only a few well-chosen friends.

By the following month the Queen album had a title – *Innuendo* – and was scheduled for a Christmas 1990 release.

When this looked in danger of being pushed back, EMI were understandably annoyed. The album's production had already taken almost two years and to miss the massive festive market would prove costly. Across the Atlantic, their relationship with the US label, Capitol Records, had been running into other kinds of difficulties. Jim Beach had been negotiating Queen's way out of their contract, and in the end Hollywood Records weighed in with a lucrative bid to sign them. The deal was clinched by early November.

But business matters paled in contrast to the mounting personal pressures that were weighing down the band. The strain of fielding the bombardment of questions from the press about Mercury's health was wearing. The rest of Queen wanted to do right by their friend, but it was becoming impossible to lie with any semblance of credibility. One day, cornered by a gaggle of gossip-hungry journalists, Brian May admitted that Mercury was suffering from strain and exhaustion – and that the years of hard living had finally caught up with him. But he denied that there was any truth in the rumours that the star had AIDS.

The next day the *Sun* carried the headline: IT'S OFFICIAL! FREDDIE IS SERIOUSLY ILL. They ran the story with a support picture that showed him staring-eyed and drawn. When Mercury saw this, he was very upset. At Garden Lodge thereafter Jim Hutton, Joe Fanelli or Peter Freestone vetted all newspapers before they got to him – but his torment didn't end there. The press hounds now smelt blood and tightened their surveillance of the fading rock star. They would tail him on his rare excursions from home and finally got what they wanted: a photograph of him emerging from the Harley Street premises of a top AIDS specialist.

Mercury's health was failing faster now. Only his stubborn determination to keep working kept him going. In early January 1991 he joined the band in Mountain Studios for a gathering with a difference. He had suffered a great deal of pain throughout the recording of *Innuendo,* which was now complete, yet he wanted to get straight back into the studio. He had also decided finally to confide in his three friends that he was dying of AIDS.

Typically, he invited no pity and simply said brusquely, 'You probably realise what my problem is' – which they did. He continued, 'Well, that's it, and I don't want it to make a difference. I don't want it to be known. I don't want to talk about it. I just want to get on and work until I can't work any more.'

For those on the receiving end of this barrage of commands, it was hard to take. Brian May later revealed, 'I don't think any of us will ever forget that day. We all went off and got quietly sick somewhere.'

A week later the title track 'Innuendo', an unusual number with its bolero-type rhythm, zoomed in at number one in the UK singles chart. Then, on 2 February, Queens *Greatest Hits* re-entered the album charts, two days before *Innuendo* was finally released. Like the single, it soared straight to the top but any pride in this achievement had been lost when they had filmed the video promo of a number entitled 'I'm Going Slightly Mad'. The experience had been heartbreaking.

As the title suggests, the song's lyrics centre on insanity and to reflect this on screen, all four band members were to portray differing exaggerated forms of madness. The shoot took place at Limehouse Studios and was directed by Hannes Rossacher and Rudi Dolezal. Mercury appeared with a bunch of enormous bananas on his head. He bounced on a pantomime gorilla's knee, playfully punching its nose and raced around in circles wearing winkle-picker shoes, with his arms arched mock-threateningly above his head.

But a terrible sadness underpinned the filming. Mercury was now so ill that a bed had been set up nearby for him to lie down on between takes. He looked skeletal – and that was with an extra layer of clothes under his suit. The marks on his face were so pronounced that in order to camouflage them, his make-up was caked on. To hide his increasing hair loss, he wore an obvious wig.

Mercury was also in acute pain. To the astonishment of the crew though, he continued to run through with them the storyboard he had worked out for the shoot. They had been pre-warned that the star had muscle problems and, in particular, a knee injury, but none of that rang true. In one scene he had to crawl along the floor in front of a long leather sofa on which the other three were seated. That scene was agonising for him, but in the final cut no one would ever know this. He even took the trouble to comfort one of the penguins that featured in the video, when it became distressed under the hot lights. For all onlookers, it was hard to hide their emotions. Hardened hacks, by contrast, hung around outside the studios, hoping to catch someone off-guard as they left. But everyone was tight-lipped, and the official word was that Mercury had thoroughly enjoyed himself. 'I'm Going Slightly Mad' was released a month later, on 4 March.

After the shoot Mercury retreated once more. Naturally, the atmosphere at home was oppressive. Joe Fanelli could see his friend wasting away and was worried about his own future after the star died. When Mercury discovered this, he resolved to buy Fanelli a house. But Fanelli wasn't the only one to entertain anxieties. Clearly Jim Hutton was aware of potentially similar problems. Hutton was under no illusions. He was aware that when Mercury died, the mansion would probably pass to Mary Austin. But at the same time his lover had expressed the wish that he should continue to live there. Personally Jim Hutton was not so sure that this was how things would work out.

Mid-May saw a third single release with 'Headlong'. It was

followed at the end of the month by filming of the poignant ballad entitled 'These Are the Days of Our Lives'. It would be their last Queen promo. As in February, it was a distressing shoot, despite Mercury's continuing bravery. Only Mercury, Taylor and Deacon took part in the filming. Brian May had been touring America, promoting Queen's new album, and he was filmed separately, and his role later integrated in the editing room.

Simon Bates recalls that 'Brian told me that when Freddie was making their last two videos he was so desperately ill that he could hardly walk, yet his eyes still sparkled, and he'd be saying, do it this way or that way.' Although almost cadaverously thin, in baggy trousers, loose silk shirt and waistcoat, he managed to remain a stylish man. Despite everything, he was professional to the end.

No one knew when the end would come. Back in Montreux, May, Deacon and Taylor were only a phone call away and ready to record at a moment's notice. Although their singer and friend battled on, he could not manage much time in the studio now. But work remained important to him, as it was the best way for him to keep his spirits from plummeting – and offered something positive to offset the sorrow of facing each day. Mary Austin later said, 'I think that fed the light inside. Life wasn't just taking him to the grave. There was something else he could make happen.'

The rest of the band's contribution had been to provide Mercury with songs to sing, and he would, in turn, provide as much material to work with after he was gone as he could produce. 'Write me anything, and I'll sing it,' he told his three friends. They never knew as they watched him leave, drained and desperate to lie down, if they would ever see him again. In the last recorded interview he gave, the star spoke of hoping to cram as much fun into life as he could in the years he had left. But, the truth was, time was measured in months now.

In August Mercury heard that Paul Prenter, the man who had betrayed him to the *Sun*, had died of AIDS. He was soon to learn, too, Jim Hutton's secret that he was HIV positive; traumatic news that devastated him. Mercury had tried driving himself hard and not giving in, but he became aware that he was living on borrowed time. In the peaceful world of his Swiss lakeside house he sought solitude to reach some vital decisions, one of which was that he didn't want to hang on longer than his body could stand.

Mike Moran remembers this painful period: 'A couple of months before Freddie died, I got a phone call from Peter Freestone asking, "Are you free on 5 September?" I said, "Yes. Why?" Peter replied, "Well, it's Freddie's birthday," and of course we had never missed one – but we hadn't thought that he would be celebrating this year. However, a handful of us went to Garden Lodge, and Freddie was still the perfect host. He didn't have long left, and he knew it, but he was very calm about it, very relaxed and very pleased to see his friends. We watched old videos, told old stories and laughed, and Freddie bravely stuck it out to the end, staying until he saw everyone off. He was amazing.

'After that, though, he didn't want people to see him, because he was so bad. He and I kept in touch by phone, but if I suggested coming over he'd say to me, "No, you don't want to see me today, dear. I'm not looking very good."'

Now a spectral figure, Mercury was so aware of his mortality that he began planning the details of his own funeral service. He had already laid out £1 million on ten houses for special friends, and now he made a will – a thirteen-page document that made the usual provisions for realising his estate, settling debts and taxes, and for the division of his wealth. He signed it on 17 September 1991 before two witnesses, and in it had appointed as executors John Libson and Henry James 'Jim'

Beach. Not long after that he was so weak that he remained in bed most days, mainly asleep.

On 28 October, Queen released the album *Greatest Hits Vol II*. A fortnight before that their fortieth single, 'The Show Must Go On' had come out. As if the lyrics were not sufficiently haunting, the song's video, which was premiered on *Top of the Pops*, looked like an obvious farewell – and only heightened fans' fears that the end was near. Officially it was still denied that anything was seriously wrong, but by then few were really fooled. Some journalists had half written their obituaries, and in all areas of the music industry the general consensus was that Freddie Mercury was dying.

Although the star's team of specialists did what they could to alleviate his suffering, his illness was an horrendous ordeal for Mercury. The AIDS virus infects brain cells and the central nervous system, which causes neurological disorders beyond the immune deficiency that renders the body effectively helpless against infection. By early November Mercury chose to come off most of his medication. His doctors advised him against this, but he was suffering blind spells and night sweats. Plagued by mouth and skin sores, he eventually needed to use breathing apparatus. Near the end he would not be able even to speak. And he had come to the point where he just wanted it all to end.

Apart from his doctors, regular visitors included Dave Clark and Mary Austin, by now pregnant again, along with Jim Hutton, Joe Fanelli and Peter Freestone. A constant vigil was kept on a rota basis at Mercury's bedside. But an unwelcome presence at Garden Lodge had lately arrived in the shape of a burgeoning press contingent. The media ignorantly had settled themselves outside the house, assembling like vultures for bad news. Sometimes their tactless talk could be heard inside the sick room, upsetting those caring for him. Mercifully Mercury himself was too ill to make out their comments.

By the third week of November the star was existing on liquids alone and had almost entirely lost the use of his muscles. On the 22nd, Jim Beach arrived to go over the terms of an official statement that Mercury is said to have wanted to issue – and had supposedly worked on personally. Roger Taylor reckons that as Mercury had often remarked that he could 'pop off at any time', he hadn't wanted to be cheated of his opportunity to make an announcement.

But Jim Hutton had no prior knowledge of this. Why, after years of obsessive secrecy, would he suddenly wish to confess all to the world? Hutton held the view that his lover was originally put under pressure to make this move. He contended that once convinced of the need to say something, Mercury then stipulated that he wanted it released worldwide – to prevent a scoop for the British gutter press.

On Saturday, 23 November, Queen's PR officer, Roxy Meade, read out an official statement outside Garden Lodge, in which she stated on behalf of Queen's lead singer that he had been tested positive for HIV and that he had AIDS. He felt it had come to the point at which he wanted his friends and fans to know the truth. And he hoped everyone would join him and his doctors in fighting to combat the killer disease. The statement made headline television news and filled newspaper front pages around the world the following day.

Sunday was a bleak day. The star's doctor had been in attendance on and off for hours. Dave Clark had arrived, and Mary Austin shuttled urgently back and forth between Garden Lodge and her home nearby. Mercury was slipping in and out of consciousness. An attempt tenderly to move his emaciated body for a change of bed linen had resulted in one of his brittle bones breaking like a dry stick. He needed help to stroke his favourite cat, which had sat sentinel all day with her doting owner.

In the past week Mercury had felt himself fading. He realised he would never leave his house alive again. Just days before, weighing very little, he had insisted on enduring the agony of being carried downstairs to take one last long look around at his beautiful home packed with treasures, crammed with memories. After that he never moved from his bed again, and both Jim Hutton and Dave Clark were in the room with Mercury, when, just before seven o'clock in the evening, he died in his sleep.

Although hardly unexpected, his death was a great shock, and grief was immense. Joe Fanelli had gone to fetch the doctor, who had been leaving to pack an overnight bag, but he was too late. Mary Austin had not long said her goodbyes to Mercury, kissing him and holding his hand as she told him she loved him and respected his bravery. He couldn't reply, and she had fled his bedroom in tears. His parents, although summoned from Feltham, had not managed to arrive in time, and Jim Beach, who had left for America directly after meeting Mercury that Friday, had to be contacted in Los Angeles.

The rest of Queen were also told, and just before midnight the news was announced publicly. There was a brief statement that read: 'Freddie Mercury died peacefully this evening at his home. His death was the result of bronchopneumonia, brought on by AIDS.' After twelve years as Mercury's personal aide, making sure he always left the house perfectly dressed, Peter Freestone provided a final service for his friend and helped with the laying out. Shortly afterwards the star's body was removed from the house and taken to a secret location in west London. There was a police escort to prevent the more aggressive members of the press from tailing them.

Reporters converged on Mary Austin at the first opportunity. Tearfully she told them that Mercury had known that the end was coming, adding, 'But he kept his sense of humour right to the end. He told me he had no regrets.'

For months the tabloid pressure on Taylor, May and Deacon had been relentless. It was so intense that, as Taylor later admitted, they had often debated among themselves whether or not they could – or should – honour their promise to the singer. But after twenty-one years together, they had bonded more than ever in the face of his illness and had kept his secret. Now unwilling to endure an interrogation from the very journalists to whom they'd repeatedly had to lie, they issued a joint press statement, expressing their overwhelming sadness at losing Mercury.

With the public announcement, distraught fans arrived in Kensington in their droves, some carrying placards, to gather outside the walled garden. Although they had feared the worst for a long time, now that Mercury had died they felt devastated. It was a kind of solace for them just to join together in their grief and stand in tribute to the star they had adored. The floral tributes flooded in, too, from mourners in all walks of life, and the Hammersmith Odeon, scene of many Queen triumphs, displayed the neon message FREDDIE MERCURY. WE WILL MISS YOU!

It had been Mercury's wish to be cremated. The twenty-five-minute service took place three days later at the West London Crematorium in Harrow Road. It was a private affair on a bitterly cold day with only a few special friends joining the star's family and relations. The ceremony was conducted in the ancient Avestan language, in accordance with the Zoroastrian faith, with both priests dressed in white robes, chanting traditional prayers. Adhering to Mercury's instructions, gospel music by Aretha Franklin was also played, as well as an aria from Verdi by Montserrat Caballé.

In the aftermath many people queued to pay their public tribute to Freddie Mercury. Elton John maintained that

'Quite simply he was one of the most important figures in rock 'n' roll in the last twenty years.'

Francis Rossi added, 'Freddie was one of the élite few who could really set a stadium alight.'

And pop pundit Paul Gambaccini declared, 'What a star! They don't make them like him any more!'

Among Mercury's friends, Sir Tim Rice said, 'His death was a great loss to music.'

While Wayne Eagling thought that 'Freddie was always extremely brave in everything he did. He was never afraid to face up to the world and what was perceived as conventional. It was a great shame that he had to go.'

But for Mike Moran it had gone much deeper: 'Freddie was such a great loss to me that I still find it very hard to get over. It's almost harder for me to get over Freddie dying than it was to get over losing my father. With parents, they're older and in some ways you expect it. But not with Freddie.'

A week later Roger Taylor and Brian May were interviewed on TV, during which they were invited to elaborate on a reference at the end of their joint press release – that the remaining band members hoped to plan a tribute to Mercury. All either would say at that stage was that it would perhaps take the form of a live concert.

On 9 December, Mercury's masterpiece 'Bohemian Rhapsody' was rereleased, this time as a double A-side, along with the hitherto unreleased 'These Are the Days of Our Lives'. As expected it stormed into the charts at number one and still stands as the only song to be number one twice over a Christmas period. It also sold in sufficient quantities by the end of the year to become the second bestselling single of 1991, behind Bryan Adams's '(Everything I Do) I Do It For You'.

This time Mercury was doing it for charity, as he had stipulated that all royalties should be donated to the Terrence

Higgins Trust. With the singer released from all pain, the future of Queen had to be in serious doubt. Closer to home, for those he left behind still trying to cope personally with his passing, other ordeals lay in store.

FIFTEEN

The Legend Lives On

Cynics say that in music it's the greatest career move in the world to die – record sales rocket and legendary status is almost always guaranteed. Certainly Freddie Mercury had no death wish and could hardly have suffered a more agonising fate, but for the next year barely a month passed without either a Queen or a solo Mercury release.

Queen's *Greatest Hits Vol I* was already multi-platinum when Hollywood Records released 'Bohemian Rhapsody'/'The Show Must Go On' as a double A-side on 6 February 1992. All its royalties were donated to the Magic Johnson Aids Foundation. Days later, it was award time again.

At the BPI Awards, held that year at the Hammersmith Odeon, 'These Are the Days of Our Lives' won the award for Best Single of 1991 – and Mercury took the posthumous award for an Outstanding Contribution to Music. Accepting this on the star's behalf, Roger Taylor announced that they were to stage a huge concert in Mercury's memory on 20 April at Wembley Stadium. It was to double as an AIDS Awareness Day, and all monies would go to charity.

Within hours of going on sale next day, all tickets for this gig, already touted as potentially the biggest show since Live Aid, sold out. In theory it was the kind of tribute Freddie Mercury would have loved. Unfortunately, as plans swung into action to organise the big day, other schemes were afoot, which friends felt would have had the star spinning in his grave.

Probate in Mercury's estate was officially granted on 13 May, but the contents of his will were known to those concerned long before. Apart from generous legacies to selected friends and Jim Hutton, the bulk of his estate was divided 50 per cent to Mary Austin, with the remainder split equally between his parents and his sister, Kashmira. As expected, Austin was the principal beneficiary. Garden Lodge, together with all contents and personal possessions free of inheritance tax, was made over to her, as was other property. What has bothered some since is what happened to the people who had for years called Garden Lodge their home.

Jim Hutton, Joe Fanelli and Peter Freestone were not kept in the dark for long. Immediately after Mercury's death, Hutton was reassured. His lover's wishes had been that he should stay on in the house for as long as he wanted. One week later, however, at a formal meeting he was advised that those wishes were not legally binding as they had not been reflected in Freddie's will. Austin, as entitled under the will, was to move in to Garden Lodge. And the three men were given three months' notice to quit.

Acrimonious arguments, some reaching the press, broke out over Hutton and the others and their move to an adjacent property in the grounds. Arrangements were made to isolate Garden Lodge. All three live-in aides were to receive legacies of £500,000 each, and in Fanelli's case, Mercury had already bought him a house in Chiswick. With a bequest of half a million pounds, Hutton could certainly find himself alternative accommodation before the ejection day of 1 March 1992. But in the eyes of some people, that was not the point.

Tony Pike, who for years had known Mercury and Hutton as a couple says, 'I was horrified to discover how it all worked out for Jim. I just *know* that Freddie would not have wanted that at all.'

And Pino Sagliocco goes further, 'It is impossible! He and Jim were like husband and wife. I cannot believe that Freddie ever wanted that.'

Unfortunately for Hutton, the person Mercury treated like a wife, at the end of the day, turned out to be Austin. Feelings have run high about the quarrels after Mercury's death, but it was the star himself who, if he had wanted his lover to stay at Garden Lodge, ought to have made proper provision for this in his will.

It could perhaps have been foreseen how things would work out here, for Mercury himself once admitted, 'All my lovers asked me why they couldn't replace Mary, but it's simply impossible. The only friend I've got is Mary, and I don't want anybody else. To me, she was my common-law wife. To me, it was a marriage. We believe in each other. That's enough for me. I couldn't fall in love with a man the same way as I have with Mary.'

During all this unpleasantness, progress continued on the Freddie Mercury Easter Tribute. A series of top acts were to be invited to take part, and as the show would go worldwide, the selection criteria was said to be based on those celebrities who had links with Mercury. However, Montserrat Caballé was glaringly absent, and Mercury had never even met some of the acts who were chosen to participate.

The task of inviting these celebrity guests had devolved on the three remaining members of Queen. Def Leppard was approached personally by Brian May, as lead singer Joe Elliott recalls. 'It was a proud moment for us to be asked,' he says. 'We felt honoured. I couldn't believe that Brian was actually asking *if* we'd appear. Blimey! I'd have swum over for it!'

While Roger Taylor had roped in heart-throb singer Paul Young: 'I knew the guys socially anyway, and one day Roger phoned me at home to say he was putting some names together with a view to staging a tribute concert to Freddie and would

I be interested in taking part. I said, yes, and a couple of months later it was confirmed.'

The idea was for each act to take lead vocal on a Queen hit, with backing from the rest of the band. Rehearsals for this took place at Bray Studios in Berkshire, where Taylor, May and Deacon put various superstars through their paces.

Easter Monday 1992 saw 72,000 people cram into Wembley Stadium. Many had camped overnight on the pavement to ensure getting in when the gates opened at 4 p.m. the following afternoon. It was officially billed as THE FREDDIE MERCURY TRIBUTE. CONCERT FOR AIDS AWARENESS, and on entry each person was supplied with a simple red ribbon to wear to symbolise their support in the fight against the disease.

While the crowds flooded in at the front, the artistes were already milling about the specially set up bar backstage. The pre-gig atmosphere was a strange brew, according to Joe Elliott: 'On the one hand it was light-hearted and up – very positive – and people were in and out of each other's trailers all the time. Unusually there were no hangers-on, only the necessary people were there, and there was a great feeling of the occasion. But, on the other hand, it was definitely sad, and later it all got a bit emotional, which was understandable.'

The show opened at 6 p.m. with a rousing address individually from Brian May, Roger Taylor and John Deacon. Then the show kicked off with Metallica, followed for the next two hours by a succession of bands, including Extreme, Def Leppard, U2 and Guns N' Roses, at which point the celebrity section took over.

With a familiar explosion of smoke bombs May, Taylor and Deacon returned and plunged into their number 'Tie Your Mother Down', whose lead vocals Joe Elliott quickly rescued from Brian May. Thereafter, each turn came on, performed their chosen number and went off. The legendary Hollywood star Elizabeth Taylor made a guest appearance in her capacity as

National Chairperson for the American Foundation for AIDS Research (AmFAR) to deliver an emotive speech about AIDS, despite a few hecklers, and there seemed to be something for everyone, from a Bowie/Annie Lennox duet of 'Under Pressure' to a revival of the old Mott the Hoople classic 'All the Young Dudes', performed by Ian Hunter and Mick Ronson – with additional backing from Joe Elliott and Bowie, who'd originally written the number, playing saxophone.

As the evening progressed, clearly some found it hard to contain their emotions. No one doubts that the event was well intentioned, but for many people the concert fell flat – and not just because, through no fault of their own, none of the guest stars could sing on a par with Freddie Mercury.

Says Bob Harris, 'I thought it showed up terribly how all the acts struggled with Freddie's songs. The only person I enjoyed was Ian Hunter. He got me up in my seat. But the others were clearly in trouble.'

While Simon Bates believes, 'It was very hard to take. They meant well, but it didn't come off. I felt it was more for the fans than anything else, but how do you do that? Do you make it a memorial or a wake? I was there, and the audience weren't at all sympathetic. It probably ended up more for the benefit of the remaining three band members. Elizabeth Taylor tried her best, but it was cringing, and Bowie was just awful.'

During his solo spot David Bowie had announced that he wanted to say a prayer for a sick friend. Fish more than echoes Bates's feelings on the incident. 'When Bowie dropped to one knee and began praying it was really embarrassing,' he says. 'I cringed in my seat and thought, Oh, my God! The tribute was very disappointing, yet it could have been something sparkling. I believe that the initial feeling behind it was genuine, but I think it was corporately hijacked, which was a great pity.'

It had nevertheless been an evening to say goodbye to one of rock's greatest entertainers, and over 500 million viewers in close to seventy countries worldwide had joined in. When it came to the finale, in a choked voice Brian May announced one of Mercury's all-time favourites. When Oscar-winning actress/singer Liza Minnelli appeared on stage, she was to lead the full line-up in a bluesy rendition of 'We Are the Champions'. At the end, before finally looking heavenwards, she shouted, 'Thanks, Freddie. We just wanted to let you know, we'll be thinking of you!'

The cheering, back-slapping and tears subsided, and when the dust had settled once more, as far as Queen as an entity was concerned, it was all over. For the rest of the band the sense of being suspended in a vacuum was real, and despite the feeling that they had sensed impending doom, the situation still left them bewildered. In his final interview, Mercury had confessed, 'In the end all the mistakes, all the excuses are down to me.' Certainly others have since expressed the view that, mingled with the band's grief was a degree of anger over their lead singer's reckless behaviour. This had cut short not only his life but also their careers – it had been a needless waste all round.

Queen's music had spanned almost two decades, but the announcement that they were to disband quickly followed the Easter tribute. Years before Mercury had declared, 'If I suddenly left, they have the mechanism in them – they'd just replace me,' but added, 'Not easy to replace me, huh?' Brian May, who once called Freddie Mercury the fire and glue that held them together, said at the time: 'It would be wrong of us to go out with another singer, pretending to be Queen,' he said. But, as had just been made painfully clear, no other singer could fill the niche that Mercury had so uniquely carved out for himself.

One-time *Old Grey Whistle Test* producer Michael Appleton agrees, 'You can assess Freddie's strength by that tribute concert. With the exception of George Michael, I think it showed, when the other artistes tried to sing those songs, just how incredibly strong Freddie had been. It also showed how one person in a band can be taken very much for granted, so much so that no one realises it until something happens to separate them.

'Freddie personally had incredible strength, ability and charisma, but still Queen aren't quite up there with the Beatles and the Rolling Stones. Those bands came in the first echelon, and Queen came along later – but I'd definitely put them at the top of the second generation along with Bruce Springsteen and U2.'

In the immediate aftermath of the concert, yet more records were released, and the AIDS issue had been given a substantial public platform. Hitherto the link between AIDS charities and the rock world had been weak, but quite quickly a number of new foundations sprang up, including the Mercury Phoenix Trust set up by Queen. Around summer 1992 the awareness brought about by Mercury's death, however, had one of its most unusual effects in America. It centred on a Catholic school, and what started as a local storm in a teacup became a matter of national debate.

Graduate students at the Sacred Heart School in Clifton, New Jersey, had selected Mercury's rock anthem 'We Are the Champions' to accompany a slide show to be screened during a commencement ceremony. The trouble began when their choice was overruled by the principal, Donald Quinlan. Students believed the decision had been made solely on the grounds that Mercury, a self-confessed bisexual, had died of AIDS, and they promptly branded it discriminatory. By mounting protests, involving firstly the local press, they ensured that the story spread quickly – to state, then national newspapers, as well as reaching TV chat shows, with the satellite music station MTV covering the dispute daily. When AIDS activist groups joined in, and arrests were made, it fuelled a fire already out of control. The hysteria, however, did not reflect the whole picture.

Donald Quinlan explains that 'Freddie Mercury's song had been selected in January, but then both the eighth grade and music teachers noted that some of the students thought Mercury was cool because he was bisexual. The teachers felt that these children idolised him, and the pupils involved began ribbing the teachers about it. I met with class representatives and asked them to write a brief summary of why a Catholic school might be opposed to this graduation song, as well as one showing why we should play it. I told them that following these write-ups we would sit down and come up with an acceptable solution.'

Quinlan couldn't have been fairer. But, instead of write-ups he began to receive visits from irate parents, supporting the students' by now rampant conviction that prejudice was at work.

The whole incident snowballed, as Quinlan admits. 'In early June the first snippet appeared, and within twenty-four hours it became a major news story,' he says. 'Every TV station in New York City came to the school and stayed for weeks. Every local station came, too, and all the New York newspapers sent reporters. There were upwards of seventy media people around the school constantly.' With headlines like HOMOSEXUAL RIGHTS UNDER SIEGE, and the rebellious pupils declaring that their school had an 'eleventh Commandment' – Thou Shalt Not Rock 'n' Roll – the result was that the graduation ceremony was cancelled, and diplomas were temporarily withheld from selected students.

Back in Britain, a month later Mercury made the news again when a Liverpool builder, John Boylan, accidentally found something of potential value. 'I had been working at the city's Sunnyside Mansions,' says Boylan, 'when boxes fell out of the ceiling leading to the cellar containing a great heap of singles. They were all of two separate numbers, but as I hadn't heard of them I threw them into the skip along with the rubbish. A couple of days later our kid was listening to Radio Merseyside, and this question came up about what record was recorded under the name Larry Lurex. When the answer was "I Can Hear Music", and that the real singer had been Freddie Mercury, he came running to me saying, "You'd better get down and get those records back quick!"

'The first thing I did was phone the Queen fan club, but they didn't believe me, and I forgot about it. About three years later a mate of mine took two to a record fair and showed them to some people, and this guy said he'd been after them for years. All of a sudden my phone started ringing with press and other folk from all over the world. Then I got a call from Norman Sheffield (of Trident Records who owned the rights). He told me to burn the records. He said that if I tried to sell them he would sue me. I didn't want any trouble.'

Along with the demos, John Boylan found what appeared to be two master tapes. When he tried to have these authenticated by Sotheby's auctioneers, however, their detailed findings, says Boylan, summarised that they were 'inconclusive'. Three years later an acetate of 'I Can Hear Music' was sold at Christie's for around £800, and Boylan's find was deemed to be bootleg copies.

But, for others, the opposite of making money out of Mercury had been preoccupying them for months. Mercury had once joked, 'I want to be buried with all my treasures, like the Pharaohs. If I can afford it, I'll have a pyramid built in Kensington. Wouldn't that be fab?'

On the eve of the first anniversary of his death, news emerged of two separate applications to the Kensington and Chelsea local authority to have, not exactly a pyramid, but a statue erected near Logan Place in his honour. Other monuments in the area ranged from those of Sir Thomas More to Peter Pan. As hundreds of fans still made the pilgrimage to Garden Lodge, the idea was to add a statue of Freddie Mercury in full voice as a focus for their devotion. One bid had been put together by a group of people fronted by Dave Clark, and supported by the Queen fan club. To assist his approach to the council, Clark had also involved the then local MP Dudley Fishburn.

'It began when Dave Clark appeared in the House of Commons and put his name in,' says Dudley Fishburn. 'The morning-coated doorman rushed up to me excitedly, saying, "Dave Clark of the Dave Clark Five is here to see you!" Dave explained that he represented a group of friends who wanted to have a statue of Freddie Mercury erected in Kensington. I immediately thought it was a great idea. I was always in favour of it, and still am, even though it all came to nothing. To me, Freddie was plainly as great a figure as those nineteenth-century generals who have statues erected to them all over the place. Many's the time when I am walking through Kensington that I've been stopped by groups of German or Japanese tourists all wanting to know where they can find Freddie Mercury's house.

'As the provision of a statue rests entirely with a local authority, I wrote to the leader of that particular authority on behalf of Dave Clark, and there followed a considerable three-way correspondence. But the idea met with a democratic decision not to allow one. I felt it was a particularly foolish decision, because although mostly these fall by the wayside through lack of money, that wasn't the case here. The finance was in place and amounted to quite a sum, so that not only would it have been erected properly but safely maintained thereafter. Their refusal didn't make sense.'

The other bid for a statue memorial came from Bill Howard, Mercury's former neighbour, who didn't have the support of any MP, nor of the Queen fan club. But he did find public enthusiasm for his plans when he conducted a street survey about them. His contention that Freddie Mercury was the biggest credit to the Kensington borough in fifty years, however, failed to cut any ice with the council, and his application, too, went into oblivion.

But the statue highlighted other problems with the suggestion that gay rights campaigners would be angered by any plans to immortalise Freddie Mercury. According to one spokesman, Mercury was never any kind of icon in the gay community, for the simple reason that he never came out. 'They are likely to hold that against him for some time,' he added.

These feelings were an extension of an ongoing debate over the timing of the announcement of the star's statement, so near to his death, that he had AIDS. While some hailed it a brave and honest act, others, including a few from the pop world, accused Mercury of betraying the gay cause. They argued that the statement's timing was far from courageous – and that he ought to have admitted to having the disease long before, thus bringing it out earlier for open discussion.

Refusing to get embroiled in this debate, the rest of Queen concentrated on perpetuating Mercury's legacy through commercial releases. In late November 1992 *The Freddie Mercury Album*, a collection of existing solo tracks, peaked at number four. Days earlier, the star's old hit 'The Great Pretender' had been revived, and the following month saw the single 'In My Defence' reach number eight. But it wasn't until the following July that of all the posthumous releases, Freddie Mercury would hit his first solo number one with the single 'Living On My Own'.

Originally from his debut solo album *Mr Bad Guy*, the star felt the song was highly characteristic of himself. In one of his more maudlin moods, he once explained why. 'I have to go around the world living in hotels,' he said. 'You can have a whole shoal of people looking after you, but in the end they all go away.'

Throughout 1994 there was much talk of a final Queen

album to include previously unreleased Mercury recordings. By early 1995 the word was that Brian May, Roger Taylor and John Deacon were busy, either in Metropolis Studios or at May's home studio, putting the finishing touches to Mercury's lyrics. They were using the same modern techniques as the three former Beatles were employing with previously un-released John Lennon tracks. The ex-Queenies were to add their contributions live in the studio to the material Mercury had managed to leave behind.

Anticipation was high among the band's worldwide legions of fans, as well as in the music industry. When the first single was announced, there was consternation when it emerged that it was to be 'Heaven For Everyone': a Roger Taylor number from his solo band the Cross's 1988 debut album *Shove It*. It had then featured Mercury as guest lead vocalist. Rerecorded, this time including input from Brian May and John Deacon, on its release in late October it still went straight in at number two.

Two weeks later the long-awaited album *Made in Heaven* emerged, and it went straight in at the top, holding off Madonna, Oasis and Elton John among others. After a career of having a tough time with the critics, it was largely acclaimed, with some reviewers even declaring that it was a pity Mercury wasn't around to enjoy what was being hailed as the best Queen album for years. It quickly went double-platinum. Despite strong competition, the album survived in the top five, weeks into 1996, unlike, to the surprise of many, the hugely hyped *The Beatles Anthology 1*, which boasted Lennon's much-vaunted unreleased recordings.

Singled out for special praise in *Made in Heaven* was the track 'A Winter's Tale'. Penned by the lakeside in Montreux, the ballad was the last song Mercury had ever written, and it was released mid-December as Queen's bid for the Christmas number one. But, for others, the album's highlight was 'Too

Much Love Will Kill You', a Brian May solo single sung with great poignancy by Mercury.

In late 1995 both Roger Taylor and Brian May paid special tribute to Mercury's last courageous working months. They revealed how, doggedly determined to push his pain-racked body to the limit, he had sometimes needed to fortify himself with a few shots of vodka before getting up to sing. The track 'Mother Love', on which the singer's vocals soar to incredible heights, was the last number he recorded.

Brian May marvelled, 'This is a man who can't really stand any more without incredible pain and is very weak. There's no flesh on his bones at all – and yet you can hear the power, the will that he's still got.' Mary Austin revealed that it had taken Mercury a very long time to accept that he had AIDS, and May believes that, even to the last, the star, his friend, thought a miracle might save him. But, of course, none had come.

When once asked how he would like people to remember him professionally, Mercury had flippantly replied, 'Oh, I don't know. Dead and gone? It's up to them. When I'm dead, who cares? I don't.' But the sleeve of *Made in Heaven*, undoubtedly Queen's most personal album, had carried the legend: 'Dedicated to the immortal spirit of Freddie Mercury'.

In the coming years, further honours followed. On 25 November 1996, in the Place du Marché, Montreux, Switzerland, overlooking Lake Geneva, a three-metre-high bronze statue of Mercury in classic pose – legs apart, mike in hand and his right fist triumphantly punching the air – was unveiled by Freddie's father, Bomi Bulsara and the opera star Montserrat Caballé. The plaque on its plinth read *Freddie Mercury Lover of Life – Singer of Songs*. The statue was the work of Czech sculptor Irena Sedlecka, and had been commissioned by May, Taylor, Deacon and Freddie's family and friends, some of whom attended the small dedication ceremony. Then, in 1999, the Royal Mail issued a Freddie Mercury stamp as part of their Millennium series. The entertainment category of this series also included stamps of the footballer Bobby Moore, actor Charlie Chaplin and a Dalek from the TV series *Doctor Who*. But Mercury's 19p stamp caused some controversy. It featured an on-stage, bare-chested Freddie in scarlet leggings but drummer Roger Taylor could also be seen in the background. According to convention, the only living people permitted to appear on a British postage stamp are members of the royal family.

Having considered himself very firmly a member of rock royalty, Freddie did not live to see his band enter the coveted Rock and Roll Hall of Fame. Queen's induction to this echelon took place on 19 March 2001 at the sixteenth annual dinner held at the Waldorf Astoria in New York. Jer Bulsara accepted her son's award at the glittering event during which fellow inductees included Paul Simon, Aerosmith and Michael Jackson.

It was around this time that news broke in Britain that there was to be a West End stage musical structured around Queen's music, called *We Will Rock You*. The multi-million-pound musical, scripted by comedian and novelist Ben Elton and directed by Christopher Renshaw, opened at the Dominion Theatre in London's Tottenham Court Road on 12 May 2002. A smash hit, it has become the theatre's longest running show which, including additional productions staged around the world, is estimated to have been seen by more than 10 million people to date. A year later, Freddie's father Bomi Bulsara died, leaving his mother and his sister Kashmira to witness how his memory continued to be kept alive.

It was perhaps inevitable that the runaway success of *We Will Rock You* would whet the appetite among Queen fans to see the band perform live once more. In the aftermath of Freddie's death there was a widespread acknowledgement, if not assumption, that there could never be Queen without Mercury at its helm. But by autumn 2004, rumours were circulating of a band reunion with one or two famous singers said to be set to step into the void. In January 2005, that someone turned out to be former Free and Bad Company lead singer Paul Rodgers, a powerful and distinctive rock front man. For diehard Freddie fans it was a bittersweet prospect – to have Queen revived as a live act but without Mercury's dominant presence. And indeed, they were big enough shoes to fill without Freddie having been voted that year as the Greatest Male Singer of All Time in an *MTV* poll.

The new band comprised Brian May, Roger Taylor, Paul Rodgers, keyboard player Spike Edney, guitarist Jamie Moses and Danny Miranda on bass. John Deacon did not participate. With everyone keen to stress that Freddie was not being replaced and that Paul Rodgers would continue to pursue a solo career, this line-up was billed as Queen and Paul Rodgers. Commencing in spring 2005, on and off over the next four years they toured or performed individual gigs around the world until, in May 2009, Paul Rodgers announced that, for the foreseeable future at least, his collaboration with Queen was over.

Far from the limelight and in a very different way, time had run out for some people whom Freddie had once counted as friends, lovers or just acquaintances, many of whom had sadly died fairly young. Freddie's long-time lover Jim Hutton had reportedly been battling cancer towards the end of his life. Succumbing to complications from broncho-pneumonia, just days shy of his sixty-first birthday, Jim died in Ireland on 1 January 2010.

Nine months later, news of a more uplifting kind arrived when, after years of rumour and speculation, a big screen biopic of Freddie Mercury was finally officially announced. Talk of this project had first surfaced in late 2006, when Johnny Depp was tipped by the media for the lead role. But then again, just months earlier, similar rumours had circulated that the versatile Kentucky-born actor was due to portray the late Michael Hutchence in a biopic of the INXS front man. All Brian May could confirm in 2006 was that discussions surrounding a biopic of Mercury were at an early stage. The meat on the bones came in September 2010.

The film was the result of a partnership between GK Films, Tribeca Productions and Queen Films and, it was revealed, the screenplay for the untitled movie would be written by Peter Morgan. Nominated for an Academy Award for his work on both *the Queen* and *Frost/Nixon*, Morgan is currently considered one of the hottest screenwriters in the business. For some people, the startling news was that the starring role had gone to Sacha Baron Cohen.

Born in 1971 in Hammersmith, London, Sacha Baron Cohen studied history at Christ's College, Cambridge, before becoming an award-winning actor, famous for his fictional comedic characters: rapper Ali G, Austrian fashion reporter Bruno and Kazakhstani journalist Borat. According to Peter Morgan, it was Cohen who approached him to write the screenplay, a prospect that did not completely grab him at first, as he thought he might be limited in how much of Mercury's famously colourful life could be encompassed with an actor in his late thirties portraying a star who had died aged forty-five. Further parameters kicked in when Peter opted to steer clear of covering Mercury's debilitating illness and harrowing death, effectively knocking out the most poignant and drastically changing years of the star's life. 'I didn't want to write about a man dying from Aids,' Morgan flatly stated.

That said, Morgan identified a very fertile period of Freddie's life that entirely energised him – from early in Queen's career up to the band's legendary performance at the historic Live Aid concert on 13 July 1985 – a period that also saw Queen embroiled in the controversy surrounding their 1984 appearance at the Sun City Super Bowl in South Africa and included the creative conflicts that set in with the band, leading to Mercury breaking away to pursue his solo projects before returning to the fold. 'I'm essentially writing about the most painful time in the band's history,' Peter stressed to the media.

Couple Sacha Baron Cohen's stock-in-trade brash comedy with Freddie's flash flamboyance and leave out the intense human tragedy of his illness and death, and it would be easy to anticipate a gag-filled depiction of a wildly outrageous rock star. But Peter Morgan emphasised from the start that he planned to pen a drama that would at times be painful in its portrayal of the reality behind the dazzling public face of Queen. Graham King of GK Films enthused to *Rolling Stone*: 'Peter Morgan is going to write an amazing script. Sacha fits the bill. All the ingredients are there.'

Both Queen and solo Freddie Mercury songs will feature in the film but it was unclear in the months following the breaking news if Sacha would be performing the songs or lip-synching to Mercury's vocals.

King called Queen's music a brand all of its own; a statement that is hard to argue with. Not only does the RIAA estimate Queen's total global record sales at 300 million, Queen is officially Britain's biggest music act, having taken that mantle from the Beatles. Although Freddie, so much the linchpin of the band, died in 1991, he manages to live on strongly through Queen's commercial success and the generations of new devotees that stream nightly out of the *We Will Rock You* stage musical at the Dominion Theatre, the entrance doors to which are dominated overhead by a figure of Freddie in full throttle.

Outwardly outrageous yet inherently insecure, Mercury had myriad unfathomable facets and to capture truly his complete essence in something like two hours of screen time will undoubtedly prove a stiff challenge. But as a colossus of rock in his own lifetime, for Freddie to be immortalised in a major motion picture will thrill Queen and film fans around the world and will propel his star to even dizzier heights that may even have satisfied the mercurial man himself.

Index